African Theatre
7

Series Editors
Martin Banham, James Gibbs,
Yvette Hutchison, Jane Plastow
& Femi Osofisan

T0313627

Reviews Editor
Jane Plastow
School of English, University of Leeds LS2 9JT, UK

Associate Editors
Eckhard Breitinger
Forststr. 3, 95488 Eckersdorf, Germany

Frances Harding
SOAS, Thornhaugh St, Russell Square, London WC1H OX9, UK

Masitha Hoeane
PO Box 23689, Bedworth Park 1940, South Africa

David Kerr
kerrdavid42@yahoo.co.uk

Amandina Lihamba
Dept of Fine & Performing Arts, PO Box 35051, University of Dar es Salaam, Tanzania

Olu Obafemi
Student Affairs Unit, PMB 1515, University of Ilorin, Ilorin, Nigeria

Titles already published in the series:
African Theatre in Development
African Theatre: Playwrights & Politics
African Theatre: Women
African Theatre: Southern Africa
African Theatre: Soyinka: Blackout, Blowout & Beyond
African Theatre: Youth
African Theatre: Companies

In production:
African Theatre: Diasporas

Articles not exceeding 5,000 words should be submitted preferably on disk (as a Word file) and always accompanied by a double-spaced hard copy. Typewritten submissions may be considered in exceptional circumstances if they follow the standard double-spaced format.

Style: Preferably use UK rather than US spellings. Italicise titles of books or plays. Use single inverted commas and double for quotes within quotes. Type notes at the end of the text on a separate sheet. Do not justify the right hand-margins.

References should follow the style of this volume (Surname date: page number) in text. All references should then be listed at the end of article in full:
Surname, name, date, *title of work* (place of publication: name of publisher)
Surname, name, date, 'title of article' in surname, initial (ed./eds) *title of work* (place of publication: publisher).
or Surname, name, date, 'title of article', *Journal*, vol., no: page numbers.

Reviewers should provide full bibliographic details, including extent, ISBN and price.

Copyright: Please ensure, where appropriate, that clearance has been obtained from copyright holders of material used. Illustrations may also be submitted if appropriate and if accompanied by full captions and with reproduction rights clearly indicated. It is the responsibility of the contributors to clear all permissions.

All submissions should be accompanied by a brief biographical profile. The editors cannot undertake to return material submitted and contributors are advised to keep a copy of all material sent in case of loss in transit.

Editorial address
African Theatre, c/o The Workshop Theatre, School of English, University of Leeds, Leeds LS2 9JT, UK • ATatWT@leeds.ac.uk

Books for Review & Review articles
Jane Plastow, Reviews Editor, *African Theatre*, School of English, University of Leeds, Leeds LS2 9JT, UK • j.e.plastow@leeds.ac.uk

African Theatre Companies

Editor
James Gibbs

Reviews Editor
Jane Plastow

James Currey

James Currey www.jamescurrey.co.uk
is an imprint of Boydell and Brewer Ltd
PO Box 9, Woodbridge, Suffolk IP12 3DF, UK
www.boydell.co.uk
and of Boydell & Brewer Inc.
668 Mt Hope Avenue, Rochester, NY 14620, USA
www.boydellandbrewer.com

British Library Cataloguing in Publication Data
African theatre
    7: Companies
    1. Theater – Africa
    I. Gibbs, James
    792'.096

ISBN 978-1-84701-500-6 (James Currey paper)

Typeset in 10/11 pt Monotype Bembo by Long House, Cumbria, UK

Contents

Notes on Contributors

Victor S. Dugga studied at the Universities of Jos, Essex and Bayreuth. He has been lecturer, creative writer and theatre director at the University of Jos since 1992. His short story 'Over the bar' won first prize in a writing contest organised by the Swiss Society for African Studies and FIFA in Zurich 2001, and his book *Creolisations in Nigerian Theatre* was published in 2002. He is Executive Director, University of Jos Advancement Office.

Manfred Loimeier studied German literature, history of art and philosophy, in Tübingen, Vienna, Basel and Berlin, and comparative literature in Bayreuth. He has been working as a journalist in Mannheim, Germany, specialising in African literatures in European languages. His publications include: *Ken Saro-Wiwa* (1996), *Sudan* (1997), *Afrikanische Literatur* (1998), *Wortwechsel* (2002), *Die Macht des Wortes* (2006) and, as editor, *Yizo Yizo* (2005). His PhD thesis was published in the Bayreuth African Studies Series in 2006 under the title *Die Macht des Wortes*.

Siri Lange holds a PhD in anthropology and her research interests include the relationship between the popular culture of Dar es Salaam and the social, political, and cultural dynamics of the city. Through her position at Chr. Michelsen Institute (CMI) she has taken part in a wide range of research projects as well as commissioned work.

Basil Jones was a co-founder of Handspring Puppet Company in 1981. He has performed in all their plays and is responsible for the financial management of the company. He co-produced *Warhorse* in association with The Royal National Theatre, which opened in London in mid-September 2007 and a revival of *Woyzeck on the Highveld*, directed by William Kentridge, that was presented at the UNIMA International Festival and Conference in Perth, Australia in April 2008. (www.handspringpuppet.co.za)

K. W. Dexter Lyndersay died while this volume was in preparation. See obituary.

Christine Matzke currently teaches African literature and theatre at the Institute of Asian and African Studies, Humboldt-University, Berlin. Her research interests include theatre and cultural production in Eritrea, and post-colonial crime fiction.

Foluke Ogunleye lectures in the Department of Dramatic Arts, Obafemi Awolowo University, Ile-Ife, Nigeria. She earned her PhD from the University of Ibadan and she has published widely in international publication outlets. Her edited works include *Theatre in Swaziland: The Past, the Present and the Future* (2005) and *African Video Film Today* (2003). She is also a playwright, actress and director. Her published plays include *Jabulile* (2005) and *The Innocent Victim* (2003).

  Patrick-Jude Oteh studied theatre arts at the University of Ibadan from Diploma to Masters levels and is currently a doctoral candidate at the same institution. He holds a Masters degree in internal law and diplomacy from the University of Jos. He has been involved with theatre projects in Italy, UK, USA, Sierra Leone, Côte D'Ivoire, and Kenya, and is involved in an initiative to bring together a group of touring theatres at the El Hamra Theatre in Tunis. He is a director and has organised the Jos Festival of Theatre since it began.

Lucy Richardson is senior lecturer in performing arts at London Metropolitan University. She has also worked extensively as an actress and director and was artistic director of Lewisham Youth Theatre and Camden Young People's Theatre. She has produced and facilitated several projects for Phakama in Southern Africa, London and South America, and has recently begun to document and write about the work.

Michael Walling is artistic director of Border Crossings and has directed numerous productions across four continents including the ENO's acclaimed workshop productions of Wagner's *Ring* . He was associate director to Peter Sellars on *Nixon in China*, and to Phyllida Lloyd on *The Handmaid's Tale* (Canada). Michael teaches regularly at Rose Bruford College, and the Central School of Speech and Drama. He has published in *Suspect* (Toronto, Alphabet City 2005) and *Peripheral Centres / Central Peripheries* (Saarbrucken, 2006). See: www.bordercrossingsblog.blogspot.com

Announcement

The Special Collections section of the Brotherton Library, University of Leeds, has acquired an archive of 'African Theatre Manuscripts and Associated Material in the Collection of Martin Banham' (July 2006). At last count there were over 120 items in this collection including working manuscripts and typescripts from a wide range of contemporary African playwrights, with a strong emphasis on Nigeria and West Africa generally, plus associated correspondence, programme material, etc. This collection can be consulted in the Brotherton Library by arrangement with the Special Collections Librarian, Brotherton Library, University of Leeds, Leeds LS2 9JT, UK.

Obituaries

Saka Acquaye, 1923–2007

Sake Acquaye, who died in February 2007 at the age of 83, had been an international-class hurdler, and was a versatile artist who made an immense contribution to the visual and performing arts in Ghana during a lifetime of service. The revival of his best known work, *The Lost Fishermen*, during the month in which he died gave the younger generation a chance to experience one of the classics of the Ghanaian theatre, a story told in music, song and dance that looked, in the heady 1960s, as if it would establish 'Ghanaian folk opera' as a national form.

Acquaye was born in Accra in 1923, and the heritage of the Ga people was always of the utmost importance to him. His formal education included important time spent at Achimota School, Accra (1943–9) and two periods in the United States (1953–9 and 1962–4) where he studied in Philadelphia and at UCLA. He took a variety of courses that included art, sculpture, opera and theatre. While there he won numerous awards, travelled widely, and made several recordings, often with his 'African Ensemble'.

He returned to Ghana permanently in 1964 and picked up his work in the theatre while continuing to sculpt and, through his contact with a wide variety of musical groups, while playing an influential role on the music scene. In addition to *The Lost Fishermen,* he was responsible for *Obadzeng Goes to Town* (published 1965), *Modzawe* (presented 1970), and *Sasabonsam* (presented 1980) that were given national and international exposure. He is also credited with the neglected *Accra After Midnight, Dantsira, Ananse to Marry the Queen Mother, Bo Mong, Ananse and the Magic Drum, Ananse in Ghostland* and *Hintinhintin*. During the 1970s and 1980s, when often away from the theatre, Acquaye made passionate interventions in cultural debates, commenting on such issues as the role of mime in drama, the social function of theatre, the importance of music in education and the need for artists to be steeped in local traditions. Over the decades, he held important positions in government bodies, produced sculptures, sometimes naturalist in form, that adorned public spaces, and was honoured with national awards.

Shortly before the celebration of Ghana's Fiftieth Independence Anniversary, Saka Acquaye, the versatile artist who had made his mark on his country's theatre, music and art, fell at the hurdle that no man can clear.

James Gibbs

Bate Besong, 1954–2007

On 7 March 2007, before an audience of nearly a thousand, Bate Besong launched his book *Disgrace: Autobiographical Narcissus*. After the function, he set off by car for Yaoundé to collect his visa from the US Embassy so that he could attend the African Literature Association Conference at the University of West Virginia. He was accompanied by Dr Hilarious Ambe, a colleague at the University of Buea, known as a critic, actor and, jointly with Besong, director of the Buea University Theatre company, and by Ni Tom Gwangwa's Kwasem, director, TV-producer and influential spokesman on anglophone Cameroonian culture. On the journey, they were involved in a head-on collision with a timber truck and all died on the spot.

Bate Besong was born in Nigeria to Cameroonian parents on 8 May 1954 and had most of his school and university education in Nigeria. He graduated from the University of Ibadan and received his PhD, with a thesis entitled *Politics and Historicity in Anglophone Cameroon Drama* from the University of Calabar (1996). A teacher and lecturer, he was appointed senior lecturer at the University of Buea in 1999.

Besong had 'returned' to Cameroon in the early 1990s and become well known as a controversial poet, playwright and intellectual. For example, the production of his *Beast of No Nation* (March, 1991) created a uproar: the play was banned, the director interrogated, and Besong detained. His 'Nigerian' outspokenness about the neo-colonial regime of Paul Biya and about the marginalisation of his community was not curbed by this kind of response and, indeed, was welcomed by anglophone political activists. His key-note address at the first conference on anglophone Cameroon writing became a manifesto for an assertive cultural policy in the anglophone provinces, and he continued to write and to speak out.

Following the accident on the Yaoundé road, anglophone Cameroon mourns three prominent intellectuals and, in Bate Besong, lost one of its most vocal spokesmen.

Eckhard Breitinger

John Conteh-Morgan, 1948–2008

We have to record, with great sadness, the death of our Associate Editor, Dr John Conteh-Morgan, on 3 March 2008. John, who previously taught at Fourah Bay College, University of Sierra Leone, went to Ohio State University in 1992, teaching French and francophone literatures. From 2003 he was editor of the leading journal *Research in African Literatures (RAL)*.

John was educated at Fourah Bay College, the Université de Besançon, and Sussex University, and held visiting academic fellowships at the University of Leeds, Harvard University and Maryville College, Tennessee.

He was an authority on the theatre of francophone Africa, his major work *Theatre and Drama in Francophone Africa* being published by Cambridge University Press in 1994. Amongst a range of other distinguished publications, he contributed a major chapter on 'Francophone Africa south of the Sahara' to *A History of Theatre in Africa* edited by Martin Banham (Cambridge University Press, 2004), and, together with Tejumola Olaniyan, he edited a brilliant collection of essays that originated in *RAL, African Drama and Performance* (Indiana University Press, 2004).

John made a major contribution to the understanding of francophone theatre in Africa. At *African Theatre* we greatly benefited from his advice and enthusiasm, and we join in sending our great sympathy to his wife Miriam and children.

The Editors

K.W. Dexter Lyndersay, 1932–2006

On 19 December 2006, Dexter Lyndersay, who should have simply been listed among the contributors to this volume, died of a heart attack in retirement in Trinidad. As a result he is, sadly, 'promoted' to an obituary.

A Fulbright Fellowship enabled Dexter to earn the BFA (Chicago's Art Institute) and the MFA (Yale) that equipped him for academic posts in Nigeria, initially at the University of Ibadan and subsequently in other parts of the Federation. In all he spent 21 years in higher education in Nigeria working as a teacher, theatre practitioner and administrator, and making an enduring impact through writing, directing and designing.

Active until very near the end, it is good to report that Dexter's vivid account of one small part of his productive life appears in this volume. Among those mentioned in the article are playwrights, scholars, musicians, stage carpenters and actors with whom he collaborated closely. The distinguished list includes some who have already joined the ancestors, some who continue to make history. Even a partial list is a roll call of major figures in the Nigerian theatre: Joel Adedeji, Demola Adeyemi, Emmanuel Avbiorokoma, Samson Amali, Biodun Jeyifo, John Gillespie, Amorelle Inanga, Sunbo Marinho, Wale Ogunyemi, Kole Omotoso, Ademola Onibon-Okuta, Sonny Oti, Tunji Oyelana, and Jimi Solanke.

Testimony to the extent of Dexter's reach into wider theatrical traditions and his impact on the Nigerian theatre is provided by the names of non-Nigerian authors whose work he brought to the stage during the mid-1970s. This list includes Ed Bullins, Athol Fugard, John Kani, Winston Ntshona, Jean Genet and Tewfik al-Hakim.

With respect and affection, the editors hope the first article of this volume will recall something of Dexter Lyndersay's energy, his generosity of spirit, and his contribution to the Nigerian theatre.

The Editors

Introduction

JAMES GIBBS

The schedule for Ghana's year-long celebrations in 2007 to mark fifty years of independence included a programme of productions of 'classic Ghanaian plays', one every month. In choosing to celebrate in this way, the committee tasked with marking the anniversary quickly found itself in the middle of debates about funding the arts and about the accessibility of performances. A host of questions were raised including: When will the money be available? (With the implication that it has been delayed!) What income, if any, is expected from ticket sales? (With the hope that some seats will be free or heavily subsidised.) Where will the productions be put on? (With the unspoken: Are you thinking only of the National Theatre in Accra as a venue?) And, perhaps most important: What scale of budgets can be submitted by directors and their business managers? Now that 2007 has passed into history and the Ghana@50 Secretariat has shut down, many of these questions are still being asked. Directors and performers are out of pocket and there is no obvious source of reimbursement for expenses they incurred in good faith.

These recurrent questions in relation to theatrical enterprises, and the attempts to answer them – in the Ghanaian context – drew attention to the fact that, down the years, the country has witnessed the emergence of a variety of different kinds of theatre organisation. In the history of the country's theatre examples can be found of expatriate amateur groups putting on plays for their friends and donating the proceeds of performances to charity. One can also find examples of middle class groups of Ghanaians for whom putting on a play was a labour of love and of cultural self-assertion, who sought no financial recompense simply hoping that the proceeds from the ticket sales would cover production costs. There are also examples of professional travelling theatre groups or 'trios' as they were sometimes called, that were part of the local capitalist economy. They were organised by entrepreneurs who invested in local talent, kept expenditure down and arranged tours to maximise profits. Tour schedules were arranged so that the 'trios' 'stormed' towns just after workers had been paid. In the education sector, there have been groups, led by F.K. Fiawoo for example, that raised money for fledgling educational institutions and others that were subsidised by well established schools, universities and colleges. There have also been, at various stages during the last fifty years, companies made up of performers on the government pay-roll. These have included Kwame Nkrumah's Workers' Brigade Concert Party and the company currently attached to the National Theatre. There have also been companies that have put on productions thanks to the support they received from the international funding organisations. Of which more later.

From the outside, Ghana has sometimes appeared to be a country that, following from Nkrumah's recognition of the role of the arts in nation building, benefited from generous state support. From inside the country, however, it has not always appeared so comfortable and mounting a production has often been a risky venture in strictly financial terms. The lesson is that close scrutiny of how theatre companies operate is an important, often neglected, aspect of theatre life in Africa that reveals situations that are obscured by distance.

In this issue of *African Theatre,* the financial realities under which drama companies operate are discussed. The papers on Nigeria take the reader on a journey down the years and across the states, starting with the late Dexter Lyndersay's account of Unibadan Masques (1974–76). In common with other authors in the volume, Lyndersay's involvement in the processes he describes gives his contribution particular authority. So does his openness, duplicated elsewhere, about the finances of the operation he was involved in running. For example, he refers to a subvention for 1974–75 of Naira 6,000. It is helpful to know that the naira was pegged in 1973 at two to the pound sterling and that the Unibadan Masques' budget, with ticket sales from performances in the 304-seater Arts Theatre, allowed the planning of a production each month. The immediacy of Lyndersay's account communicates the sense of excitement that accompanied Unibadan productions, and the reference to Dani Lyndersay, Dexter's widow, as costume designer prompts reflection on how often theatre, amateur or professional, is a family concern, dependent on personal relationships if it is to function.

At the end of his article, Lyndersay looks back on what 'worked' at Ibadan, and refers to the 1960 Masks, Orisun Theatre and the School of Drama Acting Company. We then look sideways and examine, through Foluke Ogunleye's article, what had been happening between 1967 and 1975 down the treacherous Ibadan–Ife road at the University of Ile-Ife, later Obafemi Awolowo University (or 'OAU'). Ogunleye will be familiar to readers of *African Theatre* from her examination of Ife Convocation Plays in *Playwrights and Politics* (2001), and in her contribution here she returns to what was happening before those plays. She examines the impact of Ola Rotimi through his work on the Ile-Ife campus starting by picking up on early productions, key appointments and the determination of the university's vice-chancellor that 'town and gown' should find a meeting place in the playhouse. Ogunleye has taken the title of her essay from a somewhat dismissive description of Ori Olokun Players as 'enthusiastic amateurs' that clearly rankled with Rotimi. She is particularly helpful on the subtleties of contracts and on levels of remuneration – issues that profoundly affect the operation of all theatre companies but that are particularly pertinent in those African contexts where 'traditional' accomplishments are often undervalued. For Rotimi's purposes, and for many other African directors, 'passes at Cambridge' were much less important than mastery of drum rhythms or lyrical conventions. Ogunleye's paper includes an account of the careers of members of Ori Olokun after the company ceased to exist. She shows that some members of the company were absorbed into academia while others became involved in local video production, and that yet others moved away entirely from the 'drama sector'. By close scrutiny of a small group, Ogunleye manages to draw attention to major shifts in the options open to creative Nigerians through participation in theatrical productions.

In providing a brief history of the Jos Repertory Theatre, founded in 1997, Victor S. Dugga and Patrick-Jude Oteh begin far from Ibadan and Ile-Ife. However, the long shadow of Ibadan, especially the effect of the academic drama programme offered to undergraduates there, is clearly seen. Oteh earned a BA from the University of Ibadan, but, to run a theatre company in 'the real world', he had to supplement academic knowledge with many quickly acquired skills. The success of the festivals organised by Jos Repertory Theatre in recent years has shown how well he has learned, and what a contribution the company is making to the theatre scene in Nigeria. Significantly, the paper on the Jos Repertory Theatre is entitled 'Creativity and Collaboration', and this speaks volumes about the impact of 'outside' financial backing on a struggling African theatre group. Some observers are rightly sensitive of the way support from Europe and America is affecting the operation of African theatre companies; outsiders are determining what 'scripts' are selected, and where they performed. This influence must be kept under constant observation.

The playscript, that is a regular feature of *African Theatre*, comes in this instance from Jos and is fittingly a collaborative venture and one in which diverse hands may be detected. It employs a refreshingly fluid theatrical convention in presenting a view of the history of Nigeria since 1960.

Other articles in this volume grapple with issues of creativity and collaboration through examinations of the way companies operate. The coverage takes in Tanzania, Mozambique, Lesotho, Eritrea and South Africa before ending with Ghana. In the case of Tanzania, the article is accompanied by a scenario in which, in addition to her account of how the Muungano Cultural troupe evolved and how it survives by 'entertaining the urban masses of Dar-es-Salaam', Siri Lange provides the synopsis for a performance. Included here is both the original Swahili version and Lange's English translation. Manfred Loimeier does not provide a script of *Os bandoleiros de Schiller* (a translation, transposition and adaptation of Schiller's *The Robbers*) which was created in Mozambique and then presented, in Portuguese, in German-speaking Europe as part of a programme to mark the 200th anniversary of Schiller's death. However, his account of the process by which the production emerged in Mozambique is presented almost like a play, with the cast 'performing' in scenes set on different continents.

Lucy Richardson's contribution on Project Phakama takes forward the coverage of that organisation's work that was included in *African Theatre: Youth*

(2006). From it, readers have an opportunity to understand how Phakama's distinctively democratic approach bore fruit in a remarkable production prepared and presented in Lesotho during 2004. Like Lucy Richardson, Christine Matzke is familiar to readers of *African Theatre* and her scholarly account of nearly fifteen years of the Asmara Theatre Association follows on from her contribution about women performers in the Eritrean capital that appeared in *African Theatre: Women* (2002). In this case, she draws on numerous interviews to provide a sense of the interaction between politics and theatre in Eritrea and Ethiopia. Theatre and politics play in and out of one another's shadows, until open conflict between the two countries means that artists are called to the front lines. At that point, any drama that survives becomes quite openly part of the struggle.

Basil Jones begins his article on the Handspring Puppets with the following words: 'The longevity of any theatre company is dependant on two essential ingredients: continued artistic inspiration backed up by firm and flexible funding.' This immediately picks up notes sounded elsewhere in this volume and he goes on to contribute an account that fits in with the interest in 'creativity and collaboration' developed earlier in the volume. In his account, South Africa meets Mali thanks partly to financial support from those who profit from the veins of gold that are threaded through the continent and that know no national boundaries. However, even in this case the support of several funding organisations, including European and North American cultural bodies, has been essential and is acknowledged. When Jones refers to 'flexible funding' he does not just mean a small financial reserve to cover 'The theatre's little surprises' that can be found in some budgets! During 2007, London theatre-goers were delighted and moved by the skills Handspring had developed and that they were able to see in *War Horse* presented by the National Theatre. The 'purchase' of theatrical technology honed in South Africa by a London theatre continued centuries of 'cultural exchange'.

The contribution by Michael Walling began life in a modern literary form: a blog. In it he recorded the week by week process by which a production, another collaborative one and this time involving an Anglo-Ghanaian project, began to come together. Like Lyndersay's contribution, it is personal and immediate, bringing alive the conditions under which theatre can come into being and take thinking about creativity and collaboration forward. The 'story' continued after the entries archived here. The Ghanaian team members made a huge contribution to a successful production; 'collaboration' continued after the run as Dzifa Glikpoe of the National Theatre in Accra was able to travel around the UK observing and training theatre groups. She left impressed by the professionalism of British actors only to be met on her return by one of the legacies of Ghana's year of celebrations: Myjoyonline for 28 March shouted 'Ghana @50 Secretariat fails to pay actors after anniversary performances.' The position of the actors, some of the directors, and whole theatre groups was made worse by the fact that the commissioning body, the Ghana@50 Secretariat, had closed down.

The editorial team of *African Theatre*, now strengthened by the addition of Dr Yvette Hutchinson, has been constantly aware of obligations to make the titles in the series available to the journal's 'prime constituency': those involved in studying and making theatre in Africa. The first months of 2007 saw a shift away from collaborating with Book Aid International as far as distribution to African institutions was concerned and the inauguration of a scheme operated by the Leeds University Centre for African Studies that strives to ensure that copies reach the most relevant shelves in the most suitable African libraries. We are keen to hear from readers in Africa about the effectiveness of the new system of distribution. In the meantime, as is announced after the Notes on Contributors, a wonderful example of sharing material has been set by Martin Banham who has placed his collection of unpublished African play-scripts with the Brotherton Library at University of Leeds.

James Gibbs

• • •

Note from the Publishers

James Currey Publishers have now joined Boydell & Brewer Ltd. *African Theatre* will continue to be published as an annual volume under the James Currey imprint. North and South American distribution will be available from The University of Rochester Press, 68 Mount Hope Avenue, Rochester, NY 14620-2731, USA, while UK and International distribution will be handled by Boydell & Brewer Ltd., PO Box 9, Woodbridge IP12 3DF, UK.

Unibadan Masques 1974–6
A Memoir of the First Two Years
Department of Theatre Arts Performing Company

K.W. DEXTER LYNDERSAY

Aspirations

> Dr J.A. Adedeji, Acting Head of Department [of Theatre Arts, into which the old School of Drama had evolved] and Dexter Lyndersay, Unibadan Masques' Project Director, have stated that the new Company 'should reflect the African personality – in tradition, in present-day life and in aspiration for the future. It is a Company of dedicated artists in acting, dance, music and stage-crafts who will present a variety of African concerns under different guises, i.e., a group of Masqueraders entertaining in the most complete way possible – to encourage thinking and celebration in performers and audience – together.'
>
> Quoted in University of Ibadan *Alumni Newsletter* , Vol. 1, No. 3, June 1975

There was no doubt that the University of Ibadan administration had high hopes for the success of our new acting company, for which, in its 1974–75 budget, it had voted Naira 6,000 to the Department of Theatre Arts. There was no doubt that the Arts theatregoers, drawn mainly from the campus population, were in a high state of attendance approval – we had enjoyed enthusiastic sold out houses (305 seats) from the start.

The university's *Alumni Newsletter* was cheering us on, in a half-column piece that began with the news that *Unibadan Masques* had been 'launched in November 1974 – providing an average of one production per month ...' and offered an appropriate highlight in the fact that our opening production, *Diagnosis,* had been written by a University of Ibadan (hereafter 'Unibadan') registry administrator, Emmanuel Enemute Avbiorokoma (Alumnus '59).

Under the *Unibadan Masques* logo, we had also presented an evening of performance and demonstration, titled *Three Dances of a Man & A Dance Workshop Creation*, devised by the African-American dancer and choreographer, Orville Johnson. This offering was a showcase for Mr Johnson, who not only presented three items, to recorded music, from his own solo repertoire, but showed the Arts Theatre audience how a professional non-Nigerian choreographer could work with Nigerian dancers (selected from our Theatre Arts students), using dance movements that he had seen them perform in a week-long workshop, and have them show their talent, entertainingly, in a new, refreshing way.

From the Unibadan Masques point of view, we were very pleased with the initial audience responses to what we considered to be: (a) our stated intentions for the company, (b) our encouragement of new, indigenous writing (Avbiorokoma) and (c) our introduction of an international dimension (Johnson) to our department's teaching. We were looking forward to our next presentation.

Before I accepted the project directorship of the company, I had read a typed copy of Femi Osofisan's novel *Kolera Kolej*, then awaiting publication, and I did not wait long to get his permission to adapt it for the very first large-scale offering from Unibadan Masques. I often remember the several meetings of Femi, Kole Omotoso, Biodun Jeyifo and myself in my Theatre Arts office, as I read aloud from my scribbles over the previous hours. We laughed a lot and each laugh was a vote of confidence in our decision to 'World Premiere' *Kolera Kolej* at the Arts Theatre, to give a further fillip to the new company.

Chief Wale Ogunyemi – From the files of Unibadan Masques 1975

WALE OGUNYEMI was born in Igbajo, Western State, and was educated in Ibadan. He led an amateur drama group for two years up to 1964, participating as well in productions of Players of the Dawn [a thriving Ibadan Town company] and Wole Soyinka's *1960 MASKS* [in honour of which, *Unibadan Masques* was named]. He was an employee of the Nigerian Television Service (now NBC/TV) in Lagos when he became one of the founders of *THEATRE EXPRESS*, a group of out-standing performers.

From 1963, Wale Ogunyemi has been associated with the Department of Theatre Arts, first as a member of Dance-Drama Workshops and then in 1968 as a foundation member of the then School of Drama Acting Company for which he wrote the majority of the plays. He is one of Nigeria's most prolific playwrights, having written over twenty plays for television (some adapted for the stage) and several full-length plays, among which are *KIRIJI*, *IJAYE WAR* and *LANGBODO*, the Department's National Festival Play for 1974. A skilful actor of many parts, he is best remembered for his creation of Dende, the oba's fool, in Wole Soyinka's *KONGI'S HARVEST*, a role he has played in three different stage productions and the Calpenny (Nigeria) film. Wale Ogunyemi is involved in research on the staff of the Institute of African Studies, University of Ibadan, and he is the Deputy Project Director of *UNIBADAN MASQUES*, the Performing Company of the Department of Theatre Arts.

Wale Ogunyemi died 18 December 2001, see:
http://www.guardian.co.uk/obituaries/story/0,3604,649747,00.html

Great luck came our way when we discovered that Wale Ogunyemi was available to be our deputy project director. He had no competition for the position, from anywhere. For many months, we had worked together; he as writer-director of his own plays, with Dapo Adelugba, Director of the School of Drama Acting Company, and myself, among others, as readers, audience and/or critics, over Wale's several plays about the Yoruba deities. Wale and I reached a new level of mutual interest with his script for *Aare Akogun*, which began as a student exercise in one of my classes (maybe something to do with script organization) where I suggested that each student write a version of Shakespeare's *Macbeth*, as if the events had occurred within a royal Nigerian context (the student-writer to choose the context), rather than in Scotland.

Privately, I had asked Wale to have a go at the task and he came up with *Aare Akogun* in Yoruba and English. He provided a printed translation of the Yoruba words into English – especially for the Witches' chants which he had culled from his day-job research at the Unibadan Institute of African Studies. Wale's *Aare Akogun*, directed by me, was, to some, an interesting exercise, to others, including myself, a moving experience. Its success moved me, later, to a *Macbeth* production at Calabar University, where only the Witches behaved according to Efik, Annang or Ibibio lore, while Shakespeare's words were mostly retained intact, or tweaked a bit, to serve an important point of the production, which was to reveal the long-hidden reason for the Witches' extremely wicked behaviour. It was demonstrated, as it had been before, in *Aare Akogun*, that the play's Weird Sisters, simply, vastly and irresistibly, enjoyed being evil and were, in a daring twist, a bad influence on Lady Macbeth, who, both Ibadan and Calabar students agreed, could never speak to her husband as she did, without the strongest supernatural support. In 1975 Ibadan, Wale Ogunyemi, Femi Osofisan and I (with a substantial cheering section in the wings) were preparing Femi's *Kolera Kolej* for Unibadan Masques. We were aware that we were not solely in the entertainment business; that we had a serious obligation (foremost in whatever the company embarked upon) to our students. We also had an obligation to the profession of theatre; to contribute to the development of existing forms and to encourage new creative talent in all facets of dramatic presentation.

The Unibadan Masques logo

Our logo design was the result of a challenge to the Department of Theatre Arts Design students, two of whom, Egie Iyamu and Charles Oguejiofor, were requested to merge their individual designs for the latter to complete. Lola George provided the lettering.

Advertisers' support for Unibadan Masques

We inherited the support that advertisers had long given to the Arts Theatre producers, to productions of the School of Drama and to other campus theatre practitioners. For programme advertisements, if not paid for in cash, advertisers donated materials in the required quantities, as stocks permitted, or provided services, such as 'Sameday Cleaners' generously washing or dry-cleaning all costumes used in Arts Theatre productions. Without such positive and loyal support, our expenses might have defeated many an exciting theatrical idea. Our thanks remain constant, in retrospect, to I. Mudah & Co. Ltd; Kaduna Textiles Ltd; C. Zard & Co. Ltd; FAO (Textiles); Askar of Nigeria Ltd (Paint); J. A. Odutola Plastic Foam Co. Ltd; Bata Shoes; Wiggins Teape (WA) Ltd; NIPOL Ltd (Polythene Film Bags); Bagauda Textile Mills Ltd; Great Northern Tanning Co. Ltd; Kingsway Stores and our Printers, Ibadan University Press.

Femi Osofisan's *Kolera Kolej* – with a cast of 43 and a dog

For the cast, we had no need to look beyond the university campus and Ibadan town. It was clear that we already had the Poet character in Femi Osofisan himself. He thought it would be wise for him to have an understudy and a promising theatre arts student, Demola Adeyemi, who was already cast in two roles which would not conflict logistically, took on this task.

The script called for a prologue and for the cast to demonstrate the unsuspected, hilarious aspect of the 'Kolera' disease. Symptoms were both vomiting and diarrhoea. The cast circled, exaggeratedly, alternately doubling forward and straightening up with arms-flung-wide. The duration time of this prologue was around three minutes, the maximum that an audience could be expected to tolerate.

Comic masks, which greatly facilitated the playing of more than one role by a performer, were designed by Dani Lyndersay to match her costumes and we had our trusty stage carpenters, Ezekiel Agboola and James Oluyede, construct a multi-purpose scenic unit that could be changed by cast members in full stage-lighting, from a level about 9 inches above the stage to a desk with folding legs to a two-seater living-room settee, upon which two back- and two seat-cushions could be placed, and then be reset to any shape required. [Note: Our stage carpenters also had their acting debuts, as part of the Kolera Kolej 'hockey team' of thugs, with sticks they had fashioned in their workshop.]

The story of Femi Osofisan's novel remained intact in the play and the Arts Theatre stage 'became' Kolera Kolej, a new country, mainly by reason of the dire risk to the life of anyone in contact via the campus borders that the 'Mother Country,' say, Nigeria, had hastily established, in order to isolate the new citizens' deadly disease and to prevent any spread of the infection.

The core of the satire is in the political conflicts that arise when the citizens decide that they need to hold elections to select a head of state for Kolera Kolej, a ruler who would naturally be titled 'Vice-Chancellor.' The resulting chaos is resisted mainly by the Poet and his friend, a kindred spirit, the female activist, Oyinlola. [Note: During one argument between the Poet and Oyinlola, she has to spit into his face. The performers of Unibadan Masques (and, later, of Calabar University Theatre) fully acknowledged the difficulty of faking this character-defining action at down-stage-centre, and dutifully carried it out, at every performance, so that the audience clearly saw the missile fly.] Our Musical Director, Tunji Oyelana, made significant contributions: with Bola Kehinde for the prologue drumming; his leadership of the *bata* band; his singing and guitar for the calypso; his acting as the Minister of Information; his music for the Kolera Kolej National Anthem and for Femi Osofisan's song, 'Goodnight Fatherland.' [Note: Thanks to Amorelle Inanga, music teacher of the Unibadan International School, and John Gillespie, principal of the school (and an excellent Arts Theatre Production Group actor), over a dozen young singers were chosen to record an arrangement of 'Goodnight Fatherland'.]

A new recruit to the company, Bose Ayeni, harshly called everyone to attention when she became the (Prison) Camp Attendant, near the end of the play, having relaxed us, before her sharp commands, with her seductive choreography for the Banquet Dancers. [Note: The performer who played the key role of Alhaji Dr Paramole was a mystery to me. I had never consciously seen him before he turned up at the audition, got the part, executed it with style and went away, never to be seen by me again. On request, he said his name was 'Sasraku Dupong' and that name is in the programme.] Whisper, the dog, was kindly lent to us by a campus supporter and, I believe he was allowed to keep the name in life, subsequent to the play. We thanked Michael Echeruo, for use of the untitled 1964 etching by Kevin Echeruo (1947–1969) that enhanced the poster and programme cover.

Ed Bullins' *A Son Come Home* and 'Poetry and prose of Black America'

Our efforts were becoming better known. Probably at the insistence of Professor Echeruo, Chairman of the Unibadan English Department, I was invited by the American Embassy in Lagos (USIS, the United States Information Service, incidentally, the agency that had administered my four-year Fulbright scholarship from Trinidad in 1961) to participate in what was then called the Afro-American History Week Commemoration of February, 1975, at the Whitney M. Young, Jr Library in Yaba. I was told that I could bring along whomever I wanted for the participation.

Without much time to prepare, we found a copy of *A Son Come Home,* a one-act play by African-American Ed Bullins, and a cast that included a one-off performance by a talented young man named Mofe Doyle who had an authentic American accent. There were two Theatre Arts students, Yemi Sonuga and Tolu Ighodalo, who could be coached for the needed speech music, and a young lady, Peju Oworu, an American-accented volunteer.

For other literature, I compiled poems and prose by African-Americans, to be read by my performance colleagues and myself with some traditional blues lyrics that I dared to sing (jazz fan that I had been for many years). We were invited to repeat the performance at the American consulate in Ibadan.

Meanwhile, Kole Omotoso, who had been invited by the USIS to the Commemoration at Yaba (Orville Johnson was also billed to perform), had brought us a new one-act play, *The Curse,* which was perfect for a Unibadan Masques presentation, along with *A Son Come Home,* ready, and on 'stand-by', from the USIS effort.

Ed Bullins' *A Son Come Home* showed an African-American mother (Oworu) and son (Sonuga) who, on his return home from a long time away, reminisced about years gone by, while the son's earlier self (Doyle) and his then girlfriend (Ighodalo) interspersed their long-ago conversations with that of the mother and son in the present. Each pair had its own stage space, but lines of movement inevitably crossed as the two timelines related to each other in theatrical continuity. [Note: I had met Mr Bullins at the 1969 Pan-African Arts Festival in Algiers. During an intermission of Kola Ogunmola's *The Palm-Wine Drinkard*, we had chatted about the differences and similarities of African Theatre (Ogunmola and 'Yoruba Opera,' then his only reference) and that of the African Diaspora (in our case, 'Black' American Theatre and the Theatre of Trinidad & Tobago).]

Kole Omotoso's *The Golden Curse*

Kole Omotoso's *The Curse,* described by the author as a 'Fantasy-Parable,' eventually became *The Golden Curse,* because, I confess, I couldn't resist the instant conflict (risking one with the playwright) in the latter oxymoronic title, which fitted, perfectly, the character of wealthy Chief Alagba, as played by Wale Ogunyemi, with an untypical, villainous mien.

For the role of the servant, Moyegun, we welcomed back to Ibadan the enormously varied talent of Jimi Şolanke, who, when we were inaugurated, had been committed to Ola Rotimi's famous Ori Olokun Theatre at the University of Ife. (See article by Foluke Ogunleye in this volume). Jimi had almost as long a history of Ibadan Theatre activity as Wale Ogunyemi and I have no doubt that Wale's presence with us was a strong factor in Jimi's decision to join us. [Note: Had Jimi been available to play Alhaji Dr Paramole in *Kolera Kolej*, we might have not have had the brief spark of 'Sasraku Dupong,' – from my note above.]

Jimi and Theatre Arts student Terwase Avakaa verbally tore each other apart as they electrified the Arts Theatre air with Kole Omotoso's back-and-forth streams of insults and oaths and curses, as shouted at each other by his caged characters; Moyegun, jealous of the chief's apparent favouring of Gbolaro (Avakaa), who was fearful of Moyegun's strength and cleverness, as the Chief had confided that fear to him, playing one against the other.

At the time the play began, both were angry with Chief Alagba, their master, who had tricked them into the rolling cages and locked them in. The play ended with an enactment of 'rough justice' as the circle of the 'Golden Curse' of overflowing personal affluence went from Chief Alagba to Moyegun – on its way around.

Alan Marmion, our business manager in 1974–75, had successfully applied UK-trained promotion techniques to our advertising, and he designed the Poster/Programme Cover for *The Golden Curse & A Son Come Home*, a one-act play by Ed Bullins.

1. *The Golden Curse, written by Kole Omotoso, directed by Dexter Lyndersay, rolling cages designed by Kole Omotoso; left to right Terwase Avakaa (Gbolaro), Wale Ogunyemi (Chief Alagba), Jimi Solanke (Moyegun)*

(© All photographs in this chapter courtesy Estate of Dexter Lyndersay)

Wale Ogunyemi's *The Divorce*

Our season-closing production was Wale Ogunyemi's *The Divorce* and he was to direct it. For an appropriate welcome, the atmosphere in the Arts Theatre became light; the rainy-season breezes seemed to take full advantage of the louvered side walls, as the audience was washed by their flow and, on stage, by the furious French-style farce, complete with rapid movement in and out of slammable doors, up and down the stairs of a middle-class urban dwelling (designed by Sunbo Marinho) where Jimi Solanke and newcomer Golda Tina John played Sanmi and Tayo Ajao whose marital relationship matched the con-stantly-changing physical movement around them. [Note on *The Divorce* and Wale Ogunyemi, from the files of Unibadan Masques: '… Although most of his plays are full of fun and a fine sense of humour, *The Divorce* is his first attempt at a full-length work of broad farce and is a fitting choice to close our first Theatre Season.']

The Divorce was revived for the 1975–76 season. In addition to his creation of the farce-accommodating two-storey set, the stage lighting was designed by Sunbo Marinho, a School of Drama diploma graduate, with a very high grade in my Course in Technical Theatre, who had become a good friend. [Note: Sunbo (now Dr O. Marinho,) has never rescinded his plaint that he became inebriated, for the first and only time in his life, after eating one cubic inch (all I could spare) of my mother's rum-soaked Christmas 'black' cake, sent to me from her home in Trinidad in the year that he turned up in my class to begin a long working collaboration.]

Kole Omotoso's *The Golden Curse* (revived) and Tewfik Al-Hakim's *Not a Thing Out of Place*

Other commitments of the performers in *A Son Come Home* caused us to seek another companion for *The Golden Curse* in what had proved to be a popular format for us: the 'double-bill.' It was Kole Omotoso, from his experience as Lecturer in Modern Arabic Literature in the Unibadan Department of Arabic and Islamic Studies, who introduced us to the famous Egyptian playwright, Tewfik Al-Hakim, and his one-act play, *Not a Thing Out of Place*. Again, here was a perfect match for Kole's play during its revival in the 1975–76 Theatre Season of Unibadan Masques.

Not a Thing Out of Place is a gentle comedy about a hapless barber trying to survive life's challenges. Like its chief protagonist, the play itself survived a run with *The Golden Curse* in 1975. The production was greatly enhanced by the use, before and after the performance, of the recorded music of Fred Elias, as played by The Fuad Hassan Ensemble under the title of *Music of the Bedouin Bandits,* plus the onstage music of Demola Onibon-Okuta's flute and Bisi Adeleke's dun-dun, as they walked among the market villagers.

2. The Child Factor, *written and directed by Emmanuel Avbiorokoma; left to right: Irene Orubo (Caroline), Dupe Soriyan (Anna), Tony Effah (Okarode – a medicine man)*

Jimi Solanke and Wale Ogunyemi's *Day of Deities*

Jimi Solanke's return to work with us in Ibadan facilitated a long-missed partnership between him and Wale Ogunyemi. The two got together at the first
opportunity and constructed a story of Yoruba deities and humans that offered
several opportunities for dance and music, and, of course, superb acting, by,
among others, Jimi and the gifted actor-singer-flautist-drummer-painter-
sculptor, Ademola Onibon-Okuta, who also provided single drawings of the
Deities for the poster and programme-cover, designed by Roy H. Parker.

On stage, the deities were called upon, by villagers of a morally-plagued
town. The cast list included:

> Ogun, god of war and farm implements (Segun Bankole);
> Obatala, the creator god (Olumide Bakare);
> Orunmila, god of divination (Tunji Oyelana);
> Egungun, ancestral spirit (Tony Effah);
> Osun, goddess of the sea (Jumoke Akinola);
> Sango, god of thunder and lightning (Ademola Onibon-Okuta).

With the assistance of the singer/priest (Jimi Ṣolanke), the gods gathered and
restored order. The dance-drama was directed by Wale Ogunyemi.

Emmanuel Avbiorokoma's *The Child Factor*

Returning to Unibadan Masques for the first time since his play, *Diagnosis*, had
helped to launch us in November 1974, Emmanuel Avbiorokoma, previously
writer-director of the Warri Theatre Group in what was then the Mid-west
State, directed his *The Child Factor* for us in April, 1975. The play focused on a
childless wife and on village reactions to her barrenness. The story provided a
domestic balance in our production output and fully engaged even the most
sophisticated in the audience.

Jean Genet's *The Blacks* (1975)

The only production of Jean Genet's *The Blacks* that I ever saw, before the one
I directed at Unibadan, was at the St. Mark's Playhouse in New York during
1962. I was thrilled by it. I especially remember Louis Gossett Jr. as Village and,
when I was rehearsing Jimi Solanke in the role for the *Unibadan Masques*
production in 1975, I observed myself consciously trying to shape Jimi's performance so that I would feel the same thrill that the American actor had
caused by his 1962 portrayal of Village. I got the thrill, because Jimi Solanke is
at least as dynamic a performer as Louis Gossett Jr and because, given the same
play, with a great actor and with supporting performers of the quality of Sonny
Oti playing Diouf the elements that had been put in place by the playwright
would work their theatrical magic.

I know that I used a lot more research material in *The Blacks* than the New York production had. There were so many layers to that play, that went unseen or were ignored at the St. Mark's Playhouse, that I don't wonder why I best remember that performance of Village (as, I must also recall, boosted by 'straight-man' Diouf, played to perfection by Godfrey Cambridge, behind a white female mask).

First, a thorough perusal of the clues in Genet's stage directions indicated that *The Blacks* was a 'Clown Show' within the play, staged by the 'native' actors of an African country, that was being ruled by an European administration. The 'Clown Show' was devised as a distraction for their highest-ranking European audience, so that they would not stray, for any reason, from the theatre (spellbound as they would be, in superior awe) and not be free to stumble upon and interfere with a nearby meeting of revolutionary Black citizens, sorting out an internal matter – the trial of one of their members as a traitor. The character named Newport News would be the courier between the Colonial Theatre and the revolutionaries' activity. If that entire political context was present at St Marks, I apologize for missing it.

More, the 'Clown Show' was based on the events of Mozart's *Requiem,* from which the '*Dies Irae*' featured prominently in Genet's script (and in our Ibadan performances, by courtesy of Bob Armstrong, Institute of African Studies, University of Ibadan). It was not used at St Marks.

We took Genet's advice (as did St Marks) for maintaining the colonial revolutionary context, in that, for every performance, we managed to seat Caucasian expatriates in the front row, thereby avoiding his other advice about non-whites in the audience wearing white masks.

White masks were crucial to the 'Clown Show' – for the Queen, the Governor-General, the Judge, the Bishop and the Valet. These were designed, with her usual flair, by Dani Lyndersay, as were the dolls that were displayed onstage. They, according to another Genet direction, were inanimate replicas of both the white-masked onstage colonial officials and the imagined mocked ones, sitting in the theatre audience. A new talent was displayed in an exciting programme cover and poster designed by Folake Shoga. Joel Adedeji remarked to me, during one intermission: 'This is the best one yet!' In theatre, the best one is usually the current one, and so we carried on.

John Kani, Athol Fugard and Winston Ntshona's *Sizwe Banzi is Dead*

Biodun Jeyifo, who had been fully involved, with Kole Omotoso and Femi Osofisan, in the birth of *Unibadan Masques*, directed *Sizwe Banzi is Dead,* the South African play that was an indictment of apartheid. Jimi Şolanke played the photographer Styles as well as the activist Buntu, both originally created by John Kani, while Wale Ogunyemi took the Winston Ntshona role as the comparatively passive Sizwe Banzi, whose official pass-book identity was changed after a nasty alley encounter in Johannesburg. They were both magnificent, as

3. The Blacks, *written by Jean Genet, directed by Dexter Lyndersay. Left to right: Jimi Solanke (Village); Lanre Thomas (Diouf); Diouf's Wig made by Ally Bedford*

4. The Blacks, *written by Jean Genet, direction and scenery by Dexter Lyndersay, stage lighting by Sunbo Marinho. Left to right: Olumide Bakare (Newport News); Jonathan Shibi (Revolutionary Guard); Colonial Dolls [designed & made by Ally Bedford]; Floor: Femi Osofisan (Archibald, Master of Ceremonies); Jimi Solanke (Village); Platform: Lola Ijeboi (Bobo); Bose Ayeni (Snow); Kiki Onyejekwe (Virtue); Balcony: Wale Ogunyemi (The Governor General); Zack Amata (The Valet); Esohe Omoregie (The Queen); Ikem Emodi (The Missionary); Tony Effah (The Judge). [Costumes and Masks by Dani Lyndersay]*

was Sunbo Marinho, deftly stroking an old Strand dimmer-board for best lighting – the most dramatic when Styles suddenly became a still-life photograph of himself; heralding Buntu.

I remember clearly, mainly from students in my classes, that this play was an eye-opener for many students at Ibadan.

Samson Amali's *Onugbo mlOkō*

Bob Armstrong had done extensive research into the Idoma people of what was then Benue-Plateau State, and Samson Amali, an Idoma student, had written a play which Bob asked me to look at. I read it and imagined it only as a dance-drama, for which more research would be required. We needed costume information, dance movement, and specific drumming accents in addition to Bob's good, collected recordings.

It was decided that the production would be a joint presentation of Unibadan Masques and the Institute of African Studies. A research trip was organized to Benue-Plateau State, where Dani Lyndersay took costume notes and photographs, I recorded some drumming and we shot lots more photographs. At some point, Ghanaian choreographer, Odukwe Sackeyfio, had been included in the research for the dance element, and he took notes.

Bob Armstrong arranged for our use of the Institute of African Studies courtyard, for which, I had earlier designed (and the excellent Theatre Arts carpenters, Ezekiel Agboola and James Oluyede, had built) some collapsible, portable bleacher units. These had been set up several times before and were stored under shelter on the premises.

Meanwhile, the usual auditions and rehearsals took place, the costume designs were finalized and fitted to the successful auditioners. Arrangements were made, by the Institute of African Studies, for stilt-dancers (with their costumes and masks) to be hired from Idomaland for the performance. When all was ready, the bleacher units were brought out and assembled on the courtyard grass by Ezekiel and James. A few days before opening night, the stage lighting and sound equipment were installed. We all prayed there would be no rain. Our prayers were answered.

Onugbo mlOkō was mainly a re-enactment of a village inquest into the death of Okō (Akoduye Bob-Manuel), junior brother of Onugbo (Ozuloke Adigwe), the brothers being the two top hunters of the village who were also close friends. 'It was said of them, 'if Onugbo did not see Okō he would not go. If Okō did not see Onugbo, his brother, he would not go.' But Okō, the younger brother, was more patient and gradually became a better hunter than his older brother.

When Okō was killed in a hunting accident, an inquest was convened by the village Elders, during which our audience followed the story as it unfolded. The precise deliberations of the Elders were heard over a background of authentic inquest music, recorded by Bob Armstrong at the royal enclosure of the King of Akpa, Otukpo. The verbal drama was greatly intensified by the appearance of Okō's ghost (covered from head to toe with calamine lotion) who could be seen only by Onugbo and the audience.

Sunbo Marinho and I designed the lighting for the performance, and Dani Lyndersay did the costume designs. These included animal masks, based on contemporary patterns of the Odomu (hyena) masquerade of Idomaland and were practical reproductions of the traditional masks, sculpture and artefacts found in photographs from various sources. Wherever possible, original masquerade costume materials were used, rather than the synthetic materials that had replaced them.

One of the Unibadan staff who was a dependable artist for Theatre Posters and Programme Covers was entomologist Roy H. Parker. For Avbiorokoma's *The Child Factor* (on the subject of barrenness), Roy had chilled us with his scary drawing of a non-existent child, being just out-of-reach of its silhouetted mother and father. He had also organized Ademola Onibon-Okuta's Yoruba Deity drawings for Şolanke and Ogunyemi's *Day of Deities*. For the hunting background of *Onugbo mlOkō,* he had rendered a wildlife-filled grassy plain, with close-ups of the two hunters, a kill and the white horse that was featured in the legend, and for which we had recorded *Aja* drumming at Utukpo to represent its thundering presence. [Note: I regret that I could not reciprocate Roy's favours to us by taking up the offered lead role in his planned production of *Blacula,* a stage version of the 1972 William Marshall horror-classic film.]

Femi Osofisan's *The Chattering and the Song*

The poet in Femi Osofisan came fully to the fore in his play *The Chattering and the Song,* which he directed, choreographed and composed for *Unibadan Masques* in March, 1976. In that play, where, even in dialogue that is sometimes allowed to be mundane for reasons of 'naturalness,' there was a rhythm that kept the words floating into my ear. They resonated there, while, visually, the fluidity of the movement, that took the performers from one spot on stage to another, joined up with the words in my head to hold my full attention.

I had designed the functional parts of the scenery, but the main complement to Femi's many rhythms was a backdrop by Moyo Ogundipe for the late-1880s play-within-the play. He had also provided an evocative drawing for the poster and programme cover.

It was a remarkable experience to watch what I have referred to earlier in this account as 'an obligation to the profession of theatre' that was owed by Unibadan Masques, being settled, handsomely, by the delicately interwoven forays into totally new areas of Nigerian theatre performance in *The Chattering and the Song;* ventures that, I am sure, would have fascinated an audience of international theatre practitioners.

The performers were vibrant instruments in Femi's orchestration. Jimi Şolanke in the lead as Sontri, in whose garden and storeroom, the events took place. Didi Unu Odigie (Ijayin); Femi Osofisan himself as Mokan; Irene Orubo (Funlola); Bose Ayeni (Bisi); Temitayo Taiwo (Yetunde) and Demola

Adeyemi (Leje) – all performed the play's intrinsic choreography and its intricate speech patterns with style and grace and lithe energy. Their full-view change, to other characters and costumes, for the 'flashback' scene in the late-1880s Court of the Alafin of Oyo, was seamless.

Recurring, in chorus, was a suppliant phrase, 'Iwori otura,' 'Iwori otura,' about which Yoruba words (not, as I remember, ever translated for me) my current research has suggested that, if a translation into English were attempted, it could reveal that the play's characters were seeking supernatural aid to achieve a human, and countrywide, approximation to a divine 'perfect balance'. If so, their intense, insistent entreaty, for such a spiritual condition of equilibrium, appeared to be bountifully granted, not only to the play's characters, but also to Femi Osofisan, his carefully-written play and his deft presentation of it; all crude 'chattering' having been efficiently sifted and separated away from the graceful 'song' – as the phrase was chanted, again and again, with gradually growing volume.

Conclusion

It has been an exhilarating experience, reliving those years now, conjuring up memories of events and of those talents who are still with us and those who are not. I am very happy to have been associated with Unibadan Masques for those first two years.

I learned very much over that period of time, during which I also benefited from the work of my predecessors at Unibadan, who had led similar university-oriented performing groups, beginning with Wole Soyinka and his 1960 Masks and Orisun Theatre, followed by the superb actor-director, Dapo Adelugba, who had led the School of Drama Acting Company.

My learning experience with Unibadan Masques was such that, later, I could make a convincing case, fully supported by the vice-chancellor, to the University of Calabar Senate for funding what I had termed in my proposal, a 'Teaching Support Unit,' which I had described, as often as necessary, verbally and in writing, as 'a living laboratory,' essential to our one-year-old Department of Theatre Arts.

From 1977–78, a group of performers (dancers, drummers and a seven-piece 'modern band') were hired as our Teaching Support Unit, performing regularly, with and without the participation of our academic staff and students, who had established a performance presence during the year before (in 1976–77, the University's first year of operation), as Calabar University Theatre (CUT).

Ori Olokun Theatre
& the Town & Gown Policy
'Enthusiastic amateurs, farmers, carpenters & school teachers'

FOLUKE OGUNLEYE

Introduction

The university at Ile-Ife, the cradle of Yoruba civilization and the centre of the Yoruba world, sprawls graciously among the hills outside the old town. A university is the epitome of modernization and global civilization, while Ile-Ife town is synonymous with a specific culture and an ancient tradition. The university, now 'Obafemi Awolowo University', started life at Ibadan in 1962 on the premises of Ibadan Polytechnic as the 'University College, Ife'. It became first the 'University of Ife,' and then, in May 1987, after the death of one of the founding fathers of the Nigerian nation, was given the name it now carries. Appropriately its motto is 'For Learning and Culture'.

When the university moved to Ile-Ife, it was welcomed by the locals. The Vice-Chancellor, Professor Hezekiah Oluwasanmi responded by instituting a 'town and gown' policy. In 1967, he set up and chaired a committee charged with '(fostering) a relationship with the local community and (with formulating) a policy governing that relationship' (Akinrinade 1989: 41). The policy was taken forward particularly energetically by the Institute of African Studies, a research body charged with investigating Nigerian cultures at the grassroots. Ola Rotimi, researcher, man of the theatre whose ideas are central to this chapter, provided an insight into the institute's approach. In the course of an interview with Adeniyi Coker, Rotimi recalled:

> I had travel grants, cassettes, and all sorts of equipment to go and record discussions with traditional priests. … we started looking at our past and felt we simply must redefine ourselves so we do not get merged in the general mainstream of another culture. (Rotimi 2003: 77)

It was partly in the context of this sort of search and this sort of thinking that Rotimi wrote the plays for which he is well known, including *The Gods Are Not To Blame* (1968), *Kurunmi* (1969), and *Ovonramwen Nogbaisi* (1972).

Duro Ladipo, leader of a renowned theatre company from Oṣogbo, was co-opted onto the vice-chancellor's committee and, through his connections, the

Palm Tree Hotel in Arubidi was rented establishing the university's presence right in the heart of Ile-Ife. The name of the building was derived from the symbol of the political party, the Action Group, whose headquarters it had been. In talking to Coker about the space, Rotimi referred to:

> … a courtyard, apparently for dancing, and a bandstand, which I thought could be used as some kind of proscenium stage while the raised centre area could be used for theater-in-the-round. The annex to this space had the guest rooms, and we thought when performing troupes came by they could stay for free, which again would be in consonance with the purpose of that place – to serve people and encourage artistic, theater, intellectual life between the University and the people. (ibid.: 78–9)

After securing the premises, Rotimi, 'Papa' Akinola Lasekan, a prominent artist, and Ladipo put their heads together to decide on a name. According to Rotimi,

> I said 'There is this University logo, which has the head of Olokun.' Lasekan said, 'Why don't we call it Olokun's head?' I said that was good. It sounded like Boar's Head from Elizabethan history. I said 'Why not just Ori Olokun? (ibid.: 80)

Ori Olokun Cultural Centre was formally opened on the 6th of June, 1968, and became a rallying point for art lovers, attracting local and international audiences.

The early days of Ori Olokun Centre

Michael Crowder, the first director, brought a particular vigour to the Institute of African Studies. He obtained research grants for all the fellows in the institute and sent them out into the field with a mandate to return with materials that could be presented on stage. This approach to the development of the arts culminated in annual (institute-organized) Festivals of Arts. According to artist and lecturer Agbo Folarin, Crowder was able to supplement the funds obtained from the university with money from the Ford Foundation and other donor agencies for this.

The first of the plays that grew out of Rotimi's research was *The Gods Are Not to Blame,* performed in December 1968 during the first of the arts festivals. The cast and crew on that occasion included staff and students from the university, and secondary school teachers who came with some of their students. In Kole Omotoso's somewhat dismissive terms they were 'enthusiastic amateurs … farmers or carpenters or school teachers' (1983). Margaret Oldfield, a graduate in drama and a lecturer in the English Department, helped with the diction, while Folarin, from the fine arts section of the institute, designed the set. Abiodun Adebona, of the faculty of science, acted as the business manager and the cast included Femi Robinson, a lecturer in the faculty of agriculture, and Olu Akomolafe, who later became a lecturer in the Department of Dramatic Arts. The play was well received by the town and gown audience, and this shot the Ori Olokun Centre into the limelight. Ori Olokun Theatre had begun to be recognized.

With sponsorship from the university, Rotimi was able to take *The Gods* on a week-long tour to Ghana at the beginning of 1969. They performed to enthusiastic audiences at the universities of Ghana and Cape Coast, and in public halls in Kumasi and Takoradi. Substantial work was undertaken in subsequent years and a firm international reputation established. In 1972, the Ori Olokun Theatre was selected to represent Africa at the Cultural Olympics at Munich. They took Adegoke Durojaye's allegorical, *Gbe'ku de,* a play that embodies the idea that, no matter how miserable human existence may be, man would still rather live than die. Despite this serious theme, *Gbe'ku de* was a strong piece of physical theatre, well suited to the Munich audiences.

In 1975, Professor Ojetunji Aboyade took over as vice-chancellor of the university and he spearheaded the dissolution of institutes, including the Institute of African Studies, replacing them with teaching departments. For example, the Department of Dramatic Arts was formed and was confronted by the need to absorb the Ori Olokun Players. Rotimi, who was appointed the head of the department, was called upon to design a syllabus and opted to start with a certificate course for professional theatre practitioners. It included specialist courses in theatre disciplines as well as in the practice and management of television, radio and film industries (Adebayo and Oloruntimehin 1989: 67). However, the university authorities felt a degree programme would be more appropriate, and Wole Ṣoyinka, already a professor in the Department of Comparative Literature on the campus was brought into the Department of Dramatic Arts. Although Rotimi eventually designed a degree programme, the control of the department was taken away from him. This inevitably created tension and meant periods of uncertainty for the core members of Ori Olokun Theatre whose status was not guaranteed by contracts.

In the establishment profile of the Department of Dramatic Arts approved by the university senate, Rotimi had proposed that the head of department should also head the theatre company. However, when Rotimi had to take a short leave of absence in 1976, he suggested to the vice-chancellor that the administration of the department could be split between two lecturers: Olu Akomolafe could head the academic section and Segun Akinbola the acting company. This created a precedent, which later produced a situation in which Rotimi was asked to lead the company while Ṣoyinka was put in charge of the academic section. Unhappy at this deviation from the senate-approved establishment, Rotimi quit the service of the University of Ife to take up a professorship at the University of Port Harcourt. He left behind men and women who had made a significant journey with him in Ori Olokun Theatre and it is now appropriate to look more closely at the conditions under which the company operated and at Rotimi's style of leadership.

Recruitment, retraining and rehearsals

At Crowder's suggestion, some actors with proficiency in, for example, music and fine arts had been employed for the Ori Olokun Centre in 1968. Others were taken on as research assistants, who, equipped with tape-recorders, traversed the rural areas of Yorubaland, recording traditional songs, chants and other cultural materials. Monthly wages for the artists ranged from £8 to £15, depending on the artist's proficiency or previous experience. Since the going salary for a school certificate holder in the civil service at that time was between eleven and thirteen pounds, the 'non-certificated' actors might have considered themselves quite well paid. They worked hard, and much was expected of them. According to Kola Oyewo, the working day fell into four parts: Peggy Harper took the first shift and rehearsed dance sequences with the artists between seven and nine o'clock in the morning. Akin Euba took them through music rehearsals between nine-thirty and noon. The artists would then break until five pm and during this time some of them supplemented their earnings as actors by creating tie-dye or 'adire' clothes' (Coker 2003.) Rotimi would take over in the evening and rehearse late into the night.

Rehearsals and workshops run by Rotimi were conducted in a style that has attracted criticism. For example, as soon as Rotimi entered the gallery which was situated just in front of the main auditorium, he would blow his whistle to announce his arrival and to start the rehearsal or workshop. Casts also became familiar with the sound of the whistle during rehearsals as Rotimi used it to call for a cut. Rotimi loved creating crowd scenes and he mastered the art of crowd control with techniques that might appeal to a football coach. Actor Jimi Şolanke recalls:

> Rotimi would direct a play of over fifty members of cast from the black-board by drawing on the board to tell actors and actresses where and when to position themselves on the stage. (Şolanke 2006: 5,7)

Because of this – and his whistle-blowing, Rotimi has sometimes been regarded as dictatorial in his approach. Reacting to this assertion, one of the Ori Olokun actors, Kola Oyewo, maintained that Rotimi's methods should be seen in context. Rotimi had, as Oyewo argued, to work with group that included rowdy greenhorns. In order to keep them in line, and to curb any tendency for overacting or being satisfied with mediocrity, he had to use dictatorial methods. To his credit, Rotimi was able to instil discipline into the artists. To quote Şolanke again: 'Through his workshops, [Rotimi] made playwrights out of teachers, traders, masons.'

Campus publicity for Ori Olokun performances was handled inventively and effectively. Colourful handbills and posters were printed, and each performer would be sent out, with his or her bus fare, to 'cover' a particular area of the campus. The publicity in town was even more impressive: in addition to pasting posters and distributing handbills, a bus-load of artistes would go round the town with one of them sitting on top of the bus. (Peter Fatomilola, dressed in palm fronds, was the favourite for this role.) They would all sing:

E wa wo ere Rotimi,	Come and watch Rotimi's play,
oni a dara,	today will be good,

Akuruyejo oko Oyinbo,	the short man, husband of the white woman,
oni a dara.	today will be good.

(Ogunleye, 2004)

This helped to draw many patrons to the Ori Olokun theatre.

This style of publicity was similar to that used by the Yoruba travelling theatre troupes as was the adoption of the tradition of touring. The touring circuit became a very important aspect of the programme of the Ori Olokun Players. After a play had been premiered at Ile-Ife, it would be taken to other parts of the country with performances in universities and other tertiary institutions, in town halls, hotels, palaces and cultural centres. Trips were, however, shorter than those made by the Yoruba travelling theatre troupes. The longest was undertaken in 1974, lasted three weeks, and took *The Gods* to Oṣogbo, Offa, Ilọrin, Kaduna, Zaria, Kano, Jos, Oturkpo, Nsukka, Port Harcourt, Benin and Ondo.

The tours involved extensive planning. An advance team, made up of the business manager and his assistants, would go ahead to secure performance venues and make arrangements for accommodation and food. They would then return to base and prepare posters that would be pasted up some two weeks before the performance. The technical crew, who had the use of a specially purchased Land Cruiser, also travelled to the venues in advance, setting out either on the day before a performance or very early on the day of the show depending on the distance from Ile-Ife. They set up the scenery and mounted the lights before the cast, who travelled in the company's Coaster bus, got there. When they arrived, the cast would 'walk through' the production and then rest before the performance. On tour, the cast and crew were generally well taken care of, but they had to rough it on occasions. Since it was heavily subsidized by the university, the tour did not have to make a profit and gate-fees were low, audiences large and responsive.

Rotimi realized the need to give formal training to his 'enthusiastic amateurs' and he designed an appropriate programme. When he left for Port Harcourt, some members of the company felt insecure, wondering whether they would be brushed aside as 'Rotimi's Boys'. Their fears were allayed when Ṣoyinka began to operate the Certificate Programme in Dramatic Arts, and they were all given the opportunity to enrol on that programme. Eleven of the Ori Olokun Players completed Certificates in Dramatic Arts.

In other respects, too, Ṣoyinka continued what Rotimi had started. After its premiere at Oduduwa Hall, the 1983 Convocation Play, *Requiem for a Futurologist,* was taken on a nationwide tour. One of its ports of call was the University of Port Harcourt where Rotimi had been appointed professor and head of the creative arts department. According to stage manager Tunji Ojeyemi, Rotimi sat motionless throughout the show, his eyes fixed on the programme. After the performance, he spoke to the cast and his address included the following pointed comment:

> When you get back to the University of Ife, tell them that I am glad that Rotimi's 'enthusiastic amateurs, farmers, carpenters and school teachers' are now the ones taking major roles in this production.

Staff welfare at the Ori Olokun Cultural Centre

The position of the actors within the university career structure was an important consideration. There are three levels of workers within the university: daily rated staff, temporary staff and permanent staff. As the term suggests, daily rated employees have their remuneration calculated on a daily basis. They are not regarded as regular members of staff and their appointment is not pensionable. They are not entitled to welfare packages such as the use of university medical facilities or housing. The appointment of temporary staff members is not pensionable either. However, they have some privileges, for example, they are able to use university medical facilities. Temporary appointments are usually for six months after which appointments are either confirmed or terminated. Confirmation of appointment establishes the worker as a permanent member of staff with pension rights and other perquisites.

When the Ori Olokun performers were initially employed, they were designated 'artistes in residence,' receiving pay from the university as daily-rated staff. Understandably, they were unhappy about the insecurity of their position and one night in 1976 matters came to a head. After a rehearsal with Rotimi that finished later than 11.30, Peter Fatomilola raised the issue of their status as daily rated workers, other artists voiced their displeasure and the group decided to stage a public demonstration. In a curious way, life was imitating art because this decision was influenced by the participation of the cast in *Rere Run,* a political play by Oladejo Okediji in which workers fight against a corrupt establishment. It seems that Fatomilola, who played the role of workers' leader in the play, found it easy to slip into the role of the workers' leader in real life. The next day, the actors, carrying placards, and dressed in costumes from *Rere Run,* processed to the campus, a distance of about eight kilometres, singing protest songs and asking that their appointments be regularized. They made for the office of the acting director of the institute, Wande Abimbola, who promised to look into the matter.

There was a general lull in the activities of the centre in 1976 due to Aboyade's reorganizations. As part of a general staff rationalization, which resulted to some degree from Wande Abimbola's intervention, all the thirty-two employees of the centre were asked to go home until further notice. After this announcement, Adebolu Fatunmise requested that the company should pose for a group photograph, because it seemed to him that they were all going to be laid off. Many of the workers indeed had their employment terminated, but others were 'reabsorbed', becoming the foundation members of the 'University of Ife Theatre', later 'Awovarsity Theatre'. They were initially given appointments for six months which were eventually converted to permanent appointments.

Where are they now? – Former members of the Ori Olokun Theatre

A few of the artists employed at the Ori Olokun Centre in the early days were rough characters who equated being involved in the arts with being carefree

Members of the Ori Olukun theatre company and cultural centre, 1976 (© Adbolu Fatunmise)

layabouts. Some of them smoked and drank heavily and dressed untidily. Given the links between the Palm Tree Hotel and political activities, many people mistook these artists for the political thugs who had hung about there waiting for political action. (See *The Road*.) It was not entirely surprising that there was violence when, in 1974, the dreaded tax collectors invaded the centre demanding that the artists should pay their tax. Instead of explaining that they were university workers whose tax was deducted at source, the actors took on the tax collectors and a free for all ensued. Eventually, the performers were 'invited' to the local council office where they explained their status, and the tax collectors apologized to them. The 'roughness' of some of the actors caused some members of the local community to look askance at the centre and its activities. However, attitudes changed when they heard about the beautiful performances put on, and, over the years, the artists' reputation for wildness faded away.

Theatre training can be a preparation for many different careers and this has been the experience of those who have been, at one time or another, members of the Ife company.

The most natural movement has been into one branch or other of the performing arts. For example, Gboyega Ajayi, who served with the theatre until 2003, went on to freelance as a stage, television and video artist. Laide Adewale, who played the charismatic warlord, Kurunmi in Rotimi's play of the same title, became one of the most highly-rated television and video artists in the country. He is also an independent producer. Jimi Şolanke, who was invited from Ibadan in 1974 to take the lead in Rotimi's *Ovonramwen Nogbaisi*, now plays with his own highlife band, and Peter Fatomilola, mentioned above, has now established a cultural centre in Ile-Ife town. Peter Badejo used Ife as a spring-board for an international career in the performing arts and is now world famous as a teacher of African dance and a choreographer. Some of the actors have taken the turning into the academy. For example, Tunji Ojeyemi, who joined the company in 1973, did a degree in dramatic arts at Obafemi Awolowo University (1998), and Kola Oyewo went even further: in 2005, at the age of 59, he earned a PhD in theatre arts from the University of Ibadan. He now lectures in the Department of Dramatic Arts, Obafemi Awolowo University. Just in case the traditional side of the Ife experience should be forgotten there is the example of Adebolu Fatunmise, once an actor, now a chief in Ile-Ife. A friend of the Ori Olokun Players who has taken yet another career path is Akin Onigbinde: formerly a teacher at the University of Ife staff school, he is now a highly-rated football coach and sports administrator.

Ori Olokun – the fruit of the project

I suggested earlier that the plays that were produced at the Ori Olokun Centre reflected the fruits of Rotimi's research. A university town is necessarily a polyglot community, comprising people of different backgrounds. He therefore stressed the idea of ethnic unity, especially during the Nigerian Civil War. He used what he referred to as 'inter-ethnic camaraderie or solidarity' to combat 'ethnic rivalry, bias, bigotry, paranoia, chauvinism, and extreme states of jingoism'. He did this to appeal for solidarity in the face of cultural differences (cited in Coker 2005), and ensured the audiences could see themselves reflected in the characters portrayed on stage.

The extensive use of local idioms including music, proverbs and dances turned the performances of Rotimi's plays into communal experiences for Yoruba audiences. Rotimi disliked proscenium arches. He wrote about 'theatrical apartheid' and of the arch 'separating in a most un-African manner, the spectator from the performers.' (Rotimi: 2005, 88). He revelled in directing his plays in the round, considering that this reflected the traditional style for organizing performances. It proved very satisfying both to the director and to his town and gown audience. As a director Rotimi was a stickler for details. In 1973, while directing Okediji's *Rere Run,* he took the Ori Olokun Players to N. K. Zard's construction company yard at Lagere, Ile-Ife, to study 'various idiosyncrasies of labourers at work'. According to Oyewo, this really injected naturalism into their performances (Oyewo 2003: 154). No matter whose play he was directing, Rotimi gave it his best.

Rotimi's historical plays were particularly welcomed by audiences. He claimed to have two purposes in writing these works: 'to correct some misconceptions of European historians' and to '[enlighten] our people about ourselves' (Rotimi: 2005, 90). They provided, he felt, lessons in history and also gave the people a sense of pride in their forebears. His approach was sympathetic and deliberately challenged the versions produced by the colonialists. Of special note is his preoccupation with leadership: Rotimi's tragic heroes are always portrayed as credible leaders devoted to their people.

A strong point of Rotimi's productions was the use of spectacle:

You have to address the visuals. The iconography must be clean, clear, gripping, and immediate ... arrest the hearing organs of your spectators. The assault must have the same potency visually as the auditory ... this is where things like songs instrumentation all come in the rhythm, the power of the spoken word ... The visuals ... the dynamics of dance, of mimes, gestures, of course the additives of color, through costumes, makeup, and so on. (Rotimi 2005: 83)

Furthermore, the plays also reflect a keen sense of humour. No matter how intense the tragedy might be, Rotimi still introduced humour. He disagreed with those critics who thought this mixing of genres was inappropriate and in reply to them insisted that he was reflecting an African dimension.

His audiences certainly found the productions rewarding. His final word was: 'So I say grab the audience and forget about the critic. With traditional theatre, the audience is the final arbiter; once the audience has accepted you, to hell with the others' (ibid.: 86). The desire to make an impact remained the driving force behind Rotimi's art and he elaborated on it in terms that show a rejection of critics, 'the others' and a determination to alter society. He said he was intent on 'capturing the emotional territory of the spectator' ... (it was his intention) 'to make the audience think, and if possible, act' (ibid.: 86–7).

Ori Olokun: factors that aided the demise

The last major Ori Olokun Theatre production was the premier of Rotimi's *Ovonramwen Nogbaisi* in 1974. No serious performances were offered in 1975 and the fortunes of the centre were clearly in decline at that time. What factors were responsible for this? First and foremost is the fact that, in 1975, the Institute of African Studies was dissolved under the new policy structure introduced by Aboyade. New departments of dramatic arts, fine arts, music and African languages and literature were carved out of the old institute. Under the new dispensation, the research that had been crucial to the flourishing of the Ori Olokun Cultural Centre was no longer being undertaken and funds for the Festival of Arts dried up. Thus ended one era in the annals of the performing arts at the University of Ife.

In 1975, the University of Ife became a federal establishment and, anticipating financial problems arising from the new status, Aboyade economized. (Adediran 1989: 49). As a way of cutting costs, the Ori Olokun Centre was replaced by a campus venue, Oduduwa Hall. During the lull of 1975 and early 1976, members missed performances and it was in this context that Ṣoyinka premiered *Death and the King's Horseman* in the new theatre. This was followed, at the end of 1976, by *Opera Wonyosi*. The new venue was easily accessible to members of the university community but not to the people from the town. The road to the Ori Olokun Centre became rutted and pot-holed, the 'gown wearers' turned away from it and sought their theatrical pleasures in Oduduwa Hall.

BIBLIOGRAPHY

Adebayo, A. G. and Oloruntimehin, O. (1989) 'The growth and development of the arts and the social sciences', in Omosini & Adediran (eds) *Great Ife: A History of Obafemi Awolowo University Ile-Ife 1962–1967* (Ile-Ife: OAU Press), pp. 65–88.

Adediran, Biodun, and Omosini, Olufemi (1989) 'Conception, planning and birth' in Omosini & Adediran (eds) *Great Ife: A History of Obafemi Awolowo University Ile-Ife 1962–1967* (Ile-Ife: OAU Press), pp. 3–17.

Adediran, Biodun (1989) 'The Transition to a Federal University Status, 1975-1987' in Omosini & Adediran (eds) *Great Ife: A History of Obafemi Awolowo University Ile-Ife 1962–1967* (Ile-Ife: OAU Press), pp. 46–62.

Akinrinade, Olusola (1989) 'The Era of Consolidation' in Omosini and Adediran (eds) *Great Ife: A History of Obafemi Awolowo University Ile-Ife 1962–1967* (Ile-Ife: OAU Press.), pp. 31–45.

Coker, Niyi (2005) *Ola Rotimi's African Theatre: The Development of an Indigenous Aesthetic* (New York: Edwin Mellen Press).

Nigerian Exchange Website (2000) 'A Gem Lost to Death: Ola Rotimi', September 5.

http://www.ngex.com/entertainment/pages/olarotimideath.htm (Date of Download: July 4, 2004)

Ogunleye, Foluke (ed.) (2003) *African Video Film Today* (Manzini: Academic Publishers).

Ogunleye, Foluke (2004) 'The Nigerian videofilm: A report from the front', *The Quarterly Review of Film and Video*, Vol. 21, No. 2: pp. 79–88.

Omosini, Olufemi, and Adediran, Biodun (1989) *Great Ife: A History of Obafemi Awolowo University 1962–1967* (Ile-Ife: Obafemi Awolowo University Press).

Omotoso, Kole (1983) 'Unife Theatre – A History of Continuity' in 'Unife Theatre in *Requiem for a Futurologist*', Programme notes for the production.

Oyewo, Kola (2003) 'The Yoruba video film: cinematic language and the socio-aesthetic ideal' in Ogunleye, Foluke (ed.) *African Video Film Today* (Manzini: Academic Publishers).

Rotimi, Ola, interviewed by Coker, Adeniyi, 2003, 'A director's vision for theatre in Africa: Adeniyi Coker interviews Ola Rotimi – One of Nigeria's foremost playwrights and directors', *Black Renaissance*. Summer, Vol. 5, Iss. 2: p. 77.

http://www.nyu.edu/africahouse/expressive/cokerdirectorsvision.pdf (Date of Download: January 27, 2005)

Şolanke, Jimi (2006) 'Ola Rotimi, at Home with the Gods – An Experience'. Unpublished Manuscript presented at 'Ola Rotimi's Vision and Impact with the Ori Olokun Theatre Company' a symposium organized by the Department of Dramatic Arts Students Association, July 19.

'The Rotimi Foundation Website'

http://www.rotimifoundation.org/rotimi.php?content=mission (Date of Download: February 2, 2004)

INTERVIEWS

Akomolafe, Olu, 2006: Interviewed by this writer, June 27.
Fatomilola, Peter, 2006: Interviewed by this writer, June 28 & 30.
Folarin, Agbo, 2006: Interviewed by this writer, August 15.
Ojeyemi, Tunji, 2006: Interviewed by this writer, June 26 & 29.
Oyewo, Kola, 2006: Interviewed by this writer, September 6.

APPENDIX
List of Ori Olokun plays

Date	Title	Author
1968	*The Gods Are Not to Blame*	Ola Rotimi
1969	*Kurunmi*	Ola Rotimi
1970	*Gbe'ku de*	Adegoke Durojaye
1972	*Ovonramwen Nogbaisi*	Ola Rotimi
1973	*Rere Run*	Oladejo Okediji
	Wahala	Babalola Fatunwase
1974	*Our Husband Has Gone Mad Again*	Ola Rotimi

The Muungano Cultural Troupe
Entertaining the urban masses
of Dar es Salaam

SIRI LANGE

For over twenty years, the Muungano Cultural Troupe was one of the most important cultural institutions in Dar es Salaam. Their variety shows in fenced, open-air bars, reached up to two thousand people every week and they also toured twelve countries. The group has never received any meaningful sponsorship either from the Tanzanian authorities or from foreign donors. The company, numbering close to 60 at its height in 1995, has survived on the contributions that ordinary people are willing to pay to see their performances. What do people find so attractive about these variety shows? And why has the group slowly lost its audience base? In the pages that follow, I look at the history of the company; its organisation, its relationship to the ruling party, and the way in which it, together with its audiences, create theatre performances in which family relations, gender, and the institutions of the state are constantly discussed and negotiated.[1]

Early history of the company – modelled on the national troupe

The Muungano Cultural Troupe was established in August 1980 by Norbert Chenga who still owns and manages the group. A teacher by background, Chenga grew up in Lindi in southern Tanzania, an area that is among the poorest and least 'developed' regions in the country. However, it is well known for its *ngoma* – musical events including dance and mime.

When he started Muungano, Chenga was an administrator with the National Performing Arts Company (NPAC) that had been active from the time of independence to 1980, and was an umbrella for a number of subgroups, including an *ngoma* troupe and a theatre company. NPAC was disbanded in August 1980 mainly for economic reasons, but there is little doubt that, as Michael Eneza has argued, the interest in creating a national culture had diminished in the years since independence. Swahili as a national language united the country's 120 plus language groups, the one party system brought political stability, and universal primary education fostered a generation who grew up with socialism as a common goal – at least in theory. There was no need for NPAC.

27

The organisation of Muungano was influenced not only by the NPAC, but also by the cultural troupes that had been set up at various factories, schools and other institutions after independence in 1961. These troupes were meant not only to revive African 'traditions', but also to spread the message of socialism and 'villagisation', which became a national policy with the Arusha Declaration (1967). Political songs soon became a part of the nationalised neo-traditional dances, and Muungano followed this trend, replacing many of the image-laden songs in local languages with blunt propaganda for the ruling party CCM (*Chama Cha Mapinduzi*) and its policies.

To begin with, Muungano performed dances only, and the shows lasted for about an hour. In 1981 however, a rival company, DDC Kibisa, started staging short comedic skits to give the dancers time to change costumes (Plane 1996: 67). Muungano soon followed their lead. In 1984, Muungano's repertoire was further expanded to include Chinese inspired *sarakasi*, acrobatics. The following year, Muungano and some of the other companies introduced a popularised version of *taarab*. Taarab music, which originates in Zanzibar, is sung poetry accompanied by stringed instruments. Unlike *ngoma*, this musical form had not been promoted by the authorities on the mainland since it was seen as Arabic, rather than African. The latest genre to be taken up by Muungano is dance music and the so-called 'Stage Shows' where one or two solo dancers (usually female) perform to Congolese rhythms.

Muungano, then, has incorporated new cultural forms (*fani*), and, in the process, has extended its shows from one hour to four, and the number of employees from 15 to more than 50. Muungano is probably the best known, privately-owned performing company in Dar es Salaam, but it has in no way been alone at the cultural scene. According to Penina Mlama in her essay on trends in Tanzanian theatre, there were over fifty commercial cultural troupes in Dar es Salaam in 1986 (1992: 88). Many of the groups were short-lived. Typically, a successful dancer or actor would leave an established group and start up on his or her own, recruiting artists from other troupes or from rural areas. It has, however, proved hard to survive, and the number of privately-owned companies that have operated for ten years or more can be counted on the fingers of one hand.

A survey I conducted among audiences of different companies in 1992 showed that the sketches that concluded performances were the most popular items. I have argued elsewhere (Lange 2002a) that theatre pieces can be seen as embodying popular resistance against the state's appropriation of *ngoma* (Lange 2002a). With the nationalisation and politicisation of *ngoma*, this performance mode had lost it ability to comment on social issues and to criticise. *Ngoma* is still entertaining to many people, however, partly because it can bring back 'memories of home', partly due to its physicality and sexiness. Theatre, in contrast, escaped the hegemonic forces of the state, and became an arena where artists and audiences could explore the paradoxes of urban life and modernisation.

Economic organisation

Muungano Cultural Troupe has its home base at the Snake Garden Bar in Mabibo, a low-income residential area some seven kilometres from the centre of Dar es Salaam. Snake Garden, a small, fenced, open-air bar built in the mid-1980s, is situated on a plot next to Norbert Chenga's own house. The administrators of the group (*wakuu*) meet here daily. In the office there are files and newspaper clippings covering the more than twenty years that the troupe has been in existence. A secretary, employed on a full-time basis, uses an old typewriter for the group's correspondence, the artists' contracts and the programme for each week. Snake Garden is used for rehearsals and meetings, but the group seldom performs there. Apparently the people in Mabibo are not willing to pay for something that they can easily see or hear for nothing. Muungano takes its weekly show to other residential areas of the city where they have contracts with 'social halls', fenced, open-air bars, in which they perform on a given day of the week.

Sources of income

Apart from a US$ 2,500 grant from the Norwegian Agency for Development Cooperation (Norad) in the early 1980s which was used to build Snake Garden, Muungano has not received direct support from foreign donors or from the Tanzanian government. The company's primary source of income is the entrance fee to their shows, which is Tsh 1000 for adults (US$ 1.70) and 500 for children (US$ 0.80). The price is doubled during public holidays and for competitions with rival companies. Muungano's files reveal that it earns between Tsh. 110,000 and 415,000 from each of its regular shows (US$ 187 and 705). On public holidays such as Christmas Day and Idd-el-fitr, the company can earn as much as Tsh 2 million (US$ 3,400) from a single show.

In addition to bars, Muungano has a contract to perform at Bahari Beach Hotel once a week, at a fixed rate lower than its usual earnings from its regular performances (Tsh 90,000, or US$ 153). The company is occasionally hired by embassies, companies or individuals for private functions, and Muungano has also done commercials for radio and television. The most important source of extra income for the company is its involvement in educational radio drama, sponsored by US Aid in collaboration with the Ministry of Health. Although the programmes have proved very popular, Muungano has never been commissioned to produce live 'theatre for development'. One reason may be that the relevant authorities prefer to use institutions, such as the College of Arts in Bagamoyo and the Drama Department at the University of Dar es Salaam, that specialise in this form of theatre.

Members of the educated elite have a tendency to dismiss Muungano and other privately-owned theatre companies on the grounds that they are commercial. However, the Tanzanian authorities have sent Muungano to represent the country abroad. The troupe has also arranged tours independently of the government, and altogether has visited 12 different countries in Africa, Asia, Europe, and the Middle East. The tour of the Scandinavian countries in 1991, arranged by a young Danish woman who had stayed with the group, was important for the development of the company since it enabled them to buy musical instruments that were used in playing both dance music and *taarab*. A few years after their Scandinavian tour, Muungano offered a special summer course for Danes who wished to learn African dance and acrobatics. However these links have not been sustained.

Wages, advertisements and transport

Muungano artists work on annual contracts that state the monthly pay and allowances, and the financial support that can be expected in case of sickness or death. In 1997, Muungano actors, dancers and musicians were paid Tsh 25–50,000 ($42–85) per month, allowances included. This wage is comparable to that earned by unskilled workers in the formal sector, and is hard to live on. Since the artists work in the afternoon and have the mornings free, many of them supplement their incomes by preparing and selling breakfast buns or other snacks. In periods when the company cannot perform, such as during Ramadan and during the rainy seasons (long rains from mid-March to May and short rains around December), the artists risk going without pay for months. Many of the artists complain about being exploited, and gifted performers often move between troupes in search of better opportunities. The artists are encouraged to train to perform in several forms (*fani*) to avoid having too many people on the payroll. In fact, only three of the Muungano employees work solely with theatre, the rest are 'all-rounders'. Artists who are specialised in acrobatics enrich theatre by performing somersaults and other stunts during plays. This is particularly true for the comedic skits, which as a generic convention end in a comical fight. While some 'all-rounders do amazingly well in all genres, the companies need to have at least one star actor to produce plays that satisfy the audience. None of the actors has formal theatre training, but they have developed their skills through experience. Members of the audience often cheer when their favourite actors enter the scene.

Muungano has never been able to afford to buy a vehicle. It rents a truck to transport its equipment to the various venues; the artists travel individually by public transport, and a taxi is hired for the administrative personnel and the *taarab* stars. After wages, radio advertising is the company's biggest expense: the company advertise its shows on Radio One, the most popular station in Dar es Salaam. They also hire a car and use a megaphone to advertise in the neighbourhood where they are performing. During up-country tours, the company sends a group of artists around the town or village – dressed up in *vichekesho* costumes, in 'drag' (not used in the plays as such), in masks, or on stilts – to attract attention to the evening's event.

Two Theatre forms: *vichekesho* and *maigizo*

Contemporary popular theatre in Tanzania is characterised above all by syncretism. Ritual mime and drama, twentieth century Zanzibari skits, silent movies, Hindi films, school drama in the British tradition, and didactic, socialist theatre for factory workers have all fed into the kind of theatre tradition that we find today (Hussein 1971: 97; Mlama 1992: 79).

When Muungano and other privately owned troupes first incorporated theatre in their performances in the early 1980s, it was in the form of comedic skits, *vichekesho* (Lihamba 1985:157; Songoyi 1988:31). Gradually, a new and more complex form of drama called *maigizo* came into existence. *Maigizo* stems from the verb *kuiga* which means 'to imitate' or 'to act'. A specific play, however, is usually referred to as a *mchezo* (pl. *michezo*). In the case of the Muungano Cultural Troupe, the development of *maigizo* can be credited to Jayson Kami, whom the troupe hired as its theatre director in 1987. He introduced the artists to written scripts. In 1990, Muungano performed almost exclusively *maigizo* and reverted to *vichekesho* only when they had not been able to produce an *igizo* (Plane 1996: 55). In the period 1995–2000, on the other hand, the general trend for all the active companies was to have a ten to fifteen minute *kichekesho* at an early stage in the four-hour performance, and a full-length play (45–60 minutes) towards the end. *Maigizo* are often produced as serials to ensure that customers come back for the 'next instalment'.

Maigizo is considered a much more demanding genre than the improvised *vichekesho* and the full-length plays certainly need more planning and better actors. First, *maigizo* rely on written texts. Jayson Kami of Muungano is in fact the only popular playwright to produce fully developed scripts, while Bakari Mbelemba of Mandela and Ally M. Mkumbila of Muungano work with actors to create their plays on the basis of 1–2 pages of hand-written synopses. All *maigizo* have comical elements, but they tend to include melodrama, and a sad ending is twice as common as a happy one. The melodramatic element of *maigizo* is sometimes strengthened by incorporating a sad song by one of the protagonists. One example is the play *Wifi* ('Sister-in-law') in which Bracco, at the end of the play, sits on the floor, holding his dead mother, crying and lamenting. At this point, members of the audience swarm onto the stage to tip him. In another play, *Kipendacho Roho* ('Love of the Heart'), Bracco sings and dances in a happy manner clearly inspired by Hindi movies. This innovation was much appreciated by the audience. Since tips from the audience are a welcome supplement to the artists' meagre income, a playwright like Ally Mkumbila, who plays the main role (Bracco) himself, has an incentive to include songs that will encourage tipping!

Actors and audience members that I talked to all agreed that a *mchezo* should always teach something (*fundisha*). The moral lessons are generally explicit and are shown in a realistic and down to earth way. When the play is over, the intended message is often summarised over the loudspeakers. These invariably reflect the fact that Swahili drama is preoccupied by family and gender relations, and the conflicts that arise as people are pulled between traditional obligations and the wish to live a modern, urban life.

Scriptwriters: Kami and Mkumbila

Plays are composed (-*tunga*) for Muungano theatre by either Jayson Kami or 'Bracco,' but the production of them is by and large a communal process. Kami fulfils his role as scriptwriter and theatre director in addition to his full-time job in the Ministry of Planning and Land Use. His interest in drama started at secondary school. As part of the Swahili literature course, he studied plays by Penina Mlama and other Swahili playwrights and he was inspired to write plays for the school theatre group. After he had completed his studies, he directed plays for amateur groups in Iringa and Sumbawanga, where he was working as a planner. After he moved to Dar es Salaam in 1987, he was hired by Muungano. As mentioned earlier, Kami was important in the theatre history of the group as he initiated the shift from improvised *vichekesho* to written *maigizo*. He has written about 30 plays and hopes to have some of them published.

Kami distances himself from both the elite theatre and the popular improvised *vichekesho* and places his own work firmly between the two. He says that the university-based Paukwa Theatre Group has a different target audience than Muungano and claims that ordinary people do not understand the university plays. An exception is Penina Mlama's *Heshima Yangu* ('My Pride') which both he and Bakari Mbelemba of Mandela Theatre Troupe have directed for performances. In Kami's view the difference between Muungano and the other commercial troupes is that Muungano sticks to the scripts while the other groups may change a given play and its meaning (*maana*) from one day to another. Kami's scripts are laid out very like conventional Western drama with descriptions of sets and lines that are to be learned. In contrast to most Western drama, however, the scripts also include an 'announcer' (*mtangazaji*) who introduces the play, provides introductory remarks before new scenes and gives a summary of the moral message of the play when it ends. This role is played by Kami from behind the backcloth using an amplification system. While he never acts on the stage himself, he makes sure the actors stick closely to his script.

Since the group's finances do not run to having much photocopying done, Kami alone has a copy of the whole script. He sometimes asks the secretary to type it, but more often it exists as a handwritten document. During the first rehearsal for a new play, he introduces the artists to the story, gives each of them their parts on a piece of paper and asks them to memorise them. Individual actors have very different attitudes towards these written scripts. Some learn their parts by heart and follow the script word for word, while others improvise freely on the basis of the storyline. It should be said that the introduction of written scripts triggered conflicts between Kami and some of the established actors, who were illiterate. According to Kami, the star actor of the company, Mzee Small, changed the entire meaning of one of his plays. As a consequence of the conflict that arose, Small decided to leave the company and to start his own troupe. Kami permits embellishments because he knows that some of the actors are better at finding the right words than he is, but he does not tolerate altering the storyline.

Within limits, the actors adjust Kami's script to their own tastes and in response to the feedback they get from their audiences. This process is begun during rehearsals, and continues during the run of the play. The production of *Haki Ikipinda* ('Bent Justice') demonstrated to me how audience response can affect a play. The hero of the play, Police Officer Bracco, tries to arrest a wealthy drug dealer, Mr Chande. But the drug dealer sets a trap, bribes the magistrates, and Bracco ends up in jail. His wife and son finally succeed in revealing the truth. At the end of the play, Kami's script has the mother, father and son holding hands while they sing to celebrate their victory over the evil Mr Chande and the corrupt legal system. During the first performance that I watched, the actors did as they had been told by Kami. But the whole scene, with its romantic focus on a nuclear family holding hands and singing a children's song, looked somewhat out of place, and failed to catch the imagination of the audience. During subsequent performances, the actors dropped the hand-holding and the song, and Kami accepted their decision. In this instance, Kami, with his middle-class background and education, had imposed an image of 'Western style' family life and gender relations that the more 'proletarian' audience was not ready to accept. The actors were aware of this and changed an aspect of the play that they felt had failed to resonate with the audience.

Around 1993, Tanzanian theatre groups were invited to compete for a contract to produce drama for Radio Tanzania. The programmes, *Geuza Mwendo* ('Change Your Ways') and *Zinduka,* ('Wake Up'), sponsored by US AID, were to be enlightening and entertaining dramas about family planning and AIDS. Muungano won the lucrative contract. As Kami became increasingly busy writing the weekly radio scripts, the group's star actor, Ally Mkumbila, took over the main responsibility for directing Muungano's live theatre and his plays have proved very popular. Mkumbila always takes the leading role himself, be it a beggar or a successful capitalist. In Swahili popular theatre, all actors have a name which they use in all plays, regardless of the age or social status of their character. These names tend to be 'neutral' compared to the actors' personal Muslim or Christian names. Members of the audience know Ally Mkumbila as 'Bracco'.

Mkumbila's background is significantly different from Kami's and he operates differently as a playwright. In 1980, when he was 19 years old, Mkumbila joined the army as a primary school leaver, and he subsequently had great success in the army's cultural troupe. Three years later, he left the army to became a professional artist working for D.D.C. Kibisa (1983–1988), and then Bima Modern *Taarab* (1988–1993) before joining Muungano. He soon became their most popular actor, filling the gap that Mzee Small had left some years earlier.

Mkumbila does not compose full scripts but supplies one- to two-page synopses. These are written to be read out for the actors and to help them envisage the play on stage. While reading the synopsis aloud, Mkumbila occasionally embellishes the storyline to give it more flesh. The artists then create the play through improvisation. Mkumbila is more open than Kami to suggestions and alterations. In the case of *Kipendacho Roho* ('What the Heart Loves'), the storyline and the message of the play were transformed. According to the initial synopsis of the play: a wealthy female doctor, Dr Tausi, refuses two prosperous suitors, and falls in love with one of her patients, Bracco, a street vendor dressed in rags. The climax of the play is their happy wedding. The play celebrates a woman who follows her heart rather than seeking financial security. It also presents a rather unlikely 'rags to riches' story, perhaps reflecting the dreams of both the underpaid playwright and the more disadvantaged men in the audience. After having performed the first part of the play, however, Mkumbila and the other actors realised that the plot was too romantic. During the rehearsal for part two, they told me that they had decided to change the storyline. The reason they gave was that Bracco did not want to marry someone to whom he would be socially inferior (*chini*). He marries a nurse instead! The actors sensed that their audiences would not accept Dr Tausi and the romantic relationship between her and Bracco. In their eyes, this could only work if Dr Tausi was a comical figure. Ironically, the original title suited both versions of the play. But while the title originally referred to a wealthy woman who followed her heart, the staged version showed a poor man who chose love over a life of luxury (a life where he would, at the same time, lose some of his male status).

In order to fit the new version, Dr Tausi was made far more outrageous and sexually provocative than she had been in the original. Incidentally, situations in which aggressive, often mature women seduce innocent young men are common, and much appreciated features of the plays of Muungano Cultural Troupe. Elsewhere, I have argued that there are two major 'trends' or 'traditions' in Swahili popular drama. These trends perpetuate opposing ideologies concerning modernisation and change. On the one hand, there is the 'politically correct' tradition. The historical background of this tradition is the didactic *vichekesho* of the ujamaa period. Now, as then, these plays promote the abandoning of 'uncivilised' and outdated traditional practices and most of the plays in this category are sympathetic towards women. The 'anti-modern' or 'traditionalist' plays, on the other hand, criticise the changes that have come with modernisation and urbanisation, including increasing individualism and the supposedly consumerist and sexually aggressive attitudes of urban women. There is a strong tendency in these plays to blame women for what goes wrong in male–female relationships.

I see the two categories schematised above, the 'politically correct' and 'traditionalist' plays, as useful for making sense of the highly diverse ideologies and messages of Swahili popular drama. However, the two categories should not be seen as watertight. The conventions are rather sources that influence the work of playwrights and artists, and my main argument is that popular Swahili theatre as a whole can be seen as a field of discourse between these two poles. The production process of 'What the Heart Loves', the text of which is reproduced below, constituted a continuous discourse about modernisation, class and gender relations. What's more, the audience became, in a sense, co-authors of the play, since the play was changed to fit their tastes.

Challenges to viability: television and multipartism

The size and popularity of the popular theatre movement in Dar es Salaam appears to be unrivalled in other East African towns and cities. Its success can be traced to a number of factors. First, the cultural policy at independence encouraged music, dance and drama activities across ethnic and religious boundaries: NPAC provided training and acted as a model for private initiatives. Second, the fact that there was no television broadcasting in mainland Tanzania until 1993 meant that there was a big market for family entertainment. Muungano and other theatre companies tailored their performances to fit the schedules of wage workers and children, starting at 4 pm and ending when it was time for the evening meal (8 pm). Second, the variety show format meant that were was something for every taste, and Muungano proved immensely responsive to the changing preferences of its audiences.

Unfortunately, since 2002, Muungano has lost its place in the market and the company is now a shadow of what it was. Three factors stand out and will be discussed below: administrative problems, competition from television, and the ruling party's heavy subsidy of a rival company, Tanzania One Theatre. Like owners of other cultural troupes, Norbert Chenga has faced a constant dilemma regarding the balance between his wish to withdraw the troupe's surplus income for personal consumption, and the need to invest in props and salaries. The HIV/AIDS pandemic has also cost the company much. For example, it is customary for employers to cover funeral expenses and there have been several deaths.

Television broadcasting was introduced in mainland Tanzania in 1993. Initially, this did not affect the market of the cultural troupes much since few people could afford to buy sets. In fact, some theatre companies benefited since they were hired to produce television drama (Swahili Soap) – or experimented with producing videodramas. As the years passed, however, more and more people were to able to buy television sets and video play-back machines, and this appears to have had a negative effect on the companies. However, many still attend live performances where they can meet other people and interact with what's going on at stage.

Tanzania's political system and cultural policies are a major factor behind the growth of multi-ethnic and non-religious entertainment in Dar es Salaam. During the one-party system days, privately-owned cultural troupes generally had some kind of loose attachment to the state and to the ruling party. They all performed songs praising the party, and they were asked to perform for visitors and dignitaries (often for little or no monetary reward). With the introduction of multipartyism in 1992, the ruling Chama Cha Mapinduzi (CCM) feared that they would lose the support that they had enjoyed from the privately-owned troupes, and realised that performing troupes at government institutions, such as the police and the army, would have to become politically neutral. Consequently, CCM established its own cultural troupe, Tanzania One Theatre (TOT), which was provided with high quality musical instruments and three vehicles. The company was launched with much media coverage and TOTs *taarab* songs were heard on the state channel Radio Tanzania every day. TOT is led by the charismatic singer Captain Komba, who has a background in the army's cultural troupe. Several of the TOT artists were recruited from Muungano. Muungano and TOT soon entered an intense rivalry, continuing an age-old tradition in East Africa. (Askew 2002; Gunderson and Barz 2000; Lange 2002b.)

Between 1994 and 2000, the two companies arranged a number of public contests (*mashindano*), and for a while, Muungano benefitted from TOTs arrival since thousands of people attended the head-to-heads. CCM sponsored both TOT and Muungano for the competitions that were held in 1994 and 1995 when the purpose of the competition was to celebrate the jubilee of the CCM. Significantly, this was before the first multiparty election of October 1995. After the election, when it had secured another five years in power, CCM support to Muungano dried up. The company went through very difficult times and in 1996 Chenga was forced to release twelve of his artists. Large scale competitions between the two companies were held again in 1997. Since the companies compete not only in artistic excellence, but also in costumes and equipment, it has proved impossible for impoverished Muungano to keep up with the well-funded TOT. A bitter Chenga told journalists that it was wrong to compare Muungano and TOT as the latter was so heavily subsidised. He announced that he himself was a CCM supporter and that his company was ready to campaign for CCM. When the journalist from *Heko* asked him why he didn't try to get support from one of the opposition parties instead, he admitted that he had tried, but that no help had been forthcoming (Heko 1997).

Conclusion

It can be seen that the rise and fall of Muungano has been closely connected to government policies. The cultural policy after independence prepared the ground for nationalised, multi-ethnic, non-religious popular culture, and this form of entertainment proved commercially viable in Dar es Salaam. Gradually, the companies developed a new theatre form, fusing improvised skits with drama that was, to a greater or lesser extent, text based. Through plays, the companies could address issues that were of great concern to their audiences, and as a result popular theatre became an arena where artists and audiences explored their social reality *together*. The variety show format was probably an important reason for the success of Muungano and other companies since it offered something for everyone, and since the performance lasted long enough for people to feel that had had their money's worth. With the introduction of multipartism, however, things slowly became difficult for Muungano. In the end, it proved impossible to compete with the heavily subsidised Tanzania One Theatre. Unable to sustain their own playwrights and a large staff, Muungano 'shed' performers and as a result is back where they started 25 years ago – a medium sized company performing neo-traditional dance, snake shows, taarab, and comedic skits.

NOTE

1   This article is based on 18 months of fieldwork with Muungano Cultural Troupe in the period 1992–1998 and follow-up visits in the years since then. During the first nine months, I lived with one of the female artists (Pili Ikerege, alias 'Selina') and performed and toured with the company. Altogether, I have watched (or collected synopses of) close to 200 Swahili plays. The 'ethnographic present' of this chapter refers to 1998, and the exchange rates are those of that year. I wish to express my profound gratitude to Norbert Chenga and the artists of the company for letting me work with them.

BIBLIOGRAPHY

Anon. 'Baada ya mambo kumwendea vibaya Mwanza – Chenga asema yuko tayari kuipigia debe CCM.' *Heko*. 4 November. 1997.

Askew, Kelly (2002) *Performing the Nation: Swahili music and cultural politics in Tanzania*. University of Chicago Press: Chicago.

Eneza, Michael (2004) 'Traditional *ngomas*: National culture or fading distraction?' http://www.ipp.co.tz/ipp/guardian/2004/03/25/7701.html, [accessed 19.04.2006].

Fabian, Johannes (1990) *Power and Performance: Ethnographic exploration through proverbial wisdom and theater in Shaba, Zaire*. University of Wisconsin Press. Madison.

Gunderson, Frank, and Gregory Barz, eds (2000) *Mashindano! Competitive music performance in East Africa*. Dar es Salaam: Mkuki na Nyota Publishers.

Hussein, Ebrahim (1971) *On the development of theatre in East Africa*. PhD thesis, Humboldt University: Berlin.

Lange, Siri (2002a) *Managing Modernity. Gender, state and nation in the popular drama of Dar es Salaam, Tanzania*. PhD thesis, Department of Social Anthropology, University of Bergen: Bergen.

—— (2002b) 'Multipartyism, rivalry and *taarab* in Dar es Salaam.' In *Playing with identities in contemporary music in Africa*, edited by M. Palmberg and A. Kirkegaard. Nordic Africa Institute: Uppsala.

Lihamba, Amandina (1985) *Politics and Theatre in Tanzania after the Arusha Declaration 1967–1984*. PhD thesis, University of Leeds: Leeds.

Mlama, Penina (1992) 'The major trends in Tanzanian theatre.' In *On Stage. Proceedings of the Fifth International Janheinz Jahn Symposium on Theatre in Africa*, edited by U. Schild. Gottingen: Verlagsbuchhandlung.

Plane, Mark William (1996) *Fusing Oral and Literary Practices: Contemporary popular theatre in Dar es Salaam*. PhD thesis, Department of African Languages and Literature, University of Wisconsin: Madison.

Songoyi, Elias M. (1988) *Commercialization. Its impact on traditional dances*. BA thesis, University of Dar es Salaam: Dar es Salaam.

APPENDIX

Original Synopsis of Mchezo wa kuigiza – Kipendacho roho 'What the Heart Loves' Mtunzi: Ally Mkumbila – Bracco Chitosa

Sehemu ya Kwanza
Mzee Chande ni mtu mwenye mali nyingi, magari, Guest house na mifugo hapa jijini, na Coaster nae hali kadhalika. Hawa watu ni marafiki sana na wametokea kumpenda Tausi ambae ni Doctor.

I
Mzee Chande akiwa nyumbani na mkewe Tamasha wanazungumzia habari za mali zao, mara anaingia Coaster. Walisalimiana na kisha Tamasha aliwaacha na kuingia jikoni kuanda chakula. Ndipo ilikuwa nafasi ya Chande kuongelea suala la kumpenda Dr Tausi. Coaster alistuka, na kumueleza Chande aachane na habari za kumpenda Tausi kwani mimi nimekuja kwa suala la Tausi ambae ni Dr Hivyo nimekuletea barua nataka uwe mshenga wangu, kwani nataka kuoa. Mazungumzo yao yalikatishwa baada ya tamasha kurudi tena pale. Coaster aliaga. Aliuliza ni jinsi gani atasaidiwa, Chande alijibu siwezi.

II
Nyumbani Tausi anaisoma barua ambayo aliletwa na Coaster, mara Masafa aliingia na barua aliyoituma Chande. Alizisoma na kisha akacheka na huku anachambua moja baada ya nyingine. Tausi alikatishwa na hodi ya baba yake. Baba aliingia na kusalimiana, akaenda chumbani na Tausi nae alizichana barua huku anaingia chumbani kwake. Mara mshenga nae aliingia katumwa na Coaster, aliitwa Tausi, akaelezwa, Tausi alikataa. Hajaamua kuolewa, akimpata anayempenda atawaeleza.

III
Hospital Bracco anapelekwa akiwa hoi hajitambui, akiwa amebebwa mgongoni. Walipokelewa na nesi, na kisha wakaonana na Doctor, kabla haja-patiwa dawa, Bracco alimwagiwa maji na nesi ili kupunguza joto. Bracco alipatiwa kitanda akalazwa na wazee waliruhusiwa kuondoka, waje tena kesho. Chande nae alifika ofisini na kuonana na Doctor Tausi, na kuongelea mambo ya mapenzi. Lakini Dr Tausi alimjibu sina muda nipo na mgonjwa mahututi naomba utoke nje. Alipewa zawadi Tausi alizikataa. Chande akaondoka akiwa amechanganyikiwa. Doctor alianza kumwaza Bracco.

IV
Nyumbani kwa mganga, Chande anataka Tausi amkubali yeye na asimkumbuke mwanamme mwingine, na Coaster apewe kichaa ili asimtamani tena Tausi. Baada ya kuondoka na Coaster alifika kwa mganga ili Chande arogwe afe, kwa nini anamuingilia kwa mpenzi wake, wakati huo Coaster hata siku moja hajaongea nae Tausi kuhusu mapenzi. Na mganga aliwasikiliza kila mmoja na ili kuwaridhisha aliwapa dawa tofauti na lengo lao, bila wao kujua.

Sehemu ya Pili

I

Wazee wanakuja kumwona Bracco, wanamkuta kalala, lakini hajambo. Mara Doctor naye anakuja anatoa dischage kwa walio na nafuu, ndipo alikutana na wazee. Wazee waliambiwa mtoto wenu leo ataondoka kurudi nyumbani, hali yake ni nzuri. Wazee walikuwa wamechanishana pesa za matibabu na malazi, walipompa Dr Tausi alizikataa na badala yake wakapewa risiti, kwani kila kitu kishalipia. Pia alitoa pesa akampa Bracco ili zimsaidie akiwa nyumbani. Wazee walishangaa sana, wakaondoka.

II

Bracco ameamua kufanya biashara ya dagaa, katika pita pita zake mitaani, alijikuta amepita mitaa ya Dr Tausi. Tausi alitoka nje kwa nia ya kununua dagaa, alikutana na Bracco. Ha! Bracco alistuka na alifurahi sana, akamwingiza ndani, na akamshauri aache kazi hiyo kwa nia ya kuwa yupo tayari aolewe na yeye, yuko tayari atatoa pesa yeye mwenyewe, kwani pesa kwao sio tatizo. Bracco alijitetea kuwa mimi sina uwezo. Dr alimtoa wasiwasi Bracco. Kwani hata wakati ule ulipolazwa, nilitaka kukwambia lakini nilishindwa. Na Bracco aliambiwa swala kubwa ni kuwa mshenga atafute yeye mwenyewe. Alifurahi sana, na aliondoka mbio hadi nyumbani ili kukamilishe azima yake.

III

Nyumbani kwa mzee Wema, mshenga anaingia alitoa barua ya uchumba. Mzee Wema kama kawaida yake alimwita mwanae na kumuuliza iwapo atakubali kuolewa na Bracco, Tausi alikubali kwa roho moja. Kabla ya kuitwa mtoto wao wazazi walianza kukataa kutokana na uwezo wao ni mdogo. Mzee Wema na mshenga wakapanga kabisa siku ya harusi. Na anataka iwe ya jina jake kuwa ni ndoa ya kwanza kwa binti yake. Sherehe yote gharama itakuwa kwake. Na naomba huyo mchumba aje mara moja kwanza.

IV

Nyumbani kwa mzee Kagunga, mshenga anarudisha jibu na kuelezea mambo ya harusi tayari. Wakaondoka kwenda kupene taarifa wana ndugu.

V

Mzee Wema aliwaalika watu wengi kwa kadi maalum, wakiwemo Mzee Chande, Coaster. Mzee Chande na Coaster walifika kujua ni nani anayeoa, baada ya kuona ni Bracco ndiyo anaoa, waliondoka kwa hasira, katika kipindi tofauti na bila kuaga. Baadaye mzee Wema alitoa usia alipouliza hawa watu wako wapi, alijibiwa wameondoka. Baada ya usia watu waliendelea na tafrija hadi usiku wa manane na wakaondoka. Hapa ndiyo mwisho.

What the Heart Loves
Ally Mkumbila – Bracco Chitosa
(Translation by Siri Lange)

NB. The synopsis has been translated as literally as possible. Changing tenses and so on reflect the 'oral' style that is used in play synopses. Each new scene is generally described in the present tense, but the story itself is told in the past tense, as when someone is telling a story. In the few cases where characters' lines are provided, they are in the present tense and not marked with quotation marks.

Part one
Mr Chande is a wealthy man here in the city. He has several cars, a guesthouse and livestock. Coaster is also rich. The two of them are close friends and they have both come to like Tausi, who is a doctor.

I
Mr Chande is at home with his wife Tamasha. They are discussing their various properties when Coaster enters. They greeted each other and after a while Tamasha went to the kitchen to prepare some food. This gave Chande the opportunity to discuss the fact that he likes Dr Tausi. Coaster was taken aback and told Chande to stop this talk about liking Tausi as I myself have come concerning Tausi, who is a doctor. I have brought you a letter as I want to marry and I would like you to be my go-between. Their conversation was cut off when Tamasha came back. Coaster said goodbye. He asked whether he would get help, but Chande answered I can't.

II
At home Tausi is reading the letter that was brought by Coaster. Masafa then entered with the letter from Chande. She read the letters and then she laughed and talked about how crazy they both were. Tausi was interrupted by her father who came back home. They greeted each other and the father went into another room. Tausi tore the letters into pieces and went to her room. Then Coaster's go-between arrived and Tausi was called for. Tausi rejected. She had not decided to get married. When she found someone she liked, she would inform them.

III
At the hospital Bracco is brought in in a bad state. He is being carried, half unconscious. They were received by the nurse and then they saw the doctor. Before he got medicine, Bracco was given water by the nurse to get the temperature down. Bracco got a bed and was hospitalised and his parents were allowed to leave and then come back the next day. Chande came to see Dr Tausi in her office, and to talk about love. But Dr Tausi answered him I don't have time, I have a seriously ill patient and I ask you to please go out. Tausi was

given gifts but she refused them. Chande left feeling hurt. The doctor started to think about Bracco.

IV

At the medicine man's place, Chande wants Tausi to respond to him and not to remember any other man. And he wants Coaster to get mad so that he will no longer desire Tausi. After he had left, Coaster came to the medicine man to bewitch Chande to die, as he was interfering with his love affair – although Coaster had not even once talked with Tausi about love. The medicine man listened to each of them. Just in order to satisfy them, he gave them some medicine, but without them knowing it, it was different from what they had asked for.

Part two

I

The parents come to see Bracco. They find him sleeping but well. The doctor comes to discharge the ones who have become better, and then she encountered the parents. The parents were told that your child will go back home today, his condition is good. The parents had collected money for the expenses and the hospitalisation. When they gave it to Dr Tausi, she refused to take it and instead they were given a receipt as everything had already been paid. She also gave money to Bracco so as to help him when back home. The old folk were very surprised, and then they left.

II

Bracco has decided to make a living from selling whitebait fish in the streets. During his walking around, he found himself in the street of Dr Tausi. Tausi came out to buy fish and she met with Bracco, oh! Bracco was taken aback and he was very happy. She invited him in and she advised him to quit this work, as she was ready to get married to him, she would pay the money herself, as money was no problem for her family. Bracco opposed the idea as I have no means. The doctor asked him not to worry. Because even that time when you were hospitalised, I wanted to tell you but I couldn't. And Bracco was told that the main issue for him was to find a go-between (*mshenga*). He was very happy, and he ran home to complete his luck.

III

At Mr Wema's house, the go-between arrived and presented his letter of betrothal. Mr Wema, in his usual way, called his daughter and asked her whether she would agree to get married to Bracco. Tausi agreed whole-heartedly. Bracco's parents were sceptical as they had so little means. Mr Wema and the go-between decided on a day to celebrate the wedding. And he wanted to take the whole responsibility, as it was the first marriage of his daughter. He would pay for all the expenses for the celebration. And I would like the fiancé to come here to visit first.

IV

At the home of Mr Kagunga. The go-between returned with the answer and told them that everything for the wedding was now set. They left to inform their relatives.

V

Mr Wema gave invitation cards to many people, among them Mr Chande and Coaster. Mr Chande and Coaster arrived to see who was marrying. After seeing that it was Bracco, they left in anger, each one in a different direction and without saying goodbye. Later Mr Wema asked about their whereabouts and he was told that they had left. After the ceremony people continued celebrating until late in the night and then they left. The end.

The Making of
Os bandoleiros de Schiller
An account of collaboration
on a German classic

MANFRED LOIMEIER

Act 1, scenes are set in: Teatro Avenida, Maputo (Mozambique);
Schauspielhaus, Graz (Austria); Magnet Theatre, Cape Town
(South Africa).

*Dramatis Personae: Mia Couto, Henning Mankell, Manuela Soeiro,
Evaristo Abreu and all the actors of Mutumbela Gogo and M'Bêu,
Mark Fleishman and Jennie Reznek, Claudia Romeder-Szevera*

> On a December evening the theatre was to be re-inaugurated. ... It was past ten
> o'clock by the time Dona Esmeralda was able to switch on the spotlights again and
> the first actor, who had forgotten his lines, stepped on to the stage. The performance
> turned out to be a peculiar experience. It went on until dawn the following
> morning. None of those present, perhaps least of all the actors, fully understood what
> the play was about. On the other hand, none of those in attendance ever forgot what
> they had been part of. Dona Esmeralda, finally alone on the stage at first light, was
> filled with that singular sense of joy which only those who have achieved the impos-
> sible can feel. ... She went out into the city. ... She stopped at a café, sat down at a
> table, and ordered a glass of cognac and some bread. As she pondered how she was
> going to find the money to continue to operate the theatre, she chewed on the
> bread. That was when it occurred to her that the old ticket office and the abandoned
> café in the foyer of the theatre could be revamped as a bakery. By selling bread she
> could earn the money she needed. She ate the rest of the bread, stood up, and
> returned to the theatre to start the process of cleaning up, to make room for the
> dough blender and the ovens. To obtain funds for the necessary investments, she sold
> her car to an official at the British Embassy, and three months later she opened the
> doors to the bakery. (Mankell 2006: 20–21)

This account hints at the achievement of the remarkable Manuela Soeiro,
'Dona Esmeralda' in the scene described above, who, in 1986, brought back to
life the Teatro Avenida, a colonial structure that had been abandoned when the
Portuguese left Maputo and had subsequently been used as a cinema. Since
1986, Soeiro has been the manager and artistic director of the flagship theatre

building in Mozambique. She plays a major role in the examination of the adventure in international collaboration that follows. This is focused on a Mozambican / European collaboration based on Friedrich Schiller's *The Robbers* that was premiered at the Teatro Avenida in January 2005 and subsequently toured in Germany, Switzerland and Austria.

The author of the description above also played major roles in the collaboration and is also remarkable: Swedish-born Henning Mankell has an international following for the Kurt Wallander detective novels which have been translated into 35 languages and sold over 16 million copies worldwide. The passage quoted above comes from his 1995 novel *Comédia Infantil,* translated as *Chronicler of the Winds* by Tiina Nunnally. It draws on his experiences in the Mozambican capital where, between 1986 and 2004, he spent six months of every year at the Avenida directing, providing technical and financial support. *Chronicler of the Winds* reflects his intimate knowledge of the life and work of the theatre, and his deep involvement with the actors based there.

The theatre he describes occupies a privileged place in Mozambique. It is the only building in the country that approximates to conventional European ideas of what constitutes a theatre. Rather like a smaller version of the Market Theatre, Johannesburg, it has a conventional auditorium, a proscenium-arched stage and appropriate seating arrangements. Under the leadership of Manuela Soeiro, the two companies attached to the theatre, M'Bêu and Mutumbela Gogo (founded 1986), organise workshops and function as 'Community Based Organisations' (CBOs), by, for example, producing plays about HIV/AIDS. The companies attached to the Avenida can be described as 'semi-professional' and are the best organised in Maputo, which boasts some 80 drama groups, and in the country as a whole, in which there are approximately 300. During the last twenty years, their repertoires have included well known comedies from Aristophanes to Dario Fo, and some of Mankell's own, comparatively little known, plays. Without a government subsidy, the Avenida has survived, partly thanks to the bakery referred to in the opening quotation. Productions, which run for six weeks, are put on only at the weekends, and every show has to pay for itself. The actors survive because they do not depend entirely on what they can earn at the Avenida. For example, one actor, Adelino Branco, works in television and another, Rogério Manjate who founded M'Bêu, also runs a second theatre group.

M'Bêu, which means 'the seeds' in the Ronga language, is a made up of younger actors and is deeply involved in the annual Maputo International Festivals that have brought together theatre people each August since 1999. (See video *Máscaras austrais festival de teatro de SADC,* 1997.) The festivals have received sponsorship from banks and multinational companies and M'Bêu has also generated a certain amount of money by performing at conferences organised by the government and by local and international NGOs. As part of its outreach programme, M'Bêu puts on productions that explore social and personal situations. It also organises workshops with young people in the city and in the rural areas. Furthermore, it carries out research into customs, and incorporates the results of this research into its major productions.

The name 'Mutumbela Gogo' derives from the cries of encouragement used to spur on dancers at feasts. It is also the synonym for 'carnival's masquerade'. The group was founded in 1986 and initially staged texts by Mozambican authors. It then turned to Europe for inspiration and, for example, in 1991/2 put on *Lyistrata* by Aristophanes, *Woyzek* by Georg Büchner, *Jeppe of the Hills* by Ludvig Holberg and works by Bertolt Brecht. It also contributed to Theatre for Development through Mankell's *Jeito* ('coolness'), a play about HIV/Aids. Mankell directed this play which was funded by Population Services International, a US non-profit group that was promoting the use of condoms as part of a Ministry of Health drive. They also put on other plays by Mankell, including *O homen honesto* and *Os Homens*. The first, about the difficulties faced by a man who wants to live an honest life in a corrupt world, recalls Brecht's thought-provoking *Good Woman of Setzuan*. The second also raises major issues: set on New Year's Eve in a supermarket, it concerns three people who have been locked inside the shop and who face issues of liberty and choice. It was partly thanks to Mankell that, in the mid-1990s, Mutumbela Gogo visited Europe, taking his play about street children, *Os meninos de ninguém*, to Zurich. (Manjate, email, 23 June 2006), and also visiting Sweden, Portugal, and France. This was followed in 2003 by *Butterfly Blues*, an artistic collaboration and hybrid production that began to get off the ground in 2002 when Claudia Romeder-Szevera, the literary and artistic director of the theatre in Graz, asked Mankell and Mutumbela Gogo to put together a play about African immigrants living in Europe. This was presented in 2003 as part of a special season when Graz was the European Capital of Culture. *Butterfly Blues* had its premiere on 10 January, as a co-production between Mutumbela Gogo and the Schauspielhaus Graz. The credits included:

> Author and director: Henning Mankell;
> Decor and costumes: Manuela Soeiro and Gabi Mai;
> Music: Mariana Venancio Dove and Matthias Loibner;
> Actors: Lucrecia Paco, Graça Silva, Johannes Lang, Stefan Maaß.

The performance of *Butterfly Blues* opened wide the doors for Mutumbela Gogo and the group was subsequently invited to Austria in 2004, the year in which the Danube Festival in Linz, Upper Austria, focused the tenth anniversary of the end of apartheid. Before looking at the history of the collaboration on *Os bandoleiros de Schiller* that grew out of discussions at Linz, it is useful to introduce one more important player. He is a writer with extensive experience of theatre and some of international collaboration and who was to make a decisive input into *Os bandoleiros*: Mia Couto.

The son of Portuguese immigrants, Couto was born in Beira in 1955, and briefly attended medical school in Laurenço Marques in the seventies before abandoning his studies to become a member of Frelimo. After independence was secured in 1975, he returned to university and completed a degree in

biology. A poet from an early age, Couto was always attracted to writing and
rose to become director of the national news agency (AIM) and chief editor of
the weekly magazine *Tempo*. In 1992, his novel *Sleepwalking Land* was
published and well received. He currently writes, researches and runs a
company that investigates factors affecting the environment. (See Anon 2001.)
He has long been involved with the theatre and has taken great satisfaction in
providing storylines for Mutumbela Gogo. He is on record as saying:

> Mutumbela Gogo is part of my life, … I have been part of Mutumbela Gogo since
> day one, so to say. I took part in the first meetings. It is almost like my offspring.
> (Couto: Programme 2005 (np). Interventions have been made in the English spoken
> or written by those for whom English may be a second, third, fourth language only
> when meaning might be lost.)

He expanded on this in an email:

> I have been working with Mutumbela since the beginning. Actually, I am a member
> of that theatre group. Since the beginning the methodology we are used to is the
> same: I make up the fundaments of one story and they then work to create the char-
> acters. I rejoin the actors two or three months later, to discuss the sequence of the
> text. So, one may say: improvisation is part of the process of creation between
> Mutumbela and me. (Couto 17 July 2006)

His experience of collaborative theatre projects has included working with
Mark Fleishman and Jennie Reznek on *Voices Made Night* (2001), an important
collaborative initiative that involved him in working with Mutumbela Gogo
and the South African Magnet Theatre. That, however, it is a project that falls
outside the concerns of this chapter.

Act 2, scenes are set in: Linz (Austria), Danube-Festival; Theater Rampe, Stuttgart (Germany); Schauspielhaus Vienna (Austria).

Dramatis personae: Manuela Soeiro, Margit Niederhuber, Stephan Bruckmeier, Mia Couto, Rogério Manjate, Eva Hosemann

The performance of *Butterfly Blues* in Graz brought together some of the team
that made a major contribution to the Mozambican version of Friedrich
Schiller's *The Robbers*, the production that provides the central concern for this
paper. The people who took important initiatives at Linz were:

> Manuela Soeiro from Teatro Avenida, who has already been introduced and who
> was taking part in a conference to mark the tenth anniversary of the end of apartheid;

> Margit Niederhuber from Vienna, who was involved in Mozambique from the
> 1970s onwards (Niederhuber 2006). She followed the work being done at the

Teatro Avenida and knew Couto since 1978. In 1980 she wrote a thesis about literacy campaigns in Mozambique, and, more recently, was involved in co-productions with Mozambicans working for TV and radio on gender issues and child soldiers;

Stephan Bruckmeier, a stage director who had worked at Vienna and was about to move on to Stuttgart. He was artistic director of the Danube Festival and he was interested in the possibility of a co-production with the theatre group from Maputo.

After having decided in principle to go ahead with the collaboration, Bruckmeier, as producer and director, travelled to Mozambique where he outlined his plans to the members of Mutumbela Gogo. He was able to put forward the idea of an African / Mozambican version of Schiller's *The Robbers* confident that he would be supported in the venture by Eva Hosemann of the Theater Rampe in Stuttgart and, more symbolically, by the Schauspielhaus Vienna. The Schiller link was important at this point because 2006, the scheduled date for performance, marked the 200th anniversary of Schiller's death.

Bruckmeier, who regards himself as 'a big fan of Schiller's work' (Bruckmeier 17 May 2006), was hugely impressed by the atmosphere in Maputo and he left with the feeling that he definitely wanted to work with Teatro Avenida. Coming from a country where everyone seemed to be depressed, he felt that Maputo was a city full of optimistic people. He later spoke about the feelings of renewal and transformation sweeping through Southern Africa, which could be compared to the *Sturm-und-Drang* movement in German society 200 years ago. Schiller's *Robbers* was, he thought, the ideal play for Mozambique because it dealt with liberation and could also be liberating. 'Once differences are bridged, the theatre process cannot be stopped,' says Bruckmeier.

Thus we are not doing *The Robbers* by Schiller in the original. Instead we make our involvement with and exploration of *The Robbers* into a theatre evening whose aesthetics and dramatic style are marked by the African conception of culture and theatre. Mia Couto, as an author and advisor, has served the function of a bridge between the two cultures. Thus this project presents the author Schiller and the play's timeless themes to the African audience while at the same time giving the European audience insight into the social structures and problems of this African country and into its people's modes of artistic expression.

Rogério Manjate, who has already been introduced and whose helpful comments I draw on extensively, describes the group's first encounter with Bruckmeier in the following, cautious, terms:

It was a 'meeting', in the sense that we, the actors, didn't know him or his work, and neither did he know us. At first, it was a matter of trial and error, and we were also pressed for time, because we only had five weeks, plus the Christmas period which made things a bit difficult at times. But later on, things started to improve, particularly after we travelled to Germany.

Manjate continues:

With other foreign directors, for example, it works differently. They come and see our work, and then decide to do a project with us, in which case we always involve someone/another director who is already familiar with our work. It helps to know our method, you know, the one we also used devising Os Bandoleiros: improvisiation. (Manjate 23 June 2006)

The first step having been taken, Bruckmeier, as producer, had to start fundraising in earnest. It was at this point that the contacts with the Schauspielhaus Vienna began to pay dividends. Because by this link, Buckmeier was able to get money from the Austrian Ministry for Foreign Affairs, and the same ministry undertook to cover the costs of some of the flights involved. Because of his position in the Theater Rampe in Stuttgart, Bruckmeier was able to get funding from DaimlerChrysler, a company based in Stuttgart that is playing an important part within the South African Initiative of the German economy (SAFRI). From this point on, partly thanks to the recommendations of those involved with SAFRI, it was possible to attract a range of sponsors. Requests found favour with the Austrian Embassy in Harare, the Austrian Merkur bank, the Paul Zsolnay publishing house in Vienna (publisher of the very popular German translations of Mankell's detective novels), the Bayer Arts Foundation, and the various chemical industries in Leverkusen. Support was also received from the 'Landesstiftung Baden-Württemberg', the city of Stuttgart, the German Society for Schiller, South African Airways, the Austrian Trade Union Congress (ÖGB) and the Austrian Society for Development and Corporation.

Bruckmeier stressed that, with an awareness of the situation in Mozambique, it was important to find sponsors, whose products were not associated with the former oppressors and who were making positive contributions to national development. He wanted sponsors who had good reputations. In this respect, it was important that Bayer and Daimler were funding Anti-HIV/Aids-projects. He also realised that having highly reputable sponsors would make it easier for the actors from Mozambique when they applied for visas to travel to Germany, Switzerland and Austria.

As soon as the necessary backing was in place, rehearsals started and Couto became deeply involved. He had already been approached by Soeiro and asked to begin thinking about a Mozambican adaptation of *The Robbers*. He was interested from the outset, but he could only get hold of a version of the play in Brazilian Portuguese! He felt the classical language used in it suggested people who were slightly crazy. He was also concerned about the length of the original. However, *Os bandoleiros* was always a genuine co-production, and Niederhuber, who was involved as dramaturg cut some scenes to create space for input from Couto and Mutumbela Gogo.

Couto was encouraged by the fact that this co-production was seen by Bruckmeier as a project that would involve collaboration and that the final text would be created through an extended period of collaboration:

[My] aim was to get in touch with a writer who had lived in another era, to create a dialogue between Europe and Africa. It was important to work with Schiller, send him on a journey, into a different time, a different place – to face the challenge of transporting a German classic to contemporary Mozambique. (Programme Note, 2005)

The rehearsal method adopted involved taking a scene from Schiller's original, improvising around the basic situation in it, sifting what had been discovered through improvisation and then returning to the original. But there was room for innovation. For example the Mozambican group added a scene in which a robbery actually takes place on stage. This was based on the experience of one member of the group, who on her first day in Maputo had had a bag snatched through the window of a car.

In dividing up tasks during the rehearsal period, Bruckmeier's particular responsibility was to keep Schiller's plot in mind while Couto ensured the play had a Mozambican dimension. Bruckmeier ensured the retention of *Sturm-und-Drang* elements while Couto sought for what might be regarded as parallels in the current moods of Mozambican daily life. As Bruckmeier pointed out, one looked back, while the other kept the present and future in sight. Into this process one unexpected line that Couto began to explore concerned the experience of Mozambicans who had been students and workers, the so-called 'Madjermanes,' in the German Democratic Republic (GDR) and who had had to return home after German reunification (1994). Their fate, after years in a foreign land, had been to be regarded as outsiders in the land of their birth. The experience of these Madjermanes had been brought to Couto's attention by two circumstances. The first was the impact of Moisés Rendição Pinto's story, 'How much is a 'Cabinet'?' that had won first prize in a literary contest. ('Cabinet' was a brand of cigarettes sold in the GDR.) The second was being a member of a jury given the task of awarding a literary prize for work submitted by Madjermanes. In a programme note to *Os bandoleiros*, he wrote that he 'realised' that the members of the group who travelled to the GDR had been through 'a unique collective and individual experience'. In the course of working on the production, Couto and the actors learned a great deal about this 'experience' and about German history. For his part, Bruckmeier, to his astonishment, met many people in Mozambique who spoke or understood German. These discoveries entered the play.

As Charlotte Staehelin pointed out in a perceptive review for *Tages-Anzeiger,* the production also showed self-awareness about the collaborative process. This was, she felt, apparent from the incorporation of a play-within-a-play sequence. In the course of this episode, Karl/Carlos creates scenes which show daily life in Mozambique. Of the innovation, Couto said: 'I was intending to see theatre happening on a stage. As you can understand (this theatrical convention) is a very new thing for some rural communities and the naive and at the same time sophisticated understanding of that art was something that might – in my view – create misunderstandings that could work on stage.' (Couto email 17 July 2006)

The main narrative of *Os bandoleiros,* as it emerged in the collaboration, centres on Carlos who parallels Schiller's Karl and who, in the 1980s, is awarded a fellowship to study in Eastern Germany. There he discovers the classics of German literature and the theatre. With his head full of *The Robbers*, he returns to rural Mozambique to take over the shop that had belonged to his late father. Carlos falls in love with a girl called Nadia, and for this and other reasons, is envied by his brother Francisco, Schiller's Franz. Carlos feels hemmed in by the limited horizons of his parents' village, and begins to fulfil his dream of producing *The Robbers*. His mother overhears his actors rehearsing a scene in which a robbery is being planned, and, unaware of the convention they are working in, jumps to the conclusion that her son and his friends are planning to actually rob a bank. When Carlos leaves the village for the town, Francisco begins to plot: he first turns people against Carlos and then makes overtures to Nadia. When Carlos returns for Nadia, he realises that people no longer trust him. His desire for revenge on Francisco who he knows has been working against him is then interwoven with his plans to put on *The Robbers*. (At this point, it should be noted that collaborating on the project prompted discussions between Bruckmeier, Couto and the actors about colonialism, economics and politics. Some of these discussions were incorporated in the final script.) When Francisco fears that the truth about what he has done is going to be revealed, he wants to kill Carlos. However, he dies himself before he can put his plan into action. In the closing scenes of *Os bandoleiros*, Schiller himself makes an appearance, complaining that he has been 'robbed' of his play! Then, in a shift that increases the levels on which the play operates, the mother of Carlos and Francisco enters weeping, insisting that women don't want to see plays about robbers on the stage. They want to hear the truth about their own lives as women and mothers in Mozambique.

Os bandoleiros de Schiller was given its European premiere on 10 June, 2005, in the National Theatre, Mannheim, during the Internationale Schillertage. It was then taken to Theater Rampe, Stuttgart (June 18, and June 23–25), the Theater Rigiblick, Zurich, (June 21–22), the Schauspielhaus, Vienna, (June 28–July 2), and the Kesselhaus, Berlin (November 17–19). The programme available to patrons included notes that I have already drawn on and the following list:

Director: Stephan Bruckmeier;
Text: Mia Couto;
Decor: Manuela Soeiro, Berry Bickle;
Costumes: Yolanda Thomas;
Dramaturgy : Margit Niederhuber;
Music: Simão Adriano Tembe;
Actors: Graça Silva, Rogério Manjate, Jorge Vaz, Eliot Alex, Sergio Chusane, Adelino Branquinho, Lucretia Pato.

While it was recognised that the collaboration had produced an African reading of Schiller, this did not necessarily meet with approval from the critics. Indeed, partly because it was played in Portuguese (with supertitles in German), it offered, to the overwhelming majority, little more than song and dance. Nicole C. Buck, writing in the *Stuttgarter Zeitung*, caught the spirit of some of the reviews by describing the production as 'hybrid', 'clownish', 'slapstick', 'post-colonial' and 'ironic' (2005). She bemoaned the fact that, compared to the original plot, sacrifices had been made in the interests of humour.

Act 3, scene is set in: Maputo (Mozambique), Teatro Avenida.

Dramatis personae: Rogério Manjate, Mia Couto, Stephan Bruckmeier

What did those at the Mozambican end, particularly Couto and members of Mutumbela Gogo, think of the collaboration and how did the audience respond in Maputo? First of all, as far as Couto was concerned, it was important to emphasise that the production was the result of a two-way process. He said:

> Stephan (Bruckmeier) came to Maputo already linked with *Bandoleiros* project. We have discussed a lot and I found from the beginning, that there was a very productive mutual understanding. (email 17 June 2006)

It was recognised that Schiller's play was new to everybody concerned with the production in Mozambique and, of course, *Os bandoleiros* was entirely new for the Mozambican audience in the Teatro Avenida.

It must be conceded that the hybrid form did not speak directly to Mozambicans. As Manjate put it:

> In Mozambique they wanted to get the story and it was not there for them, because the play was a kind of suggestion of another story inside the other and the plot was not strength cause of it. (email 23 July 2006)

This seems to be a less than whole-hearted endorsement of the final product.

Conclusion/ Coda

Looking back over the whole collaborative project, one can conclude that a European initiative which might have been a little starry-eyed was taken up by the Mozambican collaborators with deep committment. While the result was not entirely satisfactory to either side, the production allowed the impossible to happen: it gave Mutumbela Gogo the chance to perform in Europe. In contrast to the production of Mankell's play *Butterfly Blues* in Graz in 2003, it showed it was possible to perform a play which had been Africanised by Couto and the actors of Mutumbela Gogo. *Os bandoleiros* in its new form is without doubt an African play. This play opened the door for Mutumbela Gogo as far as the German-speaking world was concerned. Created by Couto and the actors it shows the extent to which Mutumbela Gogo had begun to find a truly Mozambican voice and to take part in a cultural experiment that opened onto the outside world. The Schiller-link remained as a reminder of financial considerations: it would have been inconceivable for a 'straight' Mozambican production to have made it. Funding would have been an insoluble problem. In fact Bruckmeier said:

> It would never be possible to sell a group like Mutumbela Gogo from Mozambique with their plays here. (Telephone interview 17 May 2006)

All those involved in this co-production learnt a lot from working together. Perhaps most important, they learned just how long the chain of agents and transmitters is in a venture of this kind. Each 'link' introduces changes and the result is that something new is born, something that has elements of strangeness for absolutely everybody.

BIBLIOGRAPHY

Anon., 'A Southern Dreamscape.' *Mail and Guardian*, 9 March 2001.
Anon., 'Ein Gastarbeiter in Afrika.' *Focus*, 12 August 2002, 112–16. (On Mankell.)
Anon., 'Henning Mankell: Chronicle of a death foretold: Sweden's biggest literary export since Strindberg, has for decades led a double life.' (Review of *Chronicler of the Winds*.) http://enjoyment.independent.co.uk/books/ features/article356138.ece accessed 20 July 2006
Anon., 'Press Release', http:archiv.schauspielhaus.at/arhiv/ (then search for 'Räuber')
Becker, Kristin, *'Importierte Klassikerpflege'*, *die tageszeitung*, 15 June 2005.
Buck, Nicole C., 'Francisco hasst Carlos', *Stuttgarter Zeitung*, 20 June 2005.
Couto, Mia, *Sleepwalking Land*. Cape Town: Double Storey, 2006. (Originally published in Mozambican Portuguese as *Terra sonâmbula*, 1992.)
Lanon, Philippe, 'Le fjord des crocodiles', *Libération*, 12 April 2001.
Mankell, Henning, *Chronicler of the Winds*. Translated by Tiina Nunnally: London: Hervill Secker, 2006. (Originally published in Swedish as *Comédia Infantil*, 1995.)
Mergelsberg, Katja, 'Theater wird gebraucht', *Mosambik-Rundbrief*, Nr. 69, April 2006, pp. 36–8.
Niederhuber, Margit. 'Gesprächsrunde mit Stephan Bruckmeier, Mia Couto und Manuela Soeiro, Maputo, 10 January 2005'. The programme for *Os bandoleiros de Schiller/Schiller's Räuber*, Stuttgart, 2005, Margit Niederhuber,
Schweizerische Depeschenagentur (SDA/KW-HR.SFD), 'Mosambik feiert 30 Jahre Unabhängigkeit', 15 June 2005; and Mergelsberg, Katja, 'Theater wird gebraucht', *Mosambik-Rundbrief*, Nr. 69, April 2006, 36–8.
Sayagues, Mercedes, 'Mozambique: Theatre Boom', *Inter Press Service*, 19 July 1996.
Stachelin, Charlotte, 'Friedrich Schiller als ein glücklicher Zufall', *Tages-Anzeiger*, 21 June 2005.

Interviews conducted by Manfred Loimeier

Bruckmeier, Stephan, telephone-interview, 17 May 2006.
Couto, Mia, email interview, 17 July 2006.
Manjate, Rogério, email interview, 23 June 2006.
Niederhuber, Margit, telephone interview, 16 May 2006.
Other email contacts as indicated in the text.

Videos

Máscaras austrais festival de teatro de SADC
Carvalho, Sol de
Maputo : Promarte Lda.,1997
1 videocassette (56 min.); sd., col.; 1/2 in
Summary: Documentary on a theatre festival held in Maputo in 1997, featuring participants from numerous southern African countries. Includes interviews with festival organizers and participants, and segments of some of the works presented.

Comédia Infantil (1998)
Feature Film based on novel by Mankell.
Portugal – Mozambique – Sweden
Starring: Sergio Titos, João Manja, Joaquina Odete, Jaime Julio, Avelino Manhica
Directed by Solveig Nordlund

Project Phakama
Lesotho 2004
'Follow the bird'
(birds that flock are birds that learn)

LUCY RICHARDSON

Project Phakama is a cross-arts exchange network involving arts practitioners (facilitators) and young people (participants) from eleven countries and four continents. Phakama is the Khosa word for rise up, lift up, elevate.

Project Phakama was initiated in 1996 by LIFT (London International Festival of Theatre) in partnership with Sibikwa Theatre in Johannesburg with an initial month-long creative training programme for artists, teachers and arts education practitioners from each province in South Africa. The programme, facilitated by a team of LIFT-associated artists and arts educators used the workshops to explore existing arts education practice in South Africa and the UK. Training in site specific performance by the LIFT team augmented existing skills. In exchange, the South Africans brought an array of experiences to enhance the LIFT training particularly of working in conflict situations.

This exchange laid the foundation for Phakama's work. Over the last ten years the Phakama network has grown in South Africa and London and evolved a methodology for working with individuals and communities. Phakama is a registered company and charity in both South Africa and London. While it is still run mostly by volunteers in both countries and many people give time and energy for nothing, it has the structures to fund raise and it is supported, at times, both by private sponsorship and public grants. A range of participatory projects involving young people have taken place in London, Cape Town, Seshego, Dublin, Mmabatho and Johannesburg.

More recently, the Phakama network was introduced in India in a month-long project that ended with a site specific performance with the young participants. It continues to function in India via collaboration with a new university in Pune which provides space, facilitators and financial support.

In January 2003 'Phakama SADC' (Southern African Development Community) was officially launched in Lesotho. I will describe this project in more detail in this article. It involved participants and facilitators from Namibia, Botswana, Lesotho, South Africa, Mozambique, Mauritius and England. Phakama continues to operate in some of these countries, thriving in Botswana where it is based at a school.

In March 2004 Phakama was established in South America bringing together facilitators and participants from Argentina, UK and Brazil. Hosted by existing NGOs in both South American countries, and with links with local universities, we are confident that this project will be sustainable. It seems that the bigger the network and the more links with other organisations, institutions and groups the greater the likelihood of Phakama surviving.

Of course there are many such projects happening in Africa (and the other countries we work in) but it is Phakama's process of making work (which I will go on to describe) which makes it distinct. This process is reflected in all our administrative, production and networking activities. I believe that it is partly because of this commitment to collaboration, empowerment and democracy in every decision we make or action we take that Phakama survives despite its economic struggles.

At the heart of Project Phakama is the belief that, irrespective of differences in age, experiences or cultures, the makers of art can share creative responsibility equally. Therefore the approach is participant-centred: each participant's experience and imagination is the starting point for the creative process.

The work challenges notions of what theatre is, where it can happen and, most importantly, who can be involved. Phakama believes that the place, both physical and emotional, where different cultures meet is often a place of intense creativity. So Phakama brings together, in one place, diverse peoples. The project engages with local diverse communities exploring how artists can work with a range of institutions and individuals

It is not surprising that this process with its emphasis on democracy and on multiple voices emerged out of a group of South Africans, soon after the demise of apartheid. Given the chance to create their perfect and creative working environment they insisted on one where every voice is sought, every idea is used and every individual is a leader.

Through a process referred to as Give and Gain, the learning process becomes two way. Everybody has something that they can give to the project and everybody has something that they can gain, whether this is skills, knowledge or information. Through this approach, where skills and ideas can be interchanged, everyone can become both a student and a teacher.

Each project is undertaken in residency of a number of weeks. All the ideas and concepts which form the creative work emerge from the group and no one leads or directs the process. The emphasis on forms and images emerging out of an almost random and chaotic collecting of ideas, before being woven together by a group, interests me. In Africa the creation myth is often described as an ongoing process, one which unfolds. One myth in particular uses weaving as its metaphor. It describes how the universe evolved out of four elements which when woven together created a new thing.

The way in which ideas evolve and performance emerges in a Phakama project is a complex and sometimes difficult one tied in with social issues, individual and group functioning. Perhaps, however, it is at the core of both the quality of the work and it contributes to the sustainability of the organisation.

Here I am going to attempt to trace how an idea or concept '**the bird**' developed during one residency, whilst trying to describe the creative process in its context. Perhaps this may go some way to demonstrating how that process inspires facilitators and participants and allows them a sense of empowerment and ownership. The residency I describe took place in Lesotho in January 2003, with artists drawn from seven SADC countries. The performance, which took place in and around the conference centre and museum in the small country town of Morija, involved over 50 performers and was entitled *The Child I Curry*.

The project was conceived two years before it actually happened when a group of SADC artists met at another conference. They were convinced that they needed to come together to share good community practice and establish a collaborative way of working. They were also intrigued by Phakama's idea of site specific performance. Everyone raised funds for their own flights but by the time we left for Lesotho, two years later, we did not know if we had enough money for the project. We did have the confidence of the relationships that had emerged in the planning time and the enthusiasm to take that risk. Eventually, thanks to the hard work of Selloane the facilitator from Lesotho who co-ordinated the project, Save the Children provided enough money to house and make a project.

The title *The Child I Curry* was deliberately vague and ambiguous. We were not even sure what it meant when we dreamt it up. Only that it puts the child at the centre of the work and recognised the emergent process we were going to engage in. Both the young people and those of us who facilitate the work find it all too easy to jump on the problems of their lives, the things that deter them from success, and the things they must avoid. It is sometimes unclear if these things are a reality in all their lives (clearly some of them are for some of them) or if they are just received threats they have learnt to fear. We wanted to celebrate their lives and for them to celebrate themselves. If the theatre is to empower audience and performers it also needs to uplift their spirits.

One exercise helped this to happen and happily allowed the participants to introduce their town Morija, to us. It put them in the role of givers of knowledge. They were asked in small groups to discuss and choose their favourite place in Morija. Once chosen they had to find a spot in our living/rehearsal/performance space – a huge garden with small Basotho huts, outdoor kitchens, trees, swing etc. – to re-create their favourite place. So the outdoor kitchen became a museum where cultural events, singing and dancing took place with people laughing and dancing, the swing became a romantic spot on the hillside, one of the bedrooms became a waterfall (the giver of life) and the area around the tree became a mountainside.

It was during this exercise **that the bird first took flight**. One group devised a beautiful piece where they made the shapes, movements and sounds of birds they knew from the mountain. At the end of the piece the entire cast flew away behind one of the bedrooms into the countryside. These birds appeared to have hopes and dreams, and the young participants had huge smiles on their faces as they flew determinedly away.

One of the most important aspects of a Phakama project is the fact that all facilitators (and where possible participants too) are resident. There are not set working hours, the work starts at breakfast, is intense all day and then continues into the evening with discussions and planning sessions. Even after some people have collapsed into bed others are up working, making, reflecting.

It was on one of these evenings, as I wrote the plan we had agreed upon on huge A2 paper, Clinton from South Africa organised the paints, beads and glue for the next day and the facilitators from Mauritius sat chatting with us, that Sylvan, a young and quiet facilitator from Mauritius who found it hard to contribute ideas in a large group, began to fiddle with some old bits of paper. As quick as a flash his long brown fingers folded and tore **and he had made a bird**. We all dropped what we were doing. The bird was perfect. We begged him to teach us how and whilst we worked we talked about what the bird meant to us. Soon all of us knew how to make paper birds and how to make them fly. Under the stars of a warm Morija night we ran around flying our birds.

The next day Sylvan taught a group of participants how to make the paper birds and they became part of a small performance flying into the hall around the heads of the other participants and out into the garden. Those participants who had first shown us the mountain birds were delighted to see them in their first transformation into small white symbols of peace. When we came later to choosing which moments from our residency should be included in the performance (a long and sometimes painful process which involves everyone) most of the participants and facilitators remembered the paper birds.

In his article *Theatre and Social Issues in Malawi*, David Kerr (2002) argues that imperialism imposed a style of performance on Africa which did not suit it. He identifies its two features as 'individual authorship, and the separation of the audience from the performers.' (312) The popular African tradition on the other hand draws heavily on collaboration and does not respect this spectator/performer division. It is closely linked with other cultural practices of ritual and town meetings. Historically performance in Africa is not only an essential part of the culture but one which is used to explore the society. As Frances Harding points out in the introduction to her reader *The Performance Arts in Africa*:

> Performance is a preferred *form* of iteration, explication and re-enforcement of social order in a primarily oralate society … It is also a primary forum for the exploration of new ideas, a new order. (2002 7–8. Harding has an end-note on 'oralate' – 'As distinct from 'literate'.)

In Morija we agreed that we wanted the audience to be part of the performance, not just watching. We agreed that moving around, being part of a procession which used songs they knew and dances they were familiar with would begin this process. But we wanted them to contribute their ideas too. Many of them were young people, many were the parents of young people, and some worked in organisations dedicated to supporting and developing young people. What were their dreams? How did they believe we should cook the child? We talked through the possibility of wallpapering a wall of the room for them to write their ideas on: a kind of ever-growing installation in one of the halls. We talked about them having the opportunity to call out their dreams in a call-and-response during the finale songs. These ideas were not rejected even after much discussion but were written up on our own wall of ideas.

The conference centre we were working in had one wall made up of windows and glass doors. Early on in the process we found the young people were inspired by being outside. Literally they were able to breathe in the air around them and the odd rehearsal spaces under trees and around huts informed their work positively. So it became our habit to warm up indoors and discuss the tasks then to rehearse outdoors. The energy change as the doors were opened and the young people went singing and dancing out spreading across the garden was tangible. It felt that on this journey some of the creative work was done. This move to the outdoors, this 'travelling' became essential to the work.

Finally we hit upon the idea we would finally use in the performance, to involve the audience. **The birds**. Each young person makes a paper bird. Before the show begins they wander amongst the audience chatting, breaking down the relationship which sets performer and audience apart. They take their bird to friends and strangers in the audience and ask them to write their dreams for young people on it. They do. Some thoughts are profound, some funny, some simple but heart rending. The once white birds are now multi-coloured – covered in hopes and dreams. They are no longer just a symbol of peace but the carriers of dreams.

After the first song the birds lead the audience out of the open windows into the garden for the next scene. At some point during the performance they disappear only to be returned to the audience at the very end with the request 'please look after my dreams'. The audience is not only asked to contribute to the performance but also to take the performance on after the lights have been put out and the dancing is over; to take responsibility for the impact of the performance.

We need something big to lead the procession. It is quite a long way from our first site to the second and whilst the young people will sing at high energy forever and ever it needs a focus. It is not difficult to agree that a **big bird** is the answer. Clinton and a group of young people set out to make the bird out of chicken wire and material and hundreds of beads donated by a workshop in Cape Town.

The site of creativity, whilst we pore over the beaded feathers, is also the site of cultural exchange. This is where I hear of the unrest and bloodshed of 1998. Lesotho is a monarchy. However, for the 23 years preceding 1993 it was under military control. In 1998 the second elections since that time were held. The LCD (Lesotho Congress for Democracy) party had a landslide victory. Many Basotho protested that there had been widespread cheating in the elections and there followed months of protest. In 1998 the newly elected government who were losing control called upon the SADC countries to help. Troops from Botswana, Zimbabwe and South Africa entered the country and a battle between rebel Basotho and mainly South African troops resulted in bloodshed, torching and looting. It is here that one of the youngsters tells me about his involvement. He speaks of his fear but also of his belief that South Africa should not have been involved. Clinton (white South African) is working alongside us and listens in.

It is here I learn about the black cloth one of our participants is wearing around their neck which identifies them as a child in mourning. And I am able to tell them about London. Difficult to explain, in this place of great expanses of sky where you can always see a mountain, that you can never see the horizon in London, that the sky is rarely completely clear.

Food is always a talking point at Phakama. I suppose when you get together a group of people from many different countries, where one has as her staple potatoes, another yams, another cassava, another millet, there are likely to be issues. There is also always some illness because people are not used to the water or the food and because they are tired. On this particular project the discussion about food became a focus in the first training week.

Apart from the participants from South Africa and UK everybody was new to Phakama philosophy. Also the facilitators had vastly different levels of experience. Some had never worked as artists or teachers before, others were very experienced and brilliant community workers and others were professional dancers. Somehow we had to begin to work as a team and introduce the idea of a truly democratic process. At first in meetings Fabio, Clinton and I (the facilitators from South Africa and the UK) tended to do all the talking. Ideas about the work came up and every one else was silent. I know it wasn't that they didn't have ideas, but somehow they did not feel they had a right to express them. They had no ownership of the project. Meetings were short and unsatisfying. I was worried that we were in some way inhibiting them.

Then the food crisis began. Atanasio from Mozambique was sick. He threw up all night (which was unfortunate for him and for Lucky from Namibia who had to share a bed with him) and was shaking and thirsty. I was sure it was food poisoning and would pass, others were more worried. Atanasio was back with us by the afternoon but the debate about food had begun. Every single person in the room had something to say on the matter. The debate was eloquent and heated.

There were two main issues. Earlier in the week we had been fed by a woman in the village, Matatu, whose food was delicious. Some of the female facilitators had stayed with her for the first couple of days and had become very fond of her as well as her food. However for the rest of the stay we had booked into the cultural centre where we were to stay to eat. Some people wanted to continue to eat with Matatu arguing that she would lose money she was relying on. Others felt we should eat at the centre in order to keep the project together in one place and in order to centralise the money given to the village. Some had looked in the centre's kitchen and were convinced it was dirty, another had seen a dirty cup. Several commented on the serious faces of the women who cooked. Atanasio, who had been sick, spoke up. He argued that we should not accuse other countries of dirtiness and blamed his sickness on simple unfamiliarity. Eventually we voted and agreed to eat our lunch with Matatu and breakfast and supper at the centre. Everyone seemed happy with this solution and I was thrilled that we had come to the decision by what I thought was a truly democratic process.

However the next day I was summoned into the office of the centre. We were to pack our bags and leave the next day. The women in the kitchen were not happy that we were eating lunch elsewhere. Of course I apologised, assured them that it was not a personal slight and agreed to eat all our meals at the centre.

I took this report back to the meeting. We were all rather shame faced. We realised we had made the wrong decision, not included everyone in our decision-making process, and we were determined to redress it. However from this time onwards everyone contributed to meetings. Everyone felt that they had a voice and that they had a responsibility to making sure the right decisions were made. The discussions about food had empowered us all.

Lucky was the first to make the women who cooked for us smile. He came running into the kitchen before dinner one day singing and dancing. He insisted they all stand up and join him. They did, beating on saucepans and waving their hands about. Their serious faces had been more to do with not being able to understand than rudeness. The next day they brought in grass skirts which they wore to dance in and they showed Lucky how to dance. He dressed up in a skirt and we all joined in the song. Now the women were our friends. We were determined that they should open the show and Lucky made this his project.

They watched us rehearse (we saw them gathered in corners or looking out of windows). And the food got better, more salad and fruit (we only had to ask). We needed a pot so that these very women could cook a child … a curried child. They found one for us, just big enough to fit our smallest child. What were they to sing whilst they cooked? They had an idea but didn't want to preview it. We should trust them. When, on the first performance, they came sashaying out of the kitchen into the dining room big smiles on their faces and flapping their arms like wings whilst they sang a child's song about birds I wanted to cheer. **They too had found birds!** From our debate, our disharmony, our bad decisions and our prejudices had come a brilliant opening to the show.

At the end of the show after the audience have a bird back in their hand the **young people turn into birds themselves**. Flying, arms outstretched, through the crowds of audience down the hillside to their final finale positions. Somehow they do not need the paper birds any more. They have through this process become at least a bit more empowered. They are able to take responsibility for their own flight. And we have come full circle to their initial improvisation. They teach each other how to fly.

On the 5th January 2002, fourteen facilitators flew in a big bird to Johannesburg airport. We alighted in Morija for a short while leaving birds all over the place. But perhaps the most important thing of all were the newly empowered individuals and projects which flew back home. The British Council who had partly funded the project and had loved the performance agreed to give each country a small amount of seed money for their next projects – in Mauritius the caravan around the beaches; in Namibia the workshop in a home for the homeless; in Mozambique a project about sexual abuse; in South Africa work in the Western Cape. The young facilitators from Botswana, Jessica and Boipelo, fundraised extensively and established a Phakama which still operates in the most destitute regions of Botswana. Fabio came back to UK and began planning new international projects and a wonderful two year project with young refugees resident in the UK. Clinton returned to Cape Town and revived Phakama there.

The Phakama bird has spread its wings to SADC and the big bird lives on in the hearts and minds of the funders, audience and the participants of Morija, in Lesotho – known locally, appropriately, as 'The Kingdom in the Sky'.

Jessica the 19-year-old facilitator from Botswana wrote in her evaluation:

> In a nutshell, Phakama teaches its members whatever there is to learn, and because we are PHAKAMA, we are each other's tutors. You cannot get more democratic that that.

WORKS CITED

Harding, Frances (ed.) 'Introduction.' *The Performance Arts in Africa.* London, Routledge, 2002.
Kerr, David. 'Theatre and Social Issues in Malawi.' In Harding (ed.) London: Routledge, 2002, 311–20.

The Asmara Theatre Association 1961–74

Mahber Teyatr Asmera

CHRISTINE MATZKE

If you walk down *Godena Harinnet* ('Liberation Avenue') in the city centre of the Eritrean capital Asmara today – from Cinema Asmara towards September Square, *Bahti Meskerem* – you can still find the signboard of the 'Asmara Theatrical Association', *Mahber Teyatr Asmera* (Ma.Te.A.), opposite the huge crimson facade of Cinema Impero built in 1938. The signpost directs you to a dimly lit club in the basement of a large Italian house which used to be Ma.Te.A.'s home base thirty-odd years ago and was reclaimed by former members in 1993, after Eritrean independence (Figure 1). While nowadays the club is little more than a disreputable dingy bar (Treiber 2005: 132), its walls contain memories of a theatre company still considered to be the most productive and influential in Eritrea. This article traces the story of Ma.Te.A. as recollected and documented by its members and their contemporaries, from its beginning in 1961 until its gradual decline in the mid-1970s. Largely drawing on interviews and written documents from the period,[1] I will discuss its establishment, shows and tours, with particular emphasis on the female members of the association.

In order to appreciate theatre in Eritrea – which includes music, dance, and the wider performing arts – it is useful to read it against the backdrop of the region's political history. The 1960s to 1970s were difficult times for the small country in the Horn of Africa. A former Italian colony, and thereafter under British military administration, Eritrea had been federated with Ethiopia in 1952 as a self-governing entity whose promised self-rule was quickly undermined by the Ethiopian crown. During the next ten years, Eritreans not only witnessed the suspension of local newspapers and political parties, and the lowering of their flag, but also the replacement of Tigrinya and Arabic by Amharic as the official language.[2] Previous theatre associations, the *Mahber Tewasew Deqqabbat* (Ma.Te.De., Indigenous Theatre Association, 1944–56) and the short-lived *Mahber Mimihyaš Hagerawi Limdi* (Ma.M.Ha.L., Association for the Improvement of National Customs, 1957–60), had already used cultural means to express an emergent Eritrean nationalism. Yet it was Ma.Te.A. whose popular variety shows should be remembered as the acme of modern urban,

1. In 1999 Mahber Teyatr Asmera occupied the same premises as in the late 1960s.
(© *Christine Matzke*)

and clandestine political, entertainment in the twentieth century.[3]

The 1960s were characterised by civil rights movements and student protests, by bell bottoms, beehive hairdos and miniskirts. In the Eritrean capital, fashion did not lag behind the rest of the world; neither did the rising political discontent among its population. 'Kagnew Music' was broadcast from Kagnew Station, the US military base in Asmara, a strategic monitoring point for the Horn of Africa and the Arab world from the early days of the federation. The station played anything from jazz, twist, country to rock'n roll and had a great influence on modern Eritrean (and Ethiopian) music. Apart from school drama and the odd religious play, however, few theatrical activities by Eritreans were recorded at the onset of the new decade. Only for local European repertoire bands performing in clubs and bars it was business as usual. On the political stage, on the other hand, dramatic events were beginning to escalate. In 1958 the first organised Eritrean opposition to Ethiopian hegemony, the non-military Eritrean Liberation Movement (ELM), had emerged; two years later, the first armed liberation movement, the Eritrean Liberation Front (ELF), followed. In 1960 many African nations gained independence. 'Decolonisation' was in the air. On September 1, 1961 Hamid Idris Awate and his contingent of around a dozen men opened fire on Ethiopian forces in the Eritrean lowlands and became the heralds of Africa's longest war. In the same year, the Asmara Theatre Association was established. Although a coincidence, the timing was to be indicative of Ma.Te.A.'s future involvement in the struggle on the cultural frontline. Ma.Te.A. was to combine sentiments of the 'Swinging Sixties' with local theatre practices and nationalist concerns, thus lending expression to an Eritrean modernity which was youthful and carefree, and at the same time deeply troubled. For one year later, in 1962, Emperor Haile Selassie violated the federal agreement by annexing Eritrea and declaring it an 'ordinary' Ethiopian province.[4]

The beginnings of Ma.Te.A.

In late 1960, two established performers, the singer Tekabo Woldemariam ('Mario Lanza'), and Tewolde Redda, arguably Eritrea's finest guitarist, started to discuss the establishment of yet another theatre association with a more 'dynamic' character than that of Ma.M.Ha.L. This new company would be more entertaining and more educative in character.[5] 'One thing I remember', Tegbaru Teklai, a female Ma.Te.A. member in the mid-1960s recalled, 'is that they founded the association in order to develop the language [Tigrinya], to practise our culture, to express nationalism and to assert our identity' (I 1). Obviously, these radical ideas could not be expressed explicitly, but had to be couched in a repertoire blending Tigrinya, Tigre, Amharic, Arabic and European performance elements.

Two experienced entertainers, *Memhir* ('teacher') Asres Tessema and the person generally considered to be the founding father of modern Eritrean theatre, Alemayo Kahasai, were consulted, and it was agreed that invitations should be sent out to potential participants: teachers, musicians and members of previous theatre associations, most of them amateurs. A first meeting took place in the Olympic Cafeteria owned by Kahasai Michael to which a number of artists were summoned. No women were invited, though they discussed how female members could be engaged. 'There were no women at the time' (I 8), Tekabo Woldemariam excused the all-male convention. This had been the state of affairs since the establishment of local theatre associations, and confirmed not only the uneasy relationship of women to the stage, but also spoke of their lack of participation at an executive level. Women mostly performed in *suwa* houses – privately run drinking places where local millet beer, *suwa*, was served – or bars,[6] even if the 1950s had seen women participating in singing contests and as members of previous organisations (Matzke 2002).

Ma.Te.A. eventually solved the gender imbalance by inviting one *suwa* house entertainer and three novices to the stage: Ethiopia Medhanie, a divorced *suwa* publican and *barista* (waitress) became involved as the result of a personal invitation from Alemayo Kahasai; the others were Genet Teferi, Tsehainesh (X), and Hiwot Tedla, an Italo-Eritrean employed in a local sweater factory. According to musician Vittorio Bossi, 'they were selected for their conduct, body structure, and artistic performance' (I 16). With the exception of Ethiopia, however, most women were acquaintances of the founders, rather than experienced entertainers. Hiwot Tedla recalled:

> I became a member in 1961. We started along with Tewolde Redda and Alemayo Kahasai. They told us to come and participate. I was selected because I was a friend of Tewolde Redda's girlfriend. He asked me one day whether I wouldn't like to join with her. That's how I started in Ma.Te.A. (I 13)

Algenesh Kiflu, Letebrehan Dagnew and Tegbaru Teklai followed, as did Tebereh Tesfahunei who was to become a celebrated singer known locally as 'Doris Day'. Throughout Ma.Te.De.'s heyday, until the mid-1970s, women were joining and leaving the association, as were the men.[7] While most of the early women members withdrew for family reasons – chiefly marriage or pregnancy – the 1970s also saw some female artists enlisting in the liberation movements. One striking – but not surprising – fact is that many of those who stayed shared social backgrounds with the early *suwa* house entertainers, often coming from single-parent families, with little formal education, unattached, single-minded and self-supporting (Matzke 2002: 31). The engagement of women corresponded to their contributions to previous associations, comprising singing, acting and dancing on stage. None of them worked as a musician; and they had little say in the overall running of affairs. Their main aspiration was to perform well and to look attractive. Beauty pageants were in vogue at the time, singer Tebereh Tesfahunei being among those who entered and triumphed.[8] The relationship between the sexes was as equal as the time allowed it to be, but judging from the interviews the overall tone of men towards women was that of benevolently condescending admiration. In Tekabo Woldemariam's words:

> Women [in Ma.Te.A.] were kept as gold and their artistic skills were precious. If a play has no woman, it is non-existent. If there is no woman, there is no light. Therefore in music, a woman is of importance, she has to be kept properly. There was no way we could oppress them. (I 9)

In less formal interview situations, however, it transpired that despite their prominence, these women were still considered as '*baristas*', and that many carried the social stigma of divorce or coming from a broken home. It would take another decade and the experience of the armed liberation struggle for attitudes to begin to change.

Despite teething troubles, the reputation of the association grew steadily. When Ma.Te.A. began its work in the early 1960s, the members had nothing but a dimly-lit rehearsal room, some old drums and a box guitar. Initially the Association suffered from lack of funding, props and musical instruments, the sole income being a monthly membership fee of 2 Birr.[9] This raised barely enough to rent a room, let alone pay for electricity. Rehearsals took place by candlelight, which gave the group the nickname *Wolaati Shma'a*, 'to light a candle'. After the first public performance in 1961, however, members were

2. *Mahber Teyatr Asmera in 1961*
(*courtesy of Mahber Teyatr Asmera*)

able to buy matching outfits, two accordions and an electric guitar. Right from
the start great efforts were made to create a corporate image for the organisation. A Ma.Te.A. 'anthem' was sung at the beginning and end of each show.
'*Selam nay Ma.Te.A., selam*' invited peace (*selam*) and, according to *Memhir*
Asres Tessema, called for the unity of Christians and Muslims (I 18). For the
visual effects, Alemayo Kahasai and Tekabo Woldemariam designed different
European-style matching outfits in white, black and blue. These were fitted by
an Italian tailor after the latest fashion, the women wearing skirts and blazers,
the men matching suits (Figure 2). This gave them an elegant and distinguished
appearance, re-emphasised by numerous costume changes during the shows.
Ma.Te.A. members were known as 'Asmarinos' and 'Asmarinas', men and
women from the capital who took pride in their looks.[10] The dress code set
Ma.Te.A. apart from other bands and the majority of ordinary citizens; as did
the occasional naming after famous singers and Hollywood stars such as 'Mario
Lanza' and 'Doris Day'.[11] Such acts of self-fashioning helped Ma.Te.A.
members create distinct artistic identities which drew on a global modernity,
without obliterating local cultures or negating the nationalist cause (cf. Falceto
(2001: 76), A. Kebede (1976: 290), T. Tesfahunei (1999 & 2000) Wetter (2000:
318–21)).

   In order to achieve and maintain a high standard, the group initially met on
a daily basis, from 6 pm until late. 'We just liked being around each other'
Ethiopia Medhanie said of the early period that 'There wasn't any need to
make a rehearsal schedule because we came anyway. It was our world' (I 11). In

1962, meetings were reduced to three times a week because the frequent gatherings proved too demanding for the majority, a number of whom had responsible jobs or family obligations. Ma.Te.A. also drew up a code which stipulated a probationary period of six months to a year for prospective members. Applicants had to prove that they were able to meet a certain artistic standard. Discipline was strict and members could be expelled for repeated absences (I 1, I 6, I 16). While the founding fathers initially recruited (female) artists personally, applicants now started to flock to the association. In an interview Tebereh Tesfahunei recalled how she and her friend, Letebrehan Dagnew, experienced the 'casting'.[12]

> Ma.Te.A. asked both of us what our interests were. [Letebrehan] said that her voice was low. She could not sing but she could dance. Then they asked me and I told them that I could be both a singer and a dancer. They asked what sort of songs I wanted to sing. ... Buzunesh Bekele[13] had come from Addis to Asmara. When she had finished her songs, the Eritrean audience demanded her songs again and again, three or four times. I was drawn towards her and told them that I wanted to translate and repeat Buzunesh's songs. I was very young at the time and my voice had not matured. It was Tewolde Redda who agreed to my request. He told the others they would make me a singer. (I 15).

It was a providential move because by taking on Tebereh Tesfahunei, Tewolde Redda was to help mould the most popular Eritrean female singer of the 1960s. Like her lesser known Eritrean predecessors from the 1950s, she insisted on singing in her mother tongue, refusing to follow the general course of 'Amharisation' (Matzke 2002: 39–40).

The shows

Alemayo Kahasai is generally acknowledged as the 'artistic director' of Ma.Te.A., though he never formally claimed that title. Colleagues, such as Tewolde Redda and *Memhir* Asres Tessema, assisted him in his tasks. Many well known singers, writers, musicians, and comedians passed through the fertile ground of the association, among them the comedian and playwright *Memhir* Solomon Gebregziabhier, the playwright and announcer Asmerom Habtemariam, the singer Osman Abdulrahim, the lyricist and playwright Negusse Haile 'Mensa'ai' and the celebrated vocalist Yemane Gebremichael 'Baria'.[14] Rehearsals and shows were a collective effort rather than the product of an individual director, as Hiwot Tedla recalled:

> Alemayo, Tewolde [Redda] and Asres Tessema, ... all wrote dramas and helped prepare the shows. Alemayo and Tewolde worked as directors. Initially I was a singer, then I shifted to drama. They gave us the lyrics and we learnt them by heart. Then they arranged the music. Then there were dances. If the song was modern, we danced modern dances; if it was traditional, we danced accordingly. The members created dances for every song. It was a group work. (I 13).

Dances, songs, music and drama were rehearsed separately and then arranged in a two- to three-hour show, usually performed at either Cinema Asmara or Cinema Odeon. These venues in Asmara belonged to the general Cinema Administration, Astria, which charged rent for the use of their premises. The resulting entrance fee of 5 Birr was a considerable sum at the time but the patrons paid willingly. For 25 Birr per hour, the band entertained at private and public functions – weddings, beauty pageants and dance events – and regularly played at local music venues. They also made several appearances on the American Kagnew Television Station, presenting 'an hour[-long] program of traditional and modern Ethiopian music and dancing' (Anon. 4 May 1965). By the mid-1960s and early 1970s, the following arrangement was most popular with audiences: a four-hour variety show, including a twenty-minute interval, started at 8. pm after the last film screening. Essential ingredients included modern Eritrean music (mostly a blend of Tigrinya, Tigre, Amharic, European and Sudanese pieces (Falceto 2001: 72), Figure 3), a thirty-minute play, stand-up comedians or comic sketches, an acrobatic act (performed by three boys), 'traditional' (Eritrean) and 'modern' (European) dances. The latter included the boogie, the samba, the twist, and the cha-cha-cha and allowed women to show off the latest fashions, with costumes mostly belonging to Ma.Te.A. Stage design for plays was kept to the bare minimum. One or two pieces of furniture indicated the setting, while a cinema curtain served as backdrop for the entire show (Figure 4). Though always part of the programme and crucial in conveying clandestine political ideas, drama was not the most important form of performance.[15] Unlike the highly cultivated music and dance numbers, the art of acting was reduced to knockabout buffoonery and witty dialogue. Judging from recent video films featuring popular sketches – and actors – from the 1960s, actors played mostly for laughs; overacting and gurning were fairly common. There were few psychological subtleties (cf. S. Gebregziabhier 1996).

The different elements were linked by a compere whose jokes and comments ensured sufficient time for a quick change of musical instrument or costumes. The uninterrupted flow of the show is said to have left a deep impression on the audience and, after the troupe had been on tour, was repeatedly mentioned as an influence on Ethiopian presentations.[16] Ma.Te.A. supported other groups with equipment and expertise. They regularly helped out local bands with instruments and uniforms, facilitated the annual theatre show by Eritrean students on vacation from Addis Ababa, and were host to a number of artists from Ethiopia and elsewhere, including Russia. Sadly, little is recorded or remembered about their collaboration.

Ma.Te.A. developed into a thriving theatre association whose work left an indelible mark on future generations of artists. Its success lasted for almost fifteen years, until the arrival of the Ethiopian military *Derg* regime in 1974.[17] Ma.Te.A.'s reputation was built on a broad range of entertainment which addressed socially relevant issues and subtly criticised the political climate of the times. With the tightening of censorship after the demise of the federation in

3. Tegbaru Teklai and the Mahber
Teyatr Asmera band performing in
the mid-1960s.
(courtesy of Tegbaru Teklai)

4. Mahber Teyatr Asmera play, c.
1971, second from right: Asmerom
Habtemariam.
(courtesy of Asmerom Habtemariam)

1962, artists perfected the art of allegory and allusion. Under the auspices of Ma.Te.A., Eritrean nationalists of all creeds united to encode their anger against Ethiopian hegemony. While the ELF would suffer a profound internal crisis, generating the birth of the Eritrean People's Liberation Movement (EPLF) and reaching its nadir during the civil war, the cultural arena in Asmara provided a forum for the reconciliation of different interests, religions and political beliefs. This approach was later cultivated and refined by the cultural cadres of both liberation movements, a considerable number of whom had served their apprenticeship with Ma.Te.A. (cf. Iyob 1995: 102–04).

Ma.Te.A.'s success has been documented in contemporaneous reviews which hailed their performances as some of the best ever staged in Ethiopia. The much-quoted Mengistu Gedamu, an Amhara journalist, vividly conveyed the atmosphere of a 1973/4 show in the 1400-seater Haile Selassie I Theatre in Addis Ababa.[18]

> There were thousands of people crowded around the entrance to the hall. Some were saying it was sold out, others that the chairs were full. Women who had paid 25 Birr for their hairstyles found their hair disordered by the crush. The entrance fee was 5 Birr but many people were willing to pay 25 Birr to enter the hall. … On this Sunday afternoon, even though I could not understand the language (Tigrinya) or the message, I enjoyed the way the play was performed and the music enormously. In fact, it was the best I ever saw. … Alemayo Kahasai performed the Italian Toto [a famous comedian] and Tebereh Tesfahunei sang like the American Doris Day. … All the vocalists performed well. (M. Gedamu 1966 EC [1973/4]).

Beneath the amusement and light-hearted entertainment, however, nationalist sentiments were being encouraged. An introduction in Amharic to the very same show provoked querulous shouts from the (largely Eritrean) audience. Due to the tightening of Ethiopian censorship, the public now began to read politics into seemingly harmless songs, particularly those with love lyrics. 'People started to give them double meanings and connected them with politics' (T. Tesfhaunei 2000).[19] Artists also began to work in double-entendres. In the 1960s Tewolde Redda gained national fame with his song '*Sigey Habuni*' ('Give me My Torch') which alluded to the Eritrean flag.[20] Atowebrehan Segid, with '*Aslamyi Kestan*' ('You, Moslem and Christian', written by Negusse Haile around 1966/67) called on people of all religious and social creeds to unite and to disregard Ethiopian propaganda against the liberation war.[21] And Tebereh Tesfahunei won many followers with Asres Tessema's song '*Abi Hidmo*' ('*The Big Hidmo* [a traditional Tigrinya house]'). In this song she complained about lice and bed bugs in her home – which for many signified Ethiopians in Eritrea – and called for her lover in the forest – the fighter – to come to her. It is somewhat ironic that she also sang the song when she won the 'Miss Ethiopia' contest.[22]

Subtexts of comic skits were no less political. A one-directional tug-of-war, which had already been part of the Ma.Te.De. repertoire, was subsequently censored for its suggestion that Eritreans were pulling together against

Ethiopia. Solomon Gebregziabhier's comedy '*Arba'a*' (Tigrinya: 'Forty') – in which an embezzler avoids returning money by answering all queries with a nonsensical '*arba'a*' – was interpreted as inciting disobedience against the regime (Gebregziabhier 1996; Sahle, 21 November 1998: 7). And a musical sketch in which Alemayo mimed his skill of mastering various European and local instruments (played backstage by other musicians) was read as an impersonation and critique of Ethiopia. On leaving the stage, the audience noticed that Alemayo's suit only covered his front, thus implying that appearance was everything for the colonial power.

The tours

Despite Ma.Te.A.'s veiled political critique, a one-month trip through Ethiopia was organised at the end of 1966 and during part of January 1967 to great public acclaim. Previously, the company had visited Eritrean towns – Keren, Mendefera, Massawa and Decamhare – and also less accessible places, such as Agordat and Tessenei in the Western lowlands. Travelling was already quite difficult at the time, as ELF fighters operating from remoter areas were engaged in fighting the Ethiopian forces. From 1964 to 1967, Ethiopia extended her offensives from the lowland areas to the highlands and caused considerable destruction of property. For safety Ma.Te.A. kept to larger settlements and towns. Often the whole company, including the women, went on tour, at other times only one or two artists visited villages in the vicinity of Asmara to play Ma.Te.A. music on reel tapes (Pateman 1998: 118 & I 19).

In 1966, a minister in the imperial government visited Asmara to attend his sister's wedding for which the Ma.Te.A. band had been engaged. The minister enjoyed the music so much that he promised to help the artists organise a tour through the 'motherland' – Ethiopia. Three weeks before the start of the projected tour the group was notified that the Haile Selassie I Theatre had been booked and that they could also perform in towns such as Nazareth and Gondar. Frantic preparations took place and by mid-December the company was able to set off. The only female members to travel were Tebereh Tesfahunei and Tegbaru Teklai.[23] When Ma.Te.A. reached the outskirts of Addis Ababa, a grand reception awaited them; Eritrean students, members of the first Ethiopian professional theatre company, *Hager Fiqir* ('Patriotic Theatre Association'), and other performers were lining the streets.

> The Haile Selassie Theatre Group had also come! They came with their cars, with flowers, and they welcomed us when we were just approaching the town. Then we went to Addis with songs. Everywhere we saw our pictures on the wall. Even in town, in Churchill Road, there was a written banner with 'Welcome Ma.Te.A.!' And who had done it? The Eritrean students at the university. (I 17)

Two shows were mounted in the Haile Selassie I Theatre, four more in the venues of the *Hager Fiqir* and a smaller theatre. Students from Eritrea were rewarded with an exclusive show for their support, which was free of charge. With the benefit of hindsight, it is fascinating to see that among those Eritrean youngsters who had lent a helping hand were future senior cadres of the Eritrean People's Liberation Front (EPLF), the second, and eventually central, armed liberation movement which was to split off from the ELF. The students included Alemseged Tesfai, then a law student but later to distinguish himself as a playwright and head of the Division of Literature and Drama (see Plastow 1999). And Haile Woldensae 'Dru', the future Director of the EPLF Department of Political Orientation, Education and Culture.[24]

The reception for the shows was enthusiastic, but had serious consequences. When Tebereh Tesfahunei sang *Abi Hidmo* one member of the audience started to spray insecticide to get rid of the 'lice'. (The reviewer Mengistu Gedamu deeply disapproved of this act as being inhospitable towards the foreign guests, clearly unaware of its symbolic meaning (cf. Zerai 2001: 25)). Another member of the audience tied a blue Eritrean flag around Tebereh's neck, while others began to reveal the weapons they had brought to the show. 'All people had guns', Tekabo Woldemariam described the scene, 'they were flaring with national love' (I 9). Naturally, the Ethiopian authorities were unhappy; and the same minister who had invited the troupe now ordered the production to be censored. A number of songs had to go, particularly those by Atowebrehan Segid, Alamin Abduletiff ('Interview with Alamin Abduletiff'), and Tebereh Tesfahunei. 'They just censored my songs. I cried and was sick because of that. I couldn't even eat or drink' (I 15), she complained. Thereafter the tour continued outside the capital, without major interruptions.

Ma.Te.A.'s gradual decline

The profit of 11,000 Birr from the Ethiopian trip enabled Ma.Te.A. to rent new premises in a large Italian house located on Asmara's main avenue, then named after the Emperor Haile Selassie. They were now at the height of their success, but not without having had to experience the bitter reality of political repression. Early in 1967 the ELF assassinated a number of prominent officials, and this led to a major military offensive by the Ethiopian government (Markakis 1987: 121). As Tegbaru Teklai recalled 'There was extremely severe censorship' and the artists were subjected to harassment. He spoke as follows about the situation:

> They were checking piece by piece, word by word. If your song had many admirers – even if it had nothing to do with politics – you were imprisoned. For the Ethiopian security forces, Ma.Te.A. was like a political party. What Ma.Te.A. did and said – it was considered as dangerous. They saw everything in a political light. (I 15).

Tegbaru Teklai, Ethiopia Medhanie, Tewolde Redda, Negusse Haile and

Alamin Abduletiff were among the many Ma.Te.A. members who served prison sentences. Some were imprisoned for their political activities, others for their songs or simply out of spite. A second Ethiopian tour in 1971 was much more restrained than the first. Fear of repression had forced some artists, notably the civil servants, to stay behind, and the Ethiopian authorities were no longer well-disposed towards Eritreans. The liberation struggle also experienced a difficult phase because internal strife, zonal and religious polarisation caused reformist groups to split off from the ELF (Pool 2001: 51–5).

In 1973 Solomon Gebregziabhier produced a full-length drama *Zeywirres Habti* ('Uninherited Wealth') independent of Ma.Te.A. The play was a blatant allegory – an influential man (Ethiopia) forcibly marrying a wealthy widow (Eritrea) and being killed by her nine children (Eritrea's 'micro-nations') – and thus inevitably attracted attention. Solomon received warnings from the government and was forced to cancel a show in Decamhare, which had already been sold out (ECBTP 95/7; I 2, I 3, I 4, cf. Plastow (1997: 152)).

Feelings of insecurity increased when the association received further threats. Many Ma.Te.A. members decided to leave. In 1974, the year of Haile Selassie's downfall, more than 2000 people were rounded up in front of Cinema Asmara during a show and taken into custody. Solomon Gebregzhiabier was brought to the outskirts of the town, shot and left for dead; miraculously he survived the ordeal.[25] Atrocities against Eritreans continued, as did the gradual decline of the ancient Ethiopian Empire. In 1973, the 'King of Kings', His Imperial Majesty Haile Selassie, had attained his eightieth birthday, still reigning with regal pomp, but paying no heed to the suffering of his people. Growing economic problems, famine, and social unrest eventually created considerable political instability which helped the military to take over power. In September 1974 the last Ethiopian Emperor was overthrown. A 'Provisional Military Administrative Council' was established, popularly known as the *Derg* ('committee' in Amharic), which was to serve as the new government. However power struggles also continued within the *Derg*, culminating in the assassination of two high-ranking officers and the rise of Colonel Mengistu Haile Mariam as Chairman of the Council and new Ethiopian Head of State. These events signalled an immediate escalation of the conflict. In January 1975, in a rare case of collaboration, the two liberation fronts, ELF and EPLF, participated in a joint attack on Asmara. In 1976, the *Derg* embarked on a two-year annihilation campaign to crush civilian opposition by means of street executions, mass arrests and brutal torture. The crusade, known as the 'Red Terror', swept over large parts of Ethiopia and Eritrea. (Connell 1997: 17–19; Markakis 1987: 131–40).

Confronted with such atrocities, Ma.Te.A. rapidly disintegrated during the mid-1970s. Some joined new and short-lived groups: others attached themselves to established Eritrean bands or moved to Ethiopia. Tebereh Tesfahunei, Tewolde Redda and Asres Tessema were among those who left for Addis Ababa.[26] In Asmara, Asmara Radio Station was inaugurated by the Ethiopian regime in the attempt to suppress, or at least control, Eritrean music. Possession of politicised Tigrinya music was likely to be considered suspect, with records supposedly buried in people's back yards (Falceto ([booklet] Ref. 82965-2 DK 016: 22). Eritrean music survived against all odds, as names such as *Merhaba*, Venus Band, *Mekaleh Guaila*, the Black Soul Band or Star Eritrea indicate. After the disintegration of Ma.Te.A., many musical groups attempted to include sketches, and some even tried to continue clandestine political entertainment.[27] Yet they all eventually succumbed to the relentless pressure from the Ethiopian regime. Bands were now established by the government, as were some theatre groups consisting of former Ma.Te.A. members. When *kebeles* were introduced by the *Derg* – so-called 'urban dwellers associations' which controlled every Eritrean and Ethiopian neighbourhood – each was required to set up a *kinet* (or 'culture') group to produce pro-Ethiopian propaganda. Membership was by force, as was attendance at their shows (cf. EPLF 1979: 113). Tekabo Woldemariam recalled that 'many youngsters were made to play music' (I 10). In the 1980s, Alemayo Kahasai was coerced into heading one such cultural troupe made up of some of his former colleagues. None had joined willingly, but fearing punishment they obliged. Some had already served prison sentences and were kept under surveillance; others feared for the safety of their children. Theatre under the *Derg* regime became a sensitive issue which requires further investigation. It is evident that some artists still feel stigmatised for having 'betrayed' the nation.[28]

Previously, few Ma.Te.A. members were known to have direct links with the liberation movements, for '[t]he fact that we had 'field' influences was restricted to the knowledge of a few trusted members' (ECBTP 95/8).[29] By the mid-1970s, however, artists started to flock to the fronts. To the ELF went Negusse Haile (in 1975), Tsehaitu Beraki (in 1977), Tewolde Redda (in 1979), Yemane Gebremichael 'Baria', Bereket Mengisteab (in 1975) and Osman Abdulrahim;[30] while Tebereh Tesfahunei and Asmerom Habtemariam joined the newly established contender, the EPLF. For the next fifteen years, until de-facto independence in 1991, these were the places where Eritrean theatre arts would take a very different turn, and where performances would be more openly utilised to serve a liberationist agenda (Warwick 1997). While artists did not necessarily continue to serve as entertainers – which is another story yet to be told – the variety format cultivated by Ma.Te.A. left an indelible mark on theatre produced by the liberation movements, and continues to do so on Eritrean theatre arts in the twenty-first century (cf. Matzke and Plastow [forthcoming]).

ACKNOWLEDGEMENTS

In 2005, a longer version of this essay was presented as a lecture at the University of Asmara at the invitation of the Department of Eritrean Literatures and Languages, with financial support of the German Research Foundation (DFG). The author also gratefully acknowledges the financial support of the AHRB, *Cusanuswerk*, and the German Academic Exchange Service (DAAD) during her field research in 1999–2000. Thanks to The British Council Eritrea under its director, Negusse

Araya, for administrative and office support; to the following colleagues who worked with me as translators and research assistants in Eritrea: Mohamed Salih Ismael, Mussie Tesfagiorgis, Samson Gebregzhier, Temesgen Gebreyesus, Tesfazghi Ukubazghi, and Yakem Tesfai; to various colleagues in Berlin and Bayreuth for comments on earlier drafts, and, finally, to Rainer Voigt for help with the transliteration. This paper is for my three Eritrean *abbotat*, *Memhir* Asres Tessema, Osman Ahmed and Arefaine Tewolde; and for *Mensa'ai* in Germany.

Appendix: Ma.Te.A. Performers

Please note that these lists are incomplete. They go a short way to acknowledge those artists I was unable to include in the main body of the text.

Ca. 1961

Male members: Tewolde Redda, Tekabo Woldemariam, *Memhir* Kahasai Bezaber, *Memhir* Abebe Iyasu, Atowebrehan Segid, Tesfaldet Marcos, Jabre Mahmud, Abraha Gebretensae, Asmerom Woldentesai, Alemayo Kahasai, Asres Tessema, Tewolde 'Manchu, Abraha G/medhin, Araya Belay, Abbai Alemu.

Female members: Ethiopia Medhanie, Genet Teferi, Tsehainesh (X), Hiwot Tedla.

1965 (cf. T. G/Michael 1965)

Male members: Alemayo Kahasai (president, comedian), Tewolde Redda (vocals, musician), Tekabo Woldemariam (vocals), Asmerom Woldetensae (vocals), Asres Tessema (treasurer, musician), Araya Belay (dancer), Abebe Iyasu (comedian, drummer), Haile Tekleberhan (dancer), Solomon Gebregziabhier (comedian), Tewolde Abraha 'Manchu' (vocals, musician) Jabre Mahmud (vocals, drums), Alamin Abduletiff (vocals, dancer), Gebrehiwot Keleta (musician), Abraha Gebretensae (vocals), Tesfamichael Keleta (musician), Bashir Nur (dancer), Berhane Michael (musician), Embayo Amha (musician).

Female members: Ethiopia Medhanie (vocals, dancer), Tebereh Tesfahunei (vocals, dancer), Letebrehan Dagnew (dancer), Alganesh Kiflu (vocals, dancer), Hiwot Tedla (vocals, dancer).

Additional male members: Asmerom Habtemariam, Negusse Haile 'Mensa'ai', Sultan Yasin ('Wad Shambel').

Additional female members: Tegbaru Teklai, 'Semira', Fantaye Selassie.

NOTES

1 Please note that Eritreans are usually addressed by their (first) name, the second being the name of the father rather than a surname as in European usage. First names are also used in this article. References to Eritrean (or Ethiopian) sources in the main body of the text are given by the first letter of the authors' name, followed by their father's name and the year of publication. In the bibliography authors are listed by their father's name ('surname') first to comply with international citation systems. Tigrinya-language words are given in a simplified transliteration; personal names follow the spelling used in previous non-Tigrinya publications or preferred by the person in question. This essay is based largely on interviews with one-time performers and their contemporaries, for the most part conducted by myself in Asmara in 1999 to 2000, with some by the Eritrea Community Based Theatre Project (ECBTP) in summer 1995. Between 2001 and 2005 I undertook six further research trips to Eritrea, partly to follow up previous queries. The data was triangulated with published and unpublished sources collected by former Ma.Te.A. members, some by the Research and Documentation Centre (RDC) in Asmara. Needless to say that any errors, factual or in interpretation, are mine.

2 Today nine official languages are acknowledged in Eritrea: Tigrinya, Tigre, Arabic, Saho, Afar, Hedareb (Beja), Bilen, Kunama and Nara. Tigrinya is the most widely spoken language in the

highlands, and one of the official Eritrean working languages, together with Arabic and English. Amharic, the language of the then ruling minority in Ethiopia was never indigenous to Eritrea, but imposed by the Ethiopian government in 1956.

3 Pool (1997: 10–11), Iyob (1995: 102–04), Falceto 2001 (70, 72, 76). For the work of previous associations see Plastow (1997: 146–50 & 2004: 202–03), Matzke (2002: 38–42). Note that Ma.Te.De. has also been described as '*Mahber Theatre Dekabat*' and 'Natives' Theatrical Association'.

4 Markakis (1987: 106–08), Wilson (1991: 29–30), R. Iyob (1995: 99–104), Christmann (1996: 100–04), Pool (1997: 11), NUEW (1999: 16–17), Wetter (2000: 319), Falceto (2001: 76). For contemporaneous documents regarding music and entertainment at Kagnew Station see http://www.kagnewstation.com. See also Wrong (2005: 216–36). 'Kagnew' is pronounced 'Qaññew', but widely known under the first transliteration.

5 ECBTP 95/3. Tekabo Woldemariam ('Mario Lanza'), had been a member of Ma.M.Ha.L. and a participant of the two national singing contests in 1956 and 1957. He is the father of one of Eritrea's great musical talents, Yohannes 'Wad Tekabo'. On Alemayo Kahasai see Anon. (2 May 1983EC [1991]), Plastow (1997: 146).

6 Women also performed in *secreto*, unlicensed *suwa* houses, which were often located in the better Eritrean quarters of Asmara, and which also sold beer. Because of their illegal status, people called them *secreto* – secret. In the social hierarchy they ranked above *suwa* houses. Telephone conversation with Negusse Haile, 20 January 2001. For modern *secreto* and *suwa* houses see Treiber (2005: 87–90).

7 A comprehensive reconstruction of all Ma.Te.De. members has not been possible, as movement was high. For a list of performers in 1961 and 1965 see Appendix.

8 For a beautiful picture of 'Miss Asmara Expo 69' see Falceto ([booklet] Ref 82965-2 DK 016: 17). For an account see T. Tesfahunei (1999 & 2000). Within less than 12 months, Tebereh Tesfahunei brought out two autobiographies, the second being a revised and extended version of the first. Both versions were in parts contested. It is to be assumed that she employed a ghost writer, no one considering her capable of writing two full-length books without professional help after having sustained a major injury in the liberation struggle in the 1970s.

9 The Ethiopian Birr was used as currency in Eritrea until 1997, when the Nakfa was introduced. This step has been held partly responsible for the outbreak of the military conflict between the two countries in May 1998.

10 While the idea of the smartly dressed Asmara citizen has survived, 'Asmarino' today carries more negative undertones; someone who is arrogant, lazy and cunning. According to Magnus Treiber (2005: 81-3), the expression 'Asmarina' is no longer common. However, I have heard it used various times to describe a well-dressed, fashionable, attractive woman.

11 To my knowledge Sofia Ali 'Loren', a *suwa*-entertainer and participant of the First National Singing Contest in 1956 was the first singer to assume a foreign persona (cf. Matzke 2002: 40), followed by Tekabo Woldemariam 'Mario Lanza'. Both had been members of Ma.M.Ha.L.; only Tekabo continued with Ma.Te.A. It is interesting to note the Italo-(American) connection of two of the international role models: the Italian Sophia Loren (1934–) is an internationally renowned film actress; the American tenor Mario Lanza (1921-1959) was of Italian descent.

12 In her autobiographies she renders the story differently. T. Tesfanunei (1999 & 2000).

13 Buzunesh Bekele was the 'First Lady' of Ethiopian modern swing until her untimely death at the age of 54 in 1990. Falceto (2001: 100).

14 Yemane Baria passed away in 1998 and was mourned by the whole nation. *Memhir* Solomon Gebregziabhier died in spring 2001, before I was able to interview him. His work, however, is comparatively well-documented in Eritrean theatre history. See Plastow (1997: 152-3), G. Gebru (1 January 1996: 30-3), A. Sahle (21 November 1998: 7).

15 Only two printed play scripts from Ma.Te.A. have been available to me – Asres Tessema's 'The Effect of Traditional Funeral Ceremonies in Our Country' (A. Tessema 1957EC [1965/66]) and Negusse Haile's *Tsibbuq Wussane* ('A Fair Verdict') (1957EC [1969/70]). Both plays comprise social, rather than political, critique and cannot be dealt with in this context. I wish to thank Ghirmai Negash for making these plays available to me. See also G. Negash (1999: 147, 149).

16 A number of informants mentioned the uninterrupted running of the show with the help of an announcer as well as the quick change of costumes. This which was apparently unusual in Ethiopian variety shows which were said to have had longer intervals between the different acts. *Memhir* Asres Tessema also referred to the small size of their band which did not drown the singers' voices, and the sparse use of the curtain (I 17). The idea of an announcer had been copied from Italian variety shows in the 1930s and 1940s.

17 Ma.Te.A. was revived by some veteran members after independence, but was forced to suspend its activities with the onset of the 1998–2000 Ethiopian-Eritrean war when the younger generation was called to arms. There were also old animosities among the veterans regarding finances and political allegiances. I was not given access to the documents kept in their offices for these reasons. In summer 2001 heavy rains flooded the premises of Ma.Te.A. and a considerable number of papers were destroyed or damaged.

18 The show was staged as part of the Ma.Te.A. tour through Ethiopia, not, as previously mentioned, in Asmara. Cf. Plastow (1997: 150).

19 It is interesting to note that today's adolescents and youths consider – and appreciate – Ma.Te.A. songs for being 'apolitical', in contrast to contemporary Tigrinya songs which are often blatantly nationalist. Treiber (2005: 102).

20 Give me my torch, don't alienate me/Give me my torch, don't make me wait./ Please, someone, listen to me/I had a friend, but he took my torch./ Why don't you give me my torch?/ Is it a crime to claim, 'My Torch', A. Tesfai (2000: 17). Alemseged Tesfai also refers to a number of other song texts.

21 Moslem, Christian, lowlander or highlander/Ignore the advice of enemies/ Ignore it or you will just be a commodity', A. Tesfai (2000: 18). According to Negusse Haile, the song was specifically targeted at the Ethiopian propaganda which claimed that the ELF was a Muslim-Arabic (and not an all-inclusive Eritrean) organisation (I 20). Both songs can also be found in R. Iyob (1995: 103) in a different translation, and in R. Bereketeab (2000: 241).

22 Our house, the big *hidmo/* is full of *tukan* (fleas) and *qunci* (bugs)/ Here or there, my love, you have captivated me/ What was your promise that you neglect me, my love/ What was our agreement, brother, at first/ Was it not to care for one another? [Please come, my love, I will be yours and you will be mine]/ Through the forest [wilderness] your love letter comes to me/ written and signed by your hand./ You've been away for long, my love, you are cruel [you do not wait, nor remember]./ Please, my love, I am waiting for no one but you', transl. Mohamed Salih Ismail and Tesfazghi Ukubazghi from (T. Tesfahunei 1999) and the selfsame song covered by Helen Meles on her audiocassette *Ti Gezana* [Our Home: Songs of Tebereh Tesfahunei].

23 Hiwot Tedla was unable to travel because of her first pregnancy, Letebrehan Dagnew had died in the meantime, at the age of 19 shortly after having delivered a baby boy by caesarean. T. Tesfahunei (2000), I 2, I 3, I 4.

24 Haile Woldensae, Foreign Minister during the 1998–2000 Ethiopian-Eritrean war, is one of the 11 former government members detained since September 2001. See Connell (2005).

25 ECBTP 95/7, G. Gebru (1 January 1996: 30–3). See also Plastow (1997: 152–3). Negusse Haile believes that Solomon was taken while enjoying a film show in Cinema Dante (private letter to the author, December 2001). I 2, I 3, I 4.

26 Tebereh Tesfahunei produced records with Amha Records, the first private music label in Ethiopia to go against the monopoly over record production and import by the *Hager Fiqir*. Amha operated from 1969 to 1978 until its founder, Amha Eshete, went into political exile. Phillips was the only foreign record company in the 1970s. Tewolde Redda also had a private label, Yared Music Shop, which produced 45s with artists like Tsehaitu Beraki, Osman Abdulrahim, Vittorio Bossi and Hussein Mohamed Ali. Falceto ([booklet] Ref. 82965-2 DK 016: 14–16, 25), Wetter (2000: 320), cf. Ashakih (2005: 80).

27 I 14, Anon. (13 September 2000: 7). The history of bands and companies in the 1970s is yet to be written. Researchers are eagerly waiting for *Memhir* Asres Tessema's study on modern Eritrean theatre arts to be published. The book has been in print since 2005.

28 For an initial study on Eritrean theatre under the *Derg* see Plastow (1997: 152–4) & (1998: 108–09). I 2, I 3, I 4, I 7, I 12, I 16.

29 Ruth Iyob writes that 'MTA served as a recruitment center and fund-raiser' (R. Iyob 1997:

102). While this might well be the case, I was unable to find further details. To my knowledge, individual Ma.Te.A. members had already joined one of the liberation movements, or served as undercover contacts to the 'field'.
30 Tsehaitu Beraki and Bereket Mengisteab did not belong to Ma.Te.A. but were very well established singers and musicians in Eritrea, and still are. Cf. Matzke (2002: 29, 34–5).

BIBLIOGRAPHY

Please note that Eritreans are usually addressed by their (first) name, the second being the name of the father rather than a surname as in European usage. First names are also used in this article. References to Eritrean (or Ethiopian) sources in the main body of the text are given by the first letter of the authors' name, followed by their father's name and the year of publication. In the bibliography authors are listed by their father's name ('surname') first to comply with international citation systems. Tigrinya-language words are given in a simplified transliteration; personal names follow the spelling used in previous non-Tigrinya publications or preferred by the person in question. Sources published according to the old Ethiopian/Eritrean calendar are given with their original date of publication where possible, indicated with $_{EC}$, and followed by the approximate Gregorian year(s) in brackets. The Ethiopian/Eritrean New Year begins in September of the Western calendar, the years being seven or eight years earlier than in the Gregorian system. Eritrean-language sources translated by Eritrean colleagues will be given with their English titles.

Abebaw, Bedele, n.d., '"Always Smiling" (Grasmach Alemayhu Khasay)' part of a pamphlet published by the Ethiopian Ministry for Sport and Culture, n.d., ECBTP 1995.
Aberra, Khaled, 12 December 2002, 'Conversation with Memher Assress Tessema: Writer, Poet, Essayist and Lyricist', online, available at http://www.shaebia.org/artman/publish/ article_499.html, accessed 2 April 2003.
Anon., 4 May 1965, 'Asmara Theatre Association Orchestra to present program of traditional and modern Ethiopia Music on Kagnew Television', *News Bulletin*: [published daily by the United States Information Service, Asmara], n.p.
Anon., 2 May 1983$_{EC}$ [1991], 'Ato Alemayo Kahasay Passes Away', translated by Tesfazghi Ukubazghi, *Hibret* [Unity]: 1, 2.
Anon., n.d., 'Interview with Alamin Abduletiff', online, available at: http://athos.mas.vcu.edu/ mas/ faculty/ghidewon/alamin.html, accessed 5 November 1998.
Anon., Interview with Veteran Artist Sultan Yasin (Wadi Shambel)', transl. Mussie Tesfagiorgis, *Kestedeben Newspaper*, 13 September 2000.
Anon., http://kagnewstation.com, accessed 23 June 2006.
Anon., http://www.ilchichingiolo.it, accessed 10 July 2006.
Ashakih, Judith, 2005, *Gift of Incense: A Story of Love and Revolution in Ethiopia: A Story by Abubakar Ashakih as Told to and Written by Judith Ashakih* . Trenton, NJ: Red Sea Press.
Bereketeab, Redie, 2000, *Eritrea: The Making of a Nation 1890–1991*. Uppsala: University of Uppsala.
Christmann, Stefanie, 1996, *Die Freiheit haben wir nicht von den Männern: Frauen in Eritrea* . Unkel: Horlemann.
Connell, Dan, 1997, *Against All Odds: A Chronicle of the Eritrean Revolution* . 1993; Asmara: Red Sea Press.
—— 2005, *Conversations with Eritrean Political Prisoners* .Trenton, NJ: Red Sea Press.
EPLF, 1979, *Creating a Popular, Economic, Political and Military Base*. n.p.: EPLF.
Falceto, Francis, 2001, *Abyssinie Swing: A Pictorial History of Modern Ethiopian Music*. Addis Ababa: Shama Books.
—— [booklet to] *Éthiopiques 5: Tigrigna Music, Tigray/Eritrea 1970-1975*. Buda Musique, Paris. 82965-2 DK 016.
Gebregziabhier, Solomon, 1996, *Weghi Sisatat* [Talks of the Sixties]. Video. Eritrean Video Service. Asmara.

Gebru, Gebremedhin, 1 January 1996, 'An Artist Who Could Survive 24 Bullets', transl. Mussie Tesfagiorgis, *Adulis*: 30–33.

Gedamu, Mengistu, December 1966$_{EC}$ [1973/4], 'Theatre and Songs in Asmara', transl. from the Amharic by ECBTP 1995, *From What We See*, n.p.

G/Michael, Tesfai, 23 March 1965, 'Asmara Theatrical Association – Agent of Good National Tradition', *Awet* (entertainment magazine), transl. ECBTP 1995.

Haile 'Mensa'ai', Negusse, 1962$_{EC}$ [1969/70], *Tsibbuq Wussane* ('A Fair Verdict'), transl. Mussie Tesfagiorgis. Asmara: Francescana Printing Press.

—— 30 December 2001, letter to the author.

Iyob, Ruth, 1995, *The Eritrean Struggle for Independence: Domination, Resistance, Nationalism, 1941–1993*. Cambridge: Cambridge University Press.

Kebede, Ashenafi, 1976, 'Zemenawi Muzika: Modern Trends in Traditional Secular Music of Ethiopia', *The Black Perspective in Music*, 3: 289–301.

Markakis, John, 1987, *National and Class Conflict in the Horn of Africa*. Cambridge: Cambridge University Press.

Matzke, Christine, 2002, 'Of *Suwa* Houses and Singing Contests: Early Urban Women Performers in Asmara, Eritrea', *African Theatre: Women*, eds Martin Banham, James Gibbs, and Femi Osofisan, guest ed. Jane Plastow. Oxford: James Currey: 29–46.

Matzke, Christine and Jane Plastow, 2006, '*Sewit* Children's Theatre in Eritrea', *African Theatre: Youth*, eds Martin Banham, James Gibbs and Femi Osofisan, guest ed. Michael Etherton. Oxford: James Currey, 138–50.

Meles, Helen, n.d., *Fikri [Love]*, on *Ti Gezana [Our Home: Songs of Tebereh Tesfahunei]*, audiocassette, transl. Tesfazghi Ukuzbaghi.

National Union of Eritrean Women (NUEW), 1999, *Eritrea: Women and Their Tradition of Resistance*. 1985; Asmara: NUEW.

Negash, Ghirmai, 1999, *A History of Tigrinya Literature in Eritrea: The Oral and the Written, 1890–1991*, CNWS Publications, 75 (Leiden, NL: Research School of Asian, African, and Amerindian Studies. CNWS), University of Leiden.

Pateman, Roy, 1998, *Eritrea: Even the Stones are Burning*, new and rev. edn , 1990; Trenton, NJ: Red Sea Press.

Plastow, Jane, 1997, 'Theatre of Conflict in the Eritrean Independence Struggle', *New Theatre Quarterly*, 13.50: 144–54.

—— 1998, 'Uses and Abuses of Theatre for Development: Political Struggle and Development Theatre in the Ethiopia-Eritrea War', in *African Theatre for Development: Art for Self-Determination*, ed. Kamal Salhi. Exeter: Intellect: 97–113.

—— 1999, 'Alemseged Tesfai: A Playwright in Service to Eritrean Liberation', *African Theatre in Development*, eds. Martin Banham, James Gibbs, and Femi Osofisan. Oxford: James Currey: 54–60.

—— 2004, 'Ethiopia and Eritrea', in *A History of Theatre in Africa*, ed. Martin Banham. Cambridge: Cambridge University Press: 192–205.

Pool, David, 1997, *Eritrea: Towards Unity in Diversity*, Minority Rights Group International Report. London: Minority Rights Group.

—— 2001, *From Guerrillas to Government: The Eritrean People's Liberation Front*. Oxford: James Currey.

Sahle, Ammanuel, 21 November 1998, 'The Anatomy of Laughter', *Eritrea Profile*: 7.

Tesfahunei, Tebereh, 1999, *The Two Lives: Based on a True Story: Autobiography of Tebereh Tesfahunei*, translated by Mohamed Salih Ismail. [Asmara]: n.p.

—— 2000, *Short Autobiography of Tebereh Tesfahunei (Doris Day)*, translated by Mohamed Salih Ismail . [Asmara]: n.p.

Tesfai, Alemseged, 'Not By Guns Alone: The pen and the Eritrean struggle for independence', unpublished paper presented at the international conference 'Against All Odds: African Languages and Literatures into the 21st Century', 11–17 January 2000.

Tessema, Asres, 1957$_{EC}$ [1965/66], 'The effect of traditional funeral ceremonies in our country', transl. Mussie Tesfagiorgis, in *Menetser* ('An Eyeglass'). Asmara: Government Printing Press.

Treiber, Magnus, 2005, *Der Traum vom guten Leben: Die eritreische* warsay-*Generation im Asmara der zweiten Nachkriegszeit.* (Münster: LIT.)

Warwick, Paul, 1997, 'Theatre and the Eritrean struggle for freedom: the cultural troupes of the People's Liberation Front', *New Theatre Quarterly,* 13.51: 221–30.

Wetter, Andreas, 2000, 'Musik in Äthiopien: Azmaris und Armee', in Wolfgang Bender, *Sweet Mother: Moderne afrikanische Musik,* rev. Edn. Wuppertal: Edition Trickster in Peter Hammer: 314–28.

Wilson, Amrit, 1991, *The Challenge Road: Women and the Eritrean Revolution.* Trenton, NJ: Red Sea Press.

Wrong, Michela, 2005, *I Didn't Do It For You: How the World Betrayed a Small African Nation.* London: Fourth Estate.

Zerai Asghedom, Misgun, 2001, 'The Theatre Experience in Eritrea', MA dissertation, Workshop Theatre, University of Leeds.

INTERVIEWS
Eritrea Community Based Theatre Project (ECBTP) 1995

Numbers after the stroke refer to the catalogue number of the ECBTP

ECBTP 95/3   Abraha Gebretensae, Ma.Te.De.
ECBTP 95/7   Solomon Gebregziabhier, playwright, actor, comedian.
ECBTP 95/8   Tekabo Woldemariam, Abebe Iyasu, Jabre Mahmud, Ma.Te.A.

INTERVIEWS
1998–2001

Memberships of bands and theatre associations are provided. Professions, if stated, were those at the time of the interview.

Abbreviations: interviewer (int.), notes (nts), recorded (rec.), translator (ttr), transcript (tpt), unrecorded (unrec.). Christine Matzke (CM), Mohamed Salih Ismael (MSI), Mussie Tesfagiorgis (MT), Samson Gebregzhier (SG), Temesgen Gebreyesus (TG), Tesfazghi Ukubazghi (TU), Yakem Tesfai (YT).

I 1   Tegbaru Teklai, receptionist, Ma.Te.A. Rec. interview in English/Tigrinya, 8 October 1999, Asmara, Eritrea. Int.: CM, ttr/tpt: SG.

I 2   Negusse Haile 'Mensa'ai', Ma.Te.A., Merhaba, ELF. 3rd unrec. interview in German, 7 November 1999, Kassel, Germany. Int./nts: CM.

I 3   Negusse Haile 'Mensa'ai', Ma.Te.A., Merhaba, ELF. 4th unrec. interview in German, 4 December 1999, Kassel, Germany. Int./nts: CM.

I 4   Negusse Haile 'Mensa'ai', Ma.Te.A., Merhaba, ELF. 5th unrec. interview in German, 12 December 1999, Kassel, Germany. Int./nts: CM.

I 5   Female Ma.Te.A. member, 2nd unrec. conversation in German, 21 December 1999, Frankfurt/M., Germany. Int./nts: CM.

I 6   Asmerom Habtemariam, Ma.Te.A., *Mekaleh Guaila,* EPLF cultural troupe, now Ministry of Information. Rec. interview in English/Tigrinya, 31 January 2000, Asmara, Eritrea. Int.: CM, ttr/tpt: MT.

I 7   Bereket Mengisteab, singer, *Mekaleh Guaila,* ELF, PFDJ Cultural Affairs. Rec. interview in English/Tigrinya, 6 March 2000, Asmara, Eritrea. Int.: CM, ttr/tpt: TU.

I 8   Tekabo Woldemariam, Ma.M.Hal., Ma.Te.A. Rec. interview in English/Tigrinya, 11 March 2000, Asmara, Eritrea. Int.: CM, ttr: TU, tpt: TG.

I 9   Tekabo Woldemariam. 3rd rec. interview in English/Tigrinya, 15 March 2000, Asmara, Eritrea. Int.: CM, ttr: TU, tpt: MT.

I 10   Tekabo Woldemariam. 4th rec. interview in English/Tigrinya, 21 March 2000, Asmara,

Eritrea. Int.: CM, ttr: TU, tpt: MT.

I 11 Ethiopia Medhanie, Ma.Te.A. Rec. interview in English/Tigrinya, 25 March 2000, Asmara, Eritrea. Int.: CM, ttr/tpt: TU.

I 12 Ethiopia Medhanie. 2nd rec. interview in English/Tigrinya, 6 April 2000, Asmara, Eritrea. Int.: CM, ttr: TU, tpt: MT.

I 13 Hiwot Tedla, Ma.Te.A. Rec. interview, in Englis/Tigrinya, 7 April 2000. Int.: CM, ttr: TU, tpt: MT.

I 14 Aslie Tedros, drummer, *Mekaleh Guaila*. Rec. interview in English/Tigrinya, 13 April 2000, Massawa, Eritrea. Int.: CM, ttr: *Memhir* Daniel (X), tpt: MT.

I 15 Tebereh Tesfahunei, singer, Ma.Te.A. Rec. interview in English/Tigrinya, 31 July 2000, Asmara, Eritrea. Int.: CM, ttr/tpt: MT.

I 16 Vittorio Bossi, musician, Ma.Te.A. Rec. interview in English/Tigrinya, 8 August 2001, Asmara, Eritrea. Int.: CM, ttr/tpt: MSI.

I 17 Asres Tessema, musician, playwright, Ma.Te.A. Rec. interview in English, 9 August 2001, Asmara, Eritrea. Int./tpt: CM.

I 18 Asres Tessema. 2nd interview, 13 August 2001, Asmara, Eritrea. Rec. interview, in English. Int./tpt: CM.

I 19 Jabre Mahmud, owner of a snack bar, Ma.Te.A. Rec. interview in English/Tigrinya, 14 October 1999, Asmara, Eritrea. Int.: CM, ttr/tpt: YT.

I 20 Negusse Haile 'Mensa'ai', Ma.Te.A., Merhaba, ELF. Unrec. interview in German, 22 December 1998, Kassel, Germany. Int./nts: CM.

The Story of Jos Repertory Theatre
Creativity & collaboration

VICTOR S. DUGGA & PATRICK-JUDE OTEH

Jos Repertory Theatre: the beginnings

Jos Repertory Theatre (JRT) emerged in 1997 and survives, swimming against the tide. It was established in an unlikely location, Jos, in north central Nigeria, has often been visited by theatre companies from the south but is not known as a source of many productions. JRT went into the theatre business seriously in 2000 at a time many theatre companies throughout the country had folded or begun to fade. The name, 'The Jos Repertory Theatre', which has confused some, indicates a link with one of the Lagos groups, 'The Pec Repertory Theatre', which was set up by J P Clark-Bekederemo and was where JRT's founder, Patrick-Jude Oteh, did his National Service (1987). When Oteh, a graduate in drama from the University of Ibadan, moved to Jos to do postgraduate work, he found many drama enthusiasts whom he had got to know through the Nigerian Universities' Theatre Arts Festivals (NUTAF). What he felt was missing was a forum for artistic expression. Meetings first took the shape of monthly Saturday-evening gatherings for poetry recitations, drumming, play readings and general discussion. They were held at Peejay's Fast Food on Ahmadu Bello Way which Oteh ran, and the same venue hosted the monthly meetings of the Plateau State chapter of the National Association of Nigerian Theatre Arts Practitioners (NANTAP). In time 'Peejay's' became an informal cultural centre, providing refreshment for mind and body.

In this chapter, we give an account of the growth and development of the JRT which we regard as an on-going experiment that shows new ways of handling age-old problems. It reveals how a small group of enthusiasts can move beyond their immediate environment to experience globalisation, and shows how managing a theatre goes much further than putting on a play and attracting an audience. This is a story of using a flexible approach to what theatre is, of attracting financial support and of fostering international links.

Theatre companies and the theatre environment in Nigeria

At the end of the last century, the commercial theatre tradition in Nigeria that

82

has been traced to the first productions of Hubert Ogunde and that continued in the Yoruba Travelling Theatre companies, was reeling under the impact of new media. First films and television, and then the Nigeria-made videos had dealt crippling blows to the travelling theatres and many groups went out of business. At the same time several of Nigeria's universities were offering degree courses in drama and producing graduates who wanted to make careers in the theatre. However, the degree programmes were academic rather than vocational, and graduates were poorly equipped to rise to the challenge of creating theatre companies from scratch. Such ventures inevitably needed strong financial support and even the theatre troupes established and funded by the universities had fallen on hard times. In *Preliminary Readings in Theatre Research*, Chris Nwamuo maintained that the universities produced good theatre but lacked the marketing skills to establish theatre as sound business. (2005: 50–51) The environment in which the Jos Repertory Theatre emerged was also characterised by the fact that the government had set up theatre companies and arts councils but had failed to fund them. In this situation some practitioners turned to the private sector for funding. However, their requests often fell on deaf ears and negative responses nudged JRT to seek funds from international grant-givers.

Seeking an audience, finding collaborators

At the beginning, in 1997, Jos Repertory Theatre began touring productions of examination set texts to local secondary schools. Oteh found it fairly easy to persuade school principals to allow the young troupe to perform and the students were enthusiastic about being able to see performances of the plays they were reading. Gate-fees were minimal and a percentage was often paid to the host schools for the use of halls and other facilities. Through these tours, JRT actors cut their teeth and the company began to establish a reputation.

By 2000, the artistes wanted to see if they could hold their own on a larger, indeed a national, stage in Ibadan and Lagos. The opportunity came with an invitation to perform in Lagos at the MUSON Festival of Arts 2000 held at the Musical Society of Nigeria (MUSON) Centre, one of the few examples of private enterprise and corporate funding making a major contribution to the cultural scene in Nigeria. JRT entered *Queen Amina of Zazzau* by Wale Ogunyemi. The playwright readily granted the company permission to premiere the play at the festival and the festival's selection committee welcomed JRT's offer to participate because it was the first one from the northern part of Nigeria. Eager to make the best use of the opportunity, the thirty-strong company set out on the journey of over 1,000 kilometres to Lagos. Under normal circumstances the money available for the journey would have been exhausted in three days, but sacrifices were made and the group stretched their resources to survive the week-long venture.

In addition to the single performance as part of the MUSON Festival, JRT took the initiative to put in two further shows at the National Theatre of Nigeria, Iganmu. These were for the benefit of the National Association of

A note on the play

Wale Ogunyemi's version of Queen Amina is the story of the Queen of old Zaria who was on the throne at a time when men held all the power. Amina grew up with an uncle who was a warrior and was brought up with a preference for wars and conquest. When, on the death of her mother Bakwa Turunku, she became Queen, she swore an oath to the Bori cult that she was not going to be dominated by any man. In return, the cult gave her powers of conquest and domination. On the night of her initiation into the Bori cult, she chose the praying mantis as her symbol. The catch with this symbol was that if she mated with any male, she had to kill that man. If she slept with a man and did not kill him, her powers would begin to wane. Amina accepted the condition. Initially she made do with slaves and men she felt were expendable as sexual partners, but her heart was always set on Aliyu, the leader of the infantry. Her lady of the chambers, Uwa Soro was also in love with Aliyu and, on the night that Aliyu slept with Queen Amina, Uwa Soro was ready with a potion to neutralise the poison that Queen Amina usually gave her male partners. As a result, Aliyu lived to tell the story of his conquest of Queen Amina. Amina spent the rest of her life pursuing Aliyu. Eventually, realising the futility of the chase, she gave up and died. According to the legend, the Kingdom of Zazzau died with her.

Nigerian Theatre Arts Practitioners (NANTAP) and to make JRT known to the organisers of FESTINA, an ambitious theatre festival which sought to attract productions from all the regions of the country. It became obvious that NATAP needed a full-scale production so that sponsors would take them seriously. This was where JRT came in, and for its part, JRT needed a venue to showcase its work. JRT also anticipated that prospective funders and people with influence would be in their audiences.

They were right. Toyin Adewale-Gabriel, the program assistant, Media Arts and Culture of the Ford Foundation, attended the premiere of *Queen Amina of Zazzau*. She returned two days later with Aida Opoku-Mensah, the program officer, who, during a post-performance discussion, expressed her desire to see what JRT was doing in Jos. Her subsequent visit to the north had a great impact on JRT, which was, at that point, still an informal outfit operating from a small office in Peejay's Fast Foods.

Discussions followed Opoku-Mensah's visit and the upshot was that Ford Foundation made a grant to JRT of $22,000. This was for office rent, the purchase of two computers and the payment of salaries of the four members of staff. The grant also covered the costs of performances of theatre-for-development (TfD) plays in four states in the north: Plateau, Kaduna, Niger and Nasarawa. To these, JRT added Abuja, the federal capital territory.

JRT's first venture into TfD was through a devised piece entitled *Valley Cry* in support of an HIV/ AIDS education and awareness campaign. In preparing

Valley Cry, members of the troupe gathered information from various communities in Jos North Local Government and liaised with local health officials. They then wove narratives to create the play. The involvement of the troupe in this project was particularly challenging because Oteh had not been exposed to the form when a drama student. His limited experience of TfD had come from working with Chuck Mike, and the Performance Studio Theatre during his time in Lagos. JRT was also on new ground in thinking about HIV/AIDS and determining what message it should send out.

The Ford Foundation approved a grant for the second year (2003) and increased it to $36,000. Still requiring the presentation TfD pieces, Ford shifted the topic to one that fitted in with its support for public education as an election approached: good governance and accountability. JRT's management, led by Jude Oteh were happy with, this. JRT hoped to contribute to diffuse the apathy clinging to the approaching elections. Many had lost faith in the democracy that had followed the departure of General Abdusalami Abubakar. The sketch was to explain to the people in the rural areas that democracy is a hands-on experience with everybody involved. Members of the audience should be encouraged to recognise that those they elected were accountable to them. The grant included a sum to start a process of staff development for those working for JRT, of whom there were five by this time. They and their job titles were: Patrick-Jude Oteh, Artistic Director; Oluwanifemi Oteh, Program Co-ordinator; Austin Okonkwo, Production Co-ordinator; Patricia Andrew, Project Accountant, and Grace John, Administration Support. These people have worked well and the structure has remained substantially unchanged, though, at the time of writing, Patricia Andrew has left for further studies and has been replaced by Guyana Adiwu.

The same five states as in the previous project remained the target sites for performances. This time the sketch toured was entitled *Community Call,* and had a cast and crew totalling fifteen. Due to the pressures of performing in several communities within a short time, the top-down approach was used. *Community Call* was the story of a landlord who felt he was not accountable to anyone – his wives or his tenants. He consistently employed divide and rule tactics to control them all. This continued until a former civil servant came to rent one of the rooms in the house and the first thing he did was to mobilise all the tenants into one body. The first demand they made of the landlord was for water. He tried his usual tactics but they failed and he had no option but to give in. Realising their new strength, the tenants made other demands which they presented at a general meeting that included all the tenants, the landlord and his entire household. With their new found co-operative approach, those who had previously been powerless found that they could improve the circumstances in which they lived. On arrival in any of the communities, we usually employed a 'Pied Piper Approach' which culminated in the attraction of the villages to a particular spot where the sketch was presented. There was usually an interactive session after each show when the villages were given time to air their views.

In 2004, the Ford Foundation provided JRT with a grant of $100,000 for a period of eighteen months with the money being separated into two grants of

$50,000 each. By this stage, JRT had put in place a structure that worked effectively and was accountable. The amount given was what JRT requested. Part of this was for TfD work aimed at secondary schools in the five states toured in previous years. On this occasion, JRT took *Deferred Dreams*, a sketch that addressed the issue of drug abuse and HIV/AIDS to twenty-four schools. The grant covered travel costs, stage sets, equipment including a generator, accommodation and allowances for the members of the performance company. On this occasion the company numbered eighteen. The rates of remuneration varied from N15,000 to N20,000 depending on experience. In addition to the fees, each artiste was paid a daily allowance of N1,000. The *per diems* were distributed in bulk before the troupe left base along with 50 per cent of the fees while the balance of the fees was paid on return when reports had been made. Some artistes elected to collect only the daily allowances and to collect their other entitlements when they got back. In some rural areas, the troupe did not get adequate accommodation and had to make do with what was available.

There was also a capacity building component to the grant that covered training and the creation of a database of audiences and performers. It should be noted at this point that all the artists, many of whom were graduates or certificate holders from the Theatre Arts Department of the University of Jos, were on contracts of limited duration and for specific projects. The focus subsequently widened to incorporate first-timers on stage as a way of giving experience to younger members of the group. For such people, the tours to schools were very testing. During a week on the road, nerves and tempers frayed. Only the best in terms of attitude and mental orientation survived, and it was from these that JRT chose the core of its regular members.

The Ford Foundation grant was sufficiently flexible to enable JRT to engage in the performance of scripted plays such as Wole Soyinka's *Death and the King's Horseman* and Yahaya Dangana's *The Royal Chambers*. Staff development also continued and, thanks to Ford and British Council support, the core office holders have been able to attend relevant courses, workshops and seminars in Lagos and the United Kingdom. These have included courses at the Lagos Business School and the 'Performing Africa' Conference organised by Leeds University Centre For African Studies (LUCAS) in 2004. With such backing, the JRT hopes to continue to build a strong, versatile, well-informed team capable of delivering world-class productions.

Thinking locally, going international

Following the Lagos MUSON experience, JRT continued to explore avenues for growth. The Internet led to the establishment of a contact with the Library Theatre, Manchester that bore fruit, and, under the artistic directorship of Chris Honer, the Library Theatre has offered JRT two internships in the areas of programming, administration and networking. During and after the first two Jos theatre festivals, the link also provided support in the areas of audience development and marketing.

David Roberts, the governance advisor at the British Council in Abuja, approved council funding for a performance of *Queen Amina of Zazzau* in Abuja to the tune of N673,700 ($4,700). The production was very well received and opened doors for JRT in the Abuja and Kano offices of the British Council. Under the council's 'Connecting Futures' programme, Biyi Bandele and John Binnie subsequently visited Nigeria from the UK and worked with JRT. The end product was *Our House*. (See below. Ed.)

During 2004, JRT seriously addressed the fact that it was working in an area where there was no regular and substantial theatre festival, and felt the need to work towards the establishment of a Jos Festival of Theatre. Plans for this fell into shape when discussing the fourth Ford Foundation grant and money was made available by the foundation.

The First Jos Festival of Theatre, held in 2004, offered a programme that included five productions: Wole Soyinka's *Death and the King's Horseman*, Yahaya Dangana's *The Royal Chamber,* a stage adaptation of Chinua Achebe's *Things Fall Apart,* a dance drama, *My Pride,* and JRT's *Our House*. The festival lasted for five weekends with each production running for four days at the Professor Luka Bentu Indoor Theatre in Jos. The balance of plays in the programme was deliberate: *Death and the King's Horseman* and the adaptation of Achebe's novel were already familiar to many and attracted lovers of those classics. Yahaya Dangana's *The Royal Chamber* was not so well known and quite unusual. It had been commissioned to accompany the 2003 All African Games, held in Abuja. National, funding had been available for the production which made use of performers from five states who joined a JRT team. The premiere had been well received and the piece had become, in a sense, part of JRT's 'repertory'. That is to say it was 'in the repertory', one of a stock of plays that JRT could stage relatively easily at quite short notice.

The most exciting experiment in the festival was, however, the staging of JRT's devised play, *Our House,* which told the story of Nigeria from independence to date. At the start the regions come together in an alliance that seeks to bring everyone into a mutually beneficial relationship. In the coverage of the years that followed various topics, including the exploitation of oil reserves and the distribution of the oil revenues, were highlighted. Other issues raised concerned gender, unemployment, the fickleness of politicians and urban migration. The play ends on a note of optimism by suggesting that all will be well with the tottering nation if everyone unites to build a virile nation in which all can take pride.

The play was the end product of the Connecting Futures New Theatre project which had started in 2003 with Biyi Bandele and the team that JRT had assembled to identify issues affecting young people all over the nation. Participants were drawn from the six geo-political zones of Nigeria and they were in Jos for ten days identifying issues and coming up with likely topics that would be addressed in Phase Two, the scripting stage. Impressed with the production that emerged, the British Council funded a tour to some Nigerian cities and subsequently (July 2005), having introduced JRT to the Clyde Unity Theatre, Glasgow, sponsored a tour of Scotland in July 2005. On that visit to the UK, the JRT was looked after by the Clyde Unity Theatre, and worked on a joint creation entitled *My Friend Matt*. This was an adaptation of a novel from Pakistan, Adam Zameenzad's *My Friend Matt and Hena the Whore* (1988).

My Friend Matt is based on actual events that occurred in Ethiopia after Emperor Haile Selassie had been deposed, when the country was hit by famine and divided by a desperate power struggle. Tyranny of both man and nature led to urban migration and to emigration in search of a better existence. In their bid to survive, some of the migrants ended up as child soldiers; others became lorry touts or prostitutes. In the absence of the younger ones from the villages, schools closed. The elders, while hoping that the children would return, told stories of their glorious past while they waited for death in the village square.

The link with Glasgow led to JRT welcoming the Clyde Unity Theatre to the second Jos Festival of Theatre (2006). This event was supported by the Ford Foundation to the tune of $100,000 but this time there were more local supporters including the Grand Cereals and Oil Mills Limited (GCOML), Coca-Cola, Guinness, Jos International Breweries (JIB), Crest Hotel and Gardens, Nigerian Film Corporation (NFC), Plateau Aids Control Agency (PLACA), African Independent Television (AIT), Alliance Francaise, Jos), and the link with Peejay's Foods continued.

Five plays and a dance drama were presented, and there were troupes and audience members from six states of Nigeria. With the exception of *My Friend Matt* which played for one night, all other plays were presented for two nights. The productions at this second festival were special because JRT had called for new directors and new playwrights to come forward. A total of fifty scripts were submitted, out of which an independent panel selected five. Three of these were premiered at the Festival: *Ajarat* by Bunmi Obasa, *Oluaiye* by Othman Alsanus and 'Meme', a dance drama choreographed by Bose Tsevende. They featured along with JRT's *Chariot Without Riders*. In encouraging new work JRT was drawing on the experiences of alternative theatres in Britain that sought to cultivate new writers. Wole Soyinka's *The Lion and the Jewel*, itself submitted to a London theatre that had requested new plays in the late 1950s, was also included in the programme and turned out to be the most popular part of the ten-day festival. Apart from the Clyde Unity Theatre, there were also representations from the London International Festival of Theatre (LIFT) which sent representatives from Project Phakama.

This contact was as a result of internship of JRT's production coordinator, Austin Okonkwo, at the LIFT offices in London in November. They wanted to see what JRT was doing and the festival provided the perfect opportunity to do this. While in Jos, it was jointly decided, in accordance with their methods, that they should become an integral part of JFT. Accordingly, they conducted workshops and led an interactive, post-performance session. The capacity building was geared towards the eventual formation of the youth wing of the Jos Repertory Theatre an idea that JRT had been considering because of the difference in ages between JRT artistes and its Glasgow partners. JRT discussed the idea with Gillian Belben, the then director of the British Council, Kano, and her opinion was that if JRT anticipated doing a lot of work with young people, it would need to start its own youth theatre. Apart from the possibility of more funding, this was a most logical step to take in order to bring on new generations of performers. LIFT, with experience of over twenty-five years in theatre work, was to be JRT's next stop in the search for collaborators, and Project Phakama came into the picture because they have abundant relevant experience with young people's theatre.

Management antics and the survival of JRT

The issues of administration, staff recruitment and retention and profitability always have to be kept in mind by theatre company managers. The same problems associated with the floating and survival of the companies persists. The experience of JRT shows that the challenge of managing a theatre company in Nigeria borders on finances more than artistic creativity.

The grants from the National Action Committee on AIDS (NACA) in 2003 and the Plateau Aids Control Agency (PLACA) in 2005 made it possible for JRT to employ a group of performers on full-time basis for a year. The artistes who took part in the NACA project were paid a monthly subsistence allowance of N7,500.00 each while those who took part in the PLACA project were paid N8,000.00 a month. This was necessary because the terms of the grants required that JRT move into communities at short notice to put on a total of more than ninety performances: fifty-one for PLACA and forty for NACA. Only a standing body of performers could guarantee availability.

At this point it should be noted that the funds it has received have ensured JRT's survival, and that they have influenced but not defined the work of the group. In the preferred professional setting, the director should choose the play to be produced. JRT has been able to determine what plays to produce even when, in some situations, the themes have been specified by funders. This can be seen in the example of *Valley Cry*.

The British Council, funded by British tax payers, supports work that involves input from the UK and that can be seen to have an impact on Britons. The challenge in working with the Council has been to align JRT's objectives with theirs. It is indisputable that without the role played by Gillian Belben, *Our House* would not have gone beyond Nigeria. A lot of deft administrative work was going on in the background which JRT was not privy to but she had the whole situation under control. For JRT, *Our House* was both a critical as well as a financial success for our young company. Each member of cast and crew was paid a subsistence of £200 for the duration of the ten day tour in the UK while accommodation, transport and part-feeding were to be arranged by Clyde Unity Theatre. Accommodation was in bed and breakfasts, or in self-catering apartments. Clyde Unity Theatre provided one meal a day.

Playwrights based in UK, Biyi Bandele and John Binnie, facilitated both the discussions in which issues for consideration were identified and the actual scripting. The narrative and the telling of it were controlled by JRT. Thanks to the funding from the British Council, some artistes were employed on the *Our*

House project for almost three years. The play that emerged is, essentially, the story of Nigeria told by Nigerians with the UK input woven into it through the participation of Biyi Bandele and John Binnie. The reviews of the performance attest to the critical success of the tour. A major review in *The Glasgow Herald* acclaimed the production as an 'African home truth'.

Several of the group of eight artistes from JRT were visiting the UK for the first time and found much that was new. For example, they visited university theatres that, they remarked, had more equipment than all theatre departments in Nigerian Universities put together. They also saw that not everyone abroad was rich. The group welcomed the opportunity to see young British people work in the theatre, and were impressed by the varity of topics they tackled and the constant experimentation. The travellers were surprised by the number of new cars – an eye opener coming from the used car depot that our country has become. But the biggest shock, coming from a nation where religion is taken very seriously, was to see that there were redundant churches and that these had been converted to clubs, pubs and even theatres.

During the tour of the UK, cast and crew were often asked questions arising from certain aspects of *Our House* especially as it relates to the Niger-Delta region and the Abacha years. The reality is that living in Nigeria, members of JRT, like other young people, are acutely aware of what Achebe called 'the trouble with Nigeria'. In a sense the follow-up to *Our House, Chariot Without Riders* took a hard look at the post-colonial state of Nigeria. It asked: What went wrong? In that play two tramps, meeting under a bridge, discuss the post-colonial state in Africa. The topics considered include poverty, bird flu, HIV/AIDS, unemployment, constitutional amendments, dictatorship, and religious tensions. The basic question they ask themselves is 'What happened to all the hopes of the colonialists and the dreams of the nationalists in the post-independence era?' It is a mark of the extent of freedom of speech in the country that the production was able to offer this radical questioning without leading to the detention of the performers. *Chariot without Riders* is an all-talk production lasting one hour which is in the manner of Samuel Beckett's *Waiting for Godot*. However, in this instance, the Godots are well known within the context of Nigerian society, and the politics of the production are clear.

As far as the Ford Foundation is concerned, the only influence they have had in terms of dictating JRT's work has been apparent when grants were being discussed. Thereafter JRT has been free to draw up its programmes. The general understanding is that the grants are intended to foster growth that will, in the long term, lead to the emergence of a sustainable, independent theatre company. We have found that the tricky part is aligning the Ford Foundation objectives with those of JRT. It is our experience that no 'funder gives you funds to chase your own dreams but if you succeed in aligning your dreams with theirs then you can begin to negotiate'. During the past six years, the funding from the Ford Foundation has enabled JRT to expand its capacity from an ad-hoc arrangement to a more structured and functional theatre organisation and to hold two regional theatre festivals that have attracted international participation. Self-sustainability is still a long way off. We have reiterated the fact that there are so many issues struggling for attention in the daily lives of the people that theatre is often relegated to the background. Takings have not been encouraging: currently the annual income from ticket sales is about N250,000.

As a small company that is striving to exist in a difficult economic and social environment, JRT has remained wary of accepting funds from organisations that might seek to erode its independence. This is principally because of the belief that any art must be created in an atmosphere of independence or it will take on the life of its funders. In searching for support, JRT's *modus operandi* has been to start early. For instance, by October of every year the plans for the next year are mostly known but there is still some flexibility. We have learned the importance of starting fund-raising early and of being prepared to change our fund-raising strategy if one avenue closes.

JRT recognises that the fund-raising aspect of the theatre business is a major part of managing a theatre company and one must foster good links. The entire Connecting Futures New Theatre project comprising *Our House* and *My Friend Matt* cost the British Council £52,000 with Connect Youth contributing £5,000 towards the project. The British Council provided a grant of £17,000 in 2004–05, and they added £35,000 for the follow-up in 2005–06. If we were asked to raise this amount locally, we doubt if it would have been possible. JRT's experience is that it is valuable to build relationships with individuals who have shown interest in the company. For instance, the support of Sue Mace, the British Council director in Kano who took over from Gillian Belben for an extended period, was very important for *My Friend Matt*.

While collaborating, relationships have to be managed delicately to satisfy all parties involved and achieve the goals of the project. JRT have found that it is easier to create ideas and find funds for them than to work with another company. On their most recent experience with the Clyde Unity Theatre, the initial contact was frosty. The difficulty started with the material woven around the Ethiopian famine and the approach of the two companies. While JRT saw the play as an African story to be realised using a distinctive African story-telling techniques, the Clyde team saw it as material that could be explored through improvisation. Their idea was that since we were working with young people, the spontaneity that improvisation required would benefit the production.

Recognising that their approaches differed, the groups worked through the initial encounter and in the following months collaborated on the script via email. Soon enough, a sound relationship was established. JRT recognised the common experience that companies working together from different cultures invariably go through phases of stress when cultural and artistic choices are made. The final product, which premiered at the Second Jos Festival of Theatre, extended the range of both companies and left all involved fulfilled. Beyond the stage production, the collaboration stimulated interaction between two groups of young people and made a deep impression on the two sides, all expressed a desire to work together again soon. It is instructive to point out that one of the fruits of this is the individual collaboration between Emmanuel Degri and Markus Montgomery Roche who have been exploring the possibility of making a record which will be a fusion of rock and roll and Afro beat. The companies planned a fourth tour.

While funds from organisations such as the Ford Foundation and the British Council are important, no theatre company can simply wait for grants. In 2005, JRT explored the possibility of collaborating with the Africa Independent Television station in Jos to mark the 45th anniversary of Nigeria's independence with a production of Wole Soyinka's *The Lion and the Jewel* and of remounting *Queen Amina of Zazzau* for the 46th independence anniversary. The presentation in 2005 was artistically satisfying, but financially unsatisfactory. Audiences were very enthusiastic, but the entry fee we felt able to ask (less than $1) meant that we could not even cover transport costs. In contrast, during the celebrations in Abuja of Professor Wole Soyinka's 70th birthday (July 2004) and of the 70th anniversary of the British Council tickets were sold at about $7. However, even at that level and with a capacity audience, the income generated only covered accommodation, transport, per diems and minimal artists' fees.

Conclusion

It can be seen that JRT started modestly in 1997 with the reading of plays and poetry and moved on to touring secondary schools with productions of set texts. It launched into business as a theatre company in 2000, and has moved forward since then. Over the years, the recognition that collaboration is essential in order to make theatre happen has enabled JRT to increase its activities and take advantage of different funding opportunities.

JRT's 2006 programme included a move back to performing in secondary schools and can be seen as turning full circle. However, JRT is not just 'back at the beginning' – over the years many miles have been travelled and many lessons have been learned. This time a new play was prepared every month and taken on tour. Through this, JRT hoped to build audiences, inspire future artists, support itself as an organisation, and provide its talented members with regular employment. The goal of being a self-sustaining company remains one to aspire towards.

BIBLIOGRAPHY

Achebe, Chinua (1983): *The Trouble with Nigeria*. London and Nairobi: Heinemann.
Asigbo, Alex (2002): 'Two faces – one voice: Towards a fruitful union between live theatre and the cinematic arts', *Performing Identities: Theatre and the State in Nigeria*, Okwori, J.Z., ed., Lagos: Society of Nigerian Theatre Artists.
Clark, Ebun (1980): *Hubert Ogunde: The Making of Nigerian Theatre*, Oxford: Oxford University Press.
Frank, Haike (2004): *Role-Play in South African Theatre*, Bayreuth: BASS 70.
Jeyifo, Biodun (1984): *The Yoruba Popular Travelling Theatre of Nigeria*, Lagos: Nigeria Magazine.
Johnson, Effiong: (2001) *Play Production Process*, Lagos: Concept Productions.
Maier, Karl (2000): *This House Has Fallen: Nigeria in Crisis*, London: Penguin Books.
Nwamuo, Chris (2005): *Preliminary Readings in Theatre Research*, Calabar: Optimist Press.

Obafemi, Olu (1996): *Contemporary Nigerian Theatre: Cultural Heritage and Social Vision*, Bayreuth: BASS 40.

Perdekamp, Gabriele Grosse (1994): 'Junction Avenue Theatre Company's *Tooth & Nail*', *Theatre and Performance in Africa*, Eckhard Breitinger, ed. Bayreuth: BASS 31.

Udoka, Arnold (2005): 'Dance and National Unity in Nigeria: The Example of the National Troupe of Nigeria,' *Nigeria Theatre Journal Vol. 8. No. 2,* Duro Oni, ed., Lagos: Society of Nigerian Theatre Artists.

Wilson, Edwin (1991): *The Theater Experience,* 5th ed., New York: McGraw Hill, Inc.

WEBOGRAPHY

Anon. 'New Theatre.' The British Council, Nigeria (on *Our House*). http://www.britishcouncil.org/nigeria-society-connectingfutures-newtheatre.htm, accessed 26 July 2006.

Adewale-Gabriel, Toyin. 'An E-Conversation with Nnorom Azuonye,' Sentinel Poetry, Online Magazine Monthly. Issue #12 (November 2003) http://www.Sentinelpoetry.Org.Uk/Magazine1103/Page17.html, Accessed 26 July 2006

Binnie, Mari 'Diary Extract', see http://www.britishcouncil.org/scotland-ezine-articles-april2006-article1.htm, Accessed 11 August 2006. This vivid account of Mari Binnie's experience with *My Friend Matt* provides testimony to the impact of the play.

Financing
Handspring Puppet Company
A South African experience

BASIL JONES

The longevity of any theatre company is dependent on two essential ingredients: continued artistic inspiration backed up by firm and flexible funding. When I was asked to contribute a piece to this issue of the Africa Theatre Series, I offered something on the financing of Handspring because this has been such a necessary aspect of our small company's enduring success.

Puppetry is a rather eccentric career choice and we never expected to make money as such. Indeed we were often surprised when we did. What you will find below is a brief account of the changing ways in which Handspring has made a living over 25 years.

Handspring Puppet Company was started by four fine arts graduates, Adrian Kohler, Jon Weinberg, Jill Joubert and Basil Jones. We knew nothing about acting and very little about theatre. Each of us had left art school somewhat unprepared for the real world and had already spent three years immersed in the realities of earning a living in the arts. Each of us had found jobs, but none felt seriously committed to what we were doing. Three of us had moved away from Cape Town, but by chance we all returned there in December 1979. We met, swapped stories and began to exchange ideas on working together to form a puppet company. Adrian Kohler had in fact been involved with puppets since childhood and since leaving art school, had first worked at the Puppet Space, at the famous Space Theatre in Cape Town.

Because of our lack of experience in the theatre we knew from the start that we had scant hope of success unless we planned well. So, once the decision to form a company had been made, we gave ourselves a year to exchange ideas and to save enough of our current salaries to survive the first six months without income.

Kohler and I were living in Botswana and working at the University of Botswana and the National Museum & Art Gallery. Twenty-five per cent of each of our salaries was commuted and due to be paid to us at the end of our contracts. We knew this would come in useful. Jill Joubert was teaching art in Cape Town and Jon Weinberg was working as a puppeteer in Pietermaritzburg.

94

So, each of us went back to our respective jobs and corresponded feverishly by letter between Maritzburg, Cape Town and Gaborone.

The company was scheduled to start work in January 1981. In July 1980, the four of us met in Gaborone and spent a week discussing how we wanted to structure both the company itself and our first year of work. Our tasks included:

- Deciding on a legal structure for the company (whether a close corporation, proprietary limited, charity etc.)
- Finding a name;
- Registering the company;
- Drafting an agreement which would set out the terms of our association, and, most importantly, the terms under which we would extricate ourselves from the association should one of us wish to leave;
- Writing a play;
- Finding premises in Cape Town, where the puppets could be made and plays rehearsed;
- Buying a truck to be used both to transport all the equipment and as a caravan;
- Finding and booking suitable venues for our first tour.

At that stage, we hadn't even agreed on a story, let alone started writing a script.

The plan was to spend six months making the puppets for our first production and making t-shirts and toys, which could be sold in foyers at interval. (We assumed that we wouldn't make enough money from ticket sales alone.) After much agony, we finally agreed on a name for the company. The famous Russian puppeteer, Sergei Obrastzov had said that 'the soul of the puppet lies in the palm of the hand'. We loved that idea and felt that 'handspring' expressed it succinctly.

By the time Adrian and I arrived in Cape Town in December 1980, Jill had found us premises. Ominously enough it was the former funeral parlour of a company called Human and Pitt. Thousands of corpses had passed through those doors and we were forced to wonder whether our newborn baby would survive such inauspicious surroundings. Nevertheless, we revelled in our spacious new studios: an office with wooden floor, a small workshop, a small storeroom with tiled walls (where the undertakers used to wash the bodies) and just enough room to rehearse. Above us was the Ark Mission for reforming alcoholics and on the balcony outside, the street kids, who slept in large cardboard boxes at night.

We had pooled our savings to buy a truck, which would become our home on the road. We fitted it out with four narrow bunk beds, one drawer each, a two-plate gas-stove and a fridge. Exactly enough money remained to pay the rent and ourselves for six months. We set about building a stage, designing puppets, making toy prototypes, and a booth from which to sell them. First drafts of the play were passed around for comment. We then planned an ambitious tour, booking town halls and theatres around the country.

Fortunately John Slemon, director of Cape Town's Baxter Theatre gave us a three-week slot in the school holidays. This was also useful because we had a booking at an established theatre gave us more credibility when speaking to officials in charge of small town venues.

Trying to be serious and adult, we held carefully minuted meetings on Monday mornings. Every budget and every schedule was revisited a hundred times. Perusing those notes today, typed on onion skin paper, I am charmed by the fact that the lower section of all the letter 'a's is red because the black-and-red typewriter ribbon was a little out of alignment for the 'a' key. Each of us had put our life's savings into the company. There were differing amounts, so quite a bit of time was spent deciding what would happen to our assets if somebody decided to leave and needed to withdraw their financial contribution.

The old Hofmeyr Theatre was closing down and, through careful negotiation and for a tiny sum, techno friends bought their lighting system and lighting bars on our behalf. The latter were used to construct our puppet stage with its lighting rig. We then bought a sound-mixing desk and speakers and in their spare time and late into many nights, these techno-angels modified the ancient lights into a system that operated 10 x 500 watt fresnels with five dimmers that could run off the power of any school hall.

Soon the script and puppets began to emerge and rehearsals began. Some time into this process, Bill Curry, the pioneering actor from the Space Theatre, visited our studio and watched a rehearsal. He noted that we didn't have a director and offered his services on condition that we didn't pay him ('You understand, I am an *actor*, not a *director*'). His offer was accepted with equal measures of humility and alacrity. Indeed, during the next five years, Curry always found time to direct us and in the process taught us all a good deal about acting.

As the time for the Baxter Theatre opening drew near, a soiree was organised for the Cape Town press in our new studios. We sent out invitations to the entire Arts Press corps and a friendly restauranteur made snacks to go with the wines. Only one of 21 journalists arrived. But there were many friends and we partied into the night. Fortunately this sole journalist, Mike van Niekerk, wrote a sunny article which, together with a prominent photo of the four of us, was published in Cape Town's morning newspaper thus heralding the birth of Handspring Puppet Company (Pty) Ltd and our forthcoming show, *The Honey Trail*. To our grateful surprise, block bookings were good and even before it opened, the show was 75 per cent full. The reviewers were more than kind and towards the end of the run we began to sell out.

After three weeks at the Baxter, *The Honey Trail* launched immediately into a tour to 23 towns around the country. It was a tumultuous honeymoon for the four of us. Indeed we discovered that working together in the day and living in the cramped truck, surrounded by sets and boxes, drying clothes and towels was a very severe test of our relationship. We were also dogged by cold, illness and awful organisation in the towns we visited. Actually, Jon had become quite ill during the Baxter season and at the last minute had to be replaced by an actor friend, who persuaded us to bring her young nephew on tour as well. By the time we reached Durban we were limping, but then chicken pox stopped us dead in our tracks. For two weeks all performances had to be cancelled. This fallow moment obliged us to rethink our way of operating. Jill had a revelation. Instead of getting schools to come to theatres – a big transport problem for them – she suggested we should take the show to schools and perform in their halls. Strictly speaking this was against departmental regulations, but school principals were able to use their discretion and some bent the rules.

This was the way we worked for the next four years. A new show would be prepared and promotional material sent to about 200 schools. About 10 per cent took the show. Each child would pay an entrance fee. (This meant that we couldn't easily perform in black schools because they simply couldn't afford to pay us and we weren't in a stable enough situation to perform for free.) In large schools the revenue could be fairly substantial. But often a smaller number than expected would turn up. There were two tours a year, one up the east coast and the other northwards, through the heart of the country to Johannesburg and Gaborone in Botswana. By the end of the year, our revenue was just enough to take us through a four-month making period, when a new show would be devised, new music composed and recorded, new puppets made and rehearsed.

At the end of the first year, however, a real problem presented itself. Jon was not at all well. It was clear that the pork pie and hamburger cuisine of life on the road was not conducive to a healthy lifestyle. Fortunately, our carefully crafted contract spelt out exactly how and when we'd pay back Jon's initial capital contribution.

Employing a replacement for Jon was a real challenge. In that s/he wouldn't be a 'founding investor' would this person be paid less than us? Have less say in the company than us? Fortunately sanity prevailed. It seemed reasonable that in such a small group everyone should earn the same and have an equal voice in company meetings. A good precedent was set.

This person was contracted for a specific show only and thus began a new phase for Handspring: employing artists on a freelance basis, whilst the founding directors were full time. From the outset, it was clear that a fully employed full-time company was a dangerous dream as it would commit us to a huge monthly salary bill, which would be impossible to generate from performances alone.

Organisations began approaching Handspring with small commissions. In our second year, we made puppets for a TV ad. The production company was happy with the result and immediately began planning a 52-episode TV series. This became *Apha Napaya* and meant Handspring's first contract, earning a modest chunk of money. Now there was enough in the bank to last six months. The company was also able to repay Jon his capital contribution.

We courted the press and sporadically, articles began to appear in newspapers and magazines.

When it came to school visits, perhaps we were overly conscientious. The school would be called beforehand to make sure that they hadn't forgotten to tell their students that we were coming. The route to the school and access to the hall and its technical capabilities, were carefully checked to ensure prompt arrival. A specially devised form became the information matrix for all aspects of each school visit noting:

- The postal and street addresses and telephone numbers;
- Principal's name and contact person;
- Dates of booking confirmation letter and the telephone follow-up;
- Number of pupils, ticket price and estimated income;
- Actual income;
- Remarks from staff;
- Remarks from pupils;
- Our own observations on the quality of our performance, how we were received, reasons for lower or higher income, etc.

These notes proved an invaluable reference when contacting the school the following year. And afterwards – always – a thank you letter. In later years, we also devised educational materials connected to each show. These were sent to the school before arrival: the story outline in comic form, the score for the music, (music and lyrics were always specially composed and recorded), activities and games.

In year four, we landed our first commission: The University of the Witwatersrand's Dental School asked Handspring to create a show for Dental Week. This was our first Handspring commission to produce a live show. It was an ideal opportunity for the company. We were given a sum of money to create the show and performances in the townships were subsidised. This meant that for the first time we had access to black students who could not afford to pay for tickets themselves. *The Mouth Trap* opened in Johannesburg and toured to primary schools in the townships. This was a period of great political turbulence. When children watching one of our performances saw a group of cars arriving in the school, they assumed it was security police and stormed outside shouting slogans, only to find they were the rather frightened Wits dental students, who'd got lost on their way to the school and were arriving late.

On 20 July 1985, a State of Emergency was declared. School principals at white schools were sent a directive by the Department of Education forbidding them to allow any people to enter school premises during school time. We would arrive at schools to find that they'd erected a 2m-high perimeter fence. Peachy-cheeked 12-year-old students were stolidly doing gate guard duty. Clearly Handspring's way of earning a living was going to have to change and a move toward the dreaded TV industry and children's programming seemed the only way to stay in the art form. The company was obliged to move to Johannesburg.

This didn't stop us from taking a big chance as a farewell to Cape Town. For many years – before even starting Handspring – we'd been wanting to do an adult theatre piece and it was now or never. To pay the theatre rental, we brought out *Gertie's Feathers*, the company's most successful show. This ran in

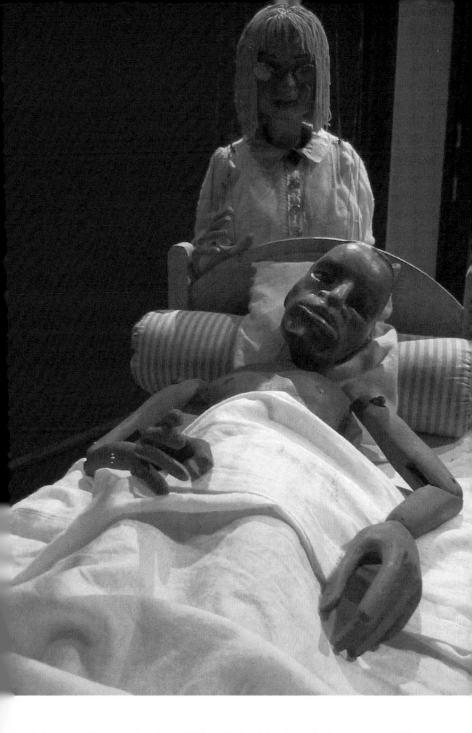

1. *Scene from* Episodes of an Easter Rising, *National Arts Festival, Grahamstown, 1985*
(reproduced with the kind permission of Handspring © Ruphin Coudyzer FPPSA – www.ruphin.com)

2. A Midsmummer Night's Dream, *Baxter Theatre, Cape Town, 1986*
(reproduced with the kind permission of Handspring)

the daytime and the adult show, *Episodes of an Easter Rising*, opened a week later, at night. The cast had extreme doubts about the wisdom of puppets for grown-ups, but the show enjoyed a rapturous welcome, first in South Africa and then at the VIIth Festival International de la Marionnette held in France. *Episodes*, the adult play, gave Handspring our first exposure abroad. Because of the cultural boycott against South Africa, we were given only one performance. This was a blessing in disguise as instead of performing, we saw many inspiring shows returning home knowing anything was possible and that even we could pull dream through into reality.

In Johannesburg the company needed a workshop, studio, and office, but rentals were high and so we decided to sell our house in Cape Town, take a loan and build. Two members of Junction Avenue had bought a piece of land on the slopes of a hill and offered half of it to us. We jumped at the opportunity. By May 1986, the building was more or less ready and we made the move.

During the transition we worked on a co-production with the Baxter Theatre. *Easter Rising's* combination of puppets and actors seemed worth taking further and this interaction seemed to lend itself to the world of fantasy. *A Midsummer Night's Dream*, became the vehicle for this. Giant puppets of Oberon and Titania held court to an airborne cloud of fairies both beautiful and ghastly. This production garnered the Vita Award for Production of the Year of a Play in the Cape.

Meanwhile as the company had no work to speak of in Johannesburg, we were asked to put together an exhibition of puppets in the Art Gallery of the University of South Africa (UNISA) in Pretoria. For a few crucial months this provided us with a modest but stable income. We borrowed puppets from everyone and every institution we knew, added our own and the result was an exhibition of about 280 puppets from South Africa, China, Tibet, Indonesia, Hungary, Germany, England. It broke attendance records and went on to several other venues including the Johannesburg and Durban Art Galleries.

Puppeteers in Johannesburg generously introduced Handspring to a company producing children's TV programmes. This was bread and butter stuff: educational, but not very well researched and rather slow in taking on board the political changes that were so urgently needed in the industry. The hours in the studio sometimes seemed interminable, but the money helped pay off the mortgage. Indeed this was the first time we began to enjoy some financial security.

However, the most important economic benefit from the TV programmes was that it effectively cross-subsidised our work on a new play with Junction Avenue Theatre Company, one of the country's few mixed race theatre groups. The play developed slowly and mainly at night as some of the cast had other jobs. The result was *Tooth and Nail* (1989), an apocalyptic prediction of the chaos about to envelop pre-election South Africa. A life-size news photographer, body wasted away in parts, bears silent witness to the violent lives of a militant schoolgirl, her sangoma mother, a prophetic trade unionist, and a trio of yuppies. On the other side of town a human-size puppet of an opera-loving madam sings duets with her human manservant. It was well received but the vision was too dark and audiences only trickled in.

In TV we slowly progressed from being manipulators of other people's puppets, to designing and manipulating our own puppets, to designing the entire TV show. The problem was that there was no research behind the scripts and no connection between broadcast and the classroom. Eventually we decided we had to produce our own series. Science education for girls had been flagged by progressive educationalists as a priority. This was the late 1980s and exiles were beginning to return to the country. One of our returning friends was a science educator. He introduced us to everyone involved in progressive education in Johannesburg and we began putting together a funding proposal. We wanted to make a series of programmes where children's ideas and thinking processes were central. In each episode a group of young friends encountered a science-related crisis, which they had to solve without adult assistance.

I produced a highly imperfect draft proposal and handed it to four people with varying types of expertise: a teacher, a successful grant recipient, a politician, an accountant. We filtered their advice, modified the proposal and gave it to another group for scrutiny and comment. Eventually about 25 professionals advised me on the document. When it was finally presented it to the Danish funders, they declared it the best grant proposal they'd received.

As part of our research, Handspring received a grant from USAID for a study tour in the States. We visited the headquarters of Sesame Street in New

York, CBS TV producers, puppet centres and attended an international science education conference in Palm Springs, where we presented a paper on our project, *Spider's Place*. By now there was a comic version of the adventure story, including a comic showing how a teacher was utilising the materials in the classroom, plus activities-based tasks for learners and a radio programme. This was backed up with a teacher development programme.

Back home our house began transforming into the headquarters of a new NGO called The Handspring Trust for Puppetry in Education. Yellow cables connected computers and the guest room and even a balcony were converted into offices where staffers organised outreach programmes in several regions. We had a board of governors, evaluators, staff leave, bonuses, remuneration packages – the works. It took five years of research and development but during 1995/96 the TV and radio programmes were finally broadcast. The trust then spent a further five years engaged in teacher development relating to the use of effective teaching strategies using the *Spider's Place* materials, but by this time it had moved to new premises and Adrian and I had resigned.

In 1990, Barney Simon, co-founder of the Market Theatre and a legend in our theatre, invited Handspring to participate in the devising of a new play. This was the first production of the Market Theatre Laboratory – which like the National Theatre Studio in London, developed new plays through a work-shopping process. The Market Theatre retained the rights and we received no royalties, but it was a wonderful opportunity for us to work with Barney. The resulting play was *Starbrites*. The political climate had changed. In the heady days after Mandela's release from prison, Simon wanted to make a fable about regeneration. A down-and-out musician, living in a shack, has his spirit rekindled by the infectious optimism of his adoring young nephew from the country.

After an 11-week season at the Market Theatre, *Starbrites* toured in 1991 to summer festivals in London and the UK, Dublin and Copenhagen. It was the second time Handspring had performed abroad and our six-week season in London was an important window for our work. That year Handspring received a special Vita Award for 'Contributions to South African Theatre' and *Starbrites* was voted 'Production of The Year of A New South African Play'.

In 1992 Handspring was approached by William Kentridge, the artist/designer working with Junction Avenue Theatre Company. He had been filming the development of his animated charcoal drawings: Draw a little, take a picture, draw some more, take a picture, rub out a bit, take a picture, etc.. He called this 'stone-age animation'. It was laborious, but the results were ravishing. The trouble was the time it took to animate a close-up of a moving hand or face. Kentridge suggested we could have puppets animate the fore-ground and he could focus on the background landscapes. We decided to tackle Büchner's *Woyzeck* as the main character seemed very like Harry, a man who lived on the street outside Kentridge's house about whom he was thinking of doing a theatre piece anyway. Also the scenes where short, cinematic and therefore appropriate for puppet theatre, a medium which benefits from laconic dialogue.

3. Busi Zokufa with Maria in Woyzeck on the Highveld, *The Market Theatre, Johannesburg 1992*

4. Woyzeck confronts Maria, The Market Theatre, Johannesburg, 1992

(both photographs reproduced with the kind permission of Handspring © Ruphin Coudyzer FPPSA – www.ruphin.com)

In this case, we approached several funders: The City of Johannesburg, The National Arts Festival, the Foundation for the Creative Arts and the German Embassy and raised R 177,000. The play premiered at the National Arts Festival in Grahamstown and thereafter was co-produced by the Market Theatre in Johannesburg, where it enjoyed a successful season. By great good fortune, the play was seen by the artistic director of Theatre der Welt and we were invited to perform in Munich the following year. Mannie Manim, executive director of the Market Theatre, offered to become our representative and was able to negotiate the deal with Theatre der Welt. This kept us focused on the work. In Munich it was seen by Thomas Petz of Art Bureau. He offered to become our European producer and to tour *Woyzeck on the Highveld*[1] in Europe.

This was a significant association. Petz was well connected in Europe and through him and Mannie Manim, *Woyzeck* travelled widely. Indeed the play saw hundreds of performances, touring to Europe, north and south America, Hong Kong, Australia and New Zealand. It was a moving and much loved production, but one of the main reasons why it toured so widely was the fact that it was economical for festivals. There were only five on stage, two technicians and (for important openings, the director). In recent years Handspring's productions have become too big for multi-venue tours.

Under the auspices of the Trust, we also participated in the establishment of the National Community Theatre For Education and Development Network, (NACTED) which developed organisational and artistic skills in the community theatre arena. This was another example of cross-subsidy, with the Trust supporting the organisation of a number of national workshops in under-developed areas.

Between 1990 and 2000, Handspring Trust received funding totalling R 4,500,000 from the governments of the USA (via USAID), Denmark (via INTERFUND) and Canada, the European Community (Via Kagiso Trust), the Rockefeller Foundation, ESKOM, the Liberty Life Foundation and the Swedish Save the Children Fund.

The success of *Woyzeck on the Highveld* and Kentridge's increasing renown as an artist, encouraged Petz to finance two more productions with Handspring and Kentridge: *Faustus in Africa* and *Ubu and the Truth Commission* (see cover photograph of this volume). Both shows premiered in Weimar as the Weimar Festival was a major funder. The South African National Arts Council provided added support to Handspring as a company with a sum of R100,000 over three years.

Now there was a marked difference in our income depending on when we were abroad or when we were in South Africa. For overseas performances we had negotiated a fee per performance. It was understood that we wouldn't do less than two performances in any city and we seldom did more than five in any one week. If the tour went to 10 cities, with a total of (say) 32 performances, we knew before departure what our income for the tour would be. However, when performing in major theatres in South Africa, Handspring had to hire the theatre, engage a publicist, print posters, and basically take on all the risk. It has

5. *Set design for* Tall Horse, *2004*

become normal for us to anticipate a loss. In fact we have sometimes made substantial losses when performing in our own country.

In 1999 we were approached by the John F. Kennedy Center to collaborate with a puppet company from Mali in the production of a play called *Tall Horse*. The story was to be centred on an historical event: the gift of a giraffe by the Pasha of Egypt to the King of France. Mali has an ancient puppetry tradition and we happily agreed. The Doris Duke Foundation in the USA provided funding for us to visit Mali and for the creative team to meet. The team included two Americans, a Malian, a Beninoise and four South Africans and we met in twice in Cape Town and in Washington. Kennedy was looking for funding for the project and I managed to interest AngloGold Ashanti (AGA), the mining house. The reason why they wanted to fund it was that they have business interests in both Mali and South Africa and probably understood both the importance and difficulty of developing a cultural dimension to these initiatives. They agreed to make a significant contribution to the Kennedy Center's $1.2m budget. Time went by. Handspring was performing *Ubu and the Truth Commission* at the Centre Pompidou in Paris when we heard that Kennedy had not managed to raise the money required and that they'd shelved the project. We were so dispirited that we didn't even call AGA to give them the news and were surprised when they called us. They were determined that we should not give up, and offered to become the sole sponsors.

This was a very complicated project and many factors made it unusually costly:

- The Malians were making their puppets in Bamako. As shipping to Cape Town would have taken far too long, the puppets had to be air freighted there. Prior to the flight they were unable to explain why the 30 puppets weighed 420kg. This averaged 14kg/puppet – far too heavy to hold above one's head for any length of time. Only once they arrived did we realise that they were made of solid wood. Weeks were spent cutting them in half, hollowing them out , and gluing them back together.
- Because of the lack of direct flights on a single airline, flights between Bamako and Cape Town cost twice the price of flying to France.
- We wanted to retain our original link with the USA for the project and we'd been introduced to a very sensitive writer from New York, but this added to our expenses and to our communication challenge.
- Language was also a problem. All complicated documents – scripts, contracts being the most obvious – had to be translated into French by professional translators. And we also needed translators to attend rehearsals. This was a budgetary line item missing from most productions.
- Our Beninoise choreographer was based in Berlin and Paris and had two agents, one in London and the other in Berlin. Communicating with them was a challenge and they drove a hard bargain in Euros. It was not easy dealing with hard-boiled experienced European agents who weren't particularly interested in the weakness of the South African Rand.

Managing such a project, required the participation of scores of personnel. It took place in three countries over four years and for a time we were overwhelmed by its many demands and many small crises. However, we felt that this collaboration between puppeteers from two sides of the African continent was a really important initiative. This is because South Africa had been through an intense period of self absorbtion. We actually knew little at first hand of the continent to the north of us. Our diplomats and businessmen were taking the lead in the re-exploration of the continent. Now it was our turn.

Indeed, the exchange was important for both companies on many levels, not least of which was the financial one. In South Africa we have a fairly articulate theatre union and a standard theatre contract, which is accepted by both the union and the producers. Handspring pays above average fees and when on tour, each member of the company whether director or assistant stage manager is paid the same. In Mali however, companies tend to be made up of family members. The head of the company is the person responsible for the wellbeing of not only the puppeteers, but of his extended family as well. Therefore remuneration tends to be more in kind than in currency. Naturally, when the two companies began comparing notes, this disparity became an issue.

In concluding, I would like to note that Handspring is now in a difficult position. The company has toured productions abroad for well over a decade. This works well from a financial point of view because South Africa's currency is weak. However, the disruption of normal social rhythms at home is considerable. Also, the shows seem to have gotten bigger and more ambitious with concomitant pressure. Thus we are now looking to find smaller, more modest projects.

ACKNOWLEDGEMENTS

I'd like to acknowledge the assistance of Estelle Randall, Tony Morphet and Nkosinathi Gaar, each of whom read this text and made valuable comments. Any errors it may contain are of course my own. (B.J.)

NOTES

1 *Woyzek on the Highveld* is an adaptation of German writer, Georg Büchner's famous play of jealousy, murder and the struggle of an individual against an uncaring society which eventually destroys him. Büchner's *Woyzek* was a German soldier in the 1800s. In this version, Woyzek is a migrant worker in 1956 Johannesburg, a landscape of barren industrialisation. The production – the first collaboration between Handspring and renowned artist and film-maker William Kentridge – brings together rod-manipulated puppets and animated film to graphically illustrate Woyzek's tortured mind as he tries to make sense of his external circumstances. http://www.handspringpuppet.co.za/html/woyz.html

REFERENCES

Miller, Mervyn. *Journey of the Tall Horse: A Story of African Theatre*. London: Oberon, 2006.
Taylor, J. *Ubu and the Truth Commission*. Cape Town: University of Cape Town Press, 1998.

VIDEO

Beata Lipman. *William Kentridge: The End of the Beginning*. David Krut Publications, 1994, ISBN: 0-9584688-4-2.

Border Crossings
Setting up a joint
Accra-London production

MICHAEL WALLING

This article is a diary of Michael Walling's research trip to Ghana in July 2005. The purpose of the visit was to establish links between UK-based Border Crossings and a Ghanaian company, with a view to a co-production in 2007. This would mark 50 years of Ghana's independence and 200 years since the banning of the trans-Atlantic slave trade. Some of the article was originally published in the form of a weblog.

Wednesday 12th July 2006

Here I sit in a sweltering internet cafe in Accra. Got in late last night after a lengthy (but not too expensive) flight via Milan and Lagos. In Lagos we just sat on the plane for 90 minutes. I was reading critical essays about Ama Ata Aidoo. Equipping myself to phone her this morning.

The purpose of this trip is to research the production we're planning for next year – her play *The Dilemma of a Ghost*. It's fifty years since this country's pioneering independence, and two hundred since the abolition of the slave trade in the British Empire – so 2007 is the time to talk about these key issues of slavery, the global economy and the African diaspora, which this play does so brilliantly. As with so many of our projects, this won't work if we just use UK-based performers. We need to find people who are alive in the traditions portrayed, in order to explore how those traditions are interacting with the predominant West. And, of course, these are the people from whom we can learn the most. Like Radhakrishna and Zhang Ruihong. [For Michael Walling's work with these actors and evolution of Border Crossings see http://bordercrossingsblog.blogspot.com]

So this trip is really in search of serendipity. Of course, talking to Ama Ata will be vital and is very exciting (we're having lunch tomorrow), but I'm also keen to see just who may be around in terms of performers, and how performance relates to the cultural traditions she's working with in the play. So much of African life is performative – just walking the streets tells you that: but how is this an expression of the spirit? Is the spirit actually still alive at all? I suspect it is.

Spend the morning at the British Council with Deputy Director Amanda

Griffiths. She's very helpful with a list of contact names. I begin the task of phoning round and making dates. This should get easier when Kofi (who minds James Gibbs' house in Madina, which I'm renting) brings me a mobile tonight. He's incredibly shy and incredibly helpful – like many Ghanaians, I think. All the cliches about danger to the white man and being treated like a walking ATM just don't seem to apply here – although the poverty is every bit as visible as in other parts of Africa I've visited. Amanda and I talk about the way in which we should be celebrating the slavery bi-centenary, and we agree that it has to be through work that re-opens the questions. There is more slavery in the world today than there has ever been. Some of it is overt – in northern Ghana, into Burkina Faso and Niger, the trade in humanity, and especially children, is booming. And some of it is covert. Populations live on tiny amounts of money to feed the luxurious lifestyle of the West; a lifestyle which cannot exist without this vast imbalance. This is slavery by another, more insidious name. The market.

If anybody is reading this for travel tips, then here's one. Most banks in Ghana don't cash travellers cheques, unless you show the purchase receipt (which I left at home, as you're supposed to!). The one which eventually worked for me was Barclays Head Office in Bank Square. I walk out with what feels like a sack of swag, but is in fact the Ghanaian equivalent of fifty quid. It will keep me fed, watered and transported for days.

Thursday 13th July

I'm writing this in what has to be the slowest internet cafe I've ever been in, just down the road from James's house in Madina. I'm making liberal use of the refresh button, as all around me young Ghanaian men are chatting to girls in America through chat-rooms. I guess it's miraculous enough that in a place this poverty-stricken we can sit here and connect with the world. At any speed at all.

Today began with a taxi ride through distinctly more salubrious bits of Accra than I saw yesterday, down to the coast and the Labadi General Hospital, next to which *Theatre for a Change* has its office. I've been keen on this organisation ever since I met its British mentor Patrick Young a few months ago: and today the general manager, Daniel Attrans, and the full staff of six are sitting round a table, notepads poised, waiting to meet me. Their work is very community-based (without being Theatre for Development, or in any way indoctrinating). They tell me about the Boal-style techniques through which they deal with issues like HIV and domestic violence. If a man performs the role of a woman being beaten, he starts to get an idea of what it might feel like. So this is a theatre about opening up imagination, and empowering people to take decisions in the social space. They're planning a workshop in James Town in a few days, working with the fishing community there. Apparently, research suggests that this community thinks of HIV less in terms of condoms and more in terms of witchcraft. I'd be excited to see this.

I only wish there was something more I could do towards this group from my end – but they're not actually doing the sort of work we do, although I feel really supportive of them. I give them a few new ideas about funders, and promise to make a bit of a noise for them (here I am doing some of it). As our chat ends, their latest volunteer walks through the door: a young man called Ryan from UCLA, where his professors include none other than Peter Sellars. [One of the patrons of Border Crossings, Ed.] Ryan was inspired to come here by (amongst other things) Peter's classes on human trafficking – which has been his subject in *Zaide* and will be ours in our Ghanaian project. A small world, or a Jungian moment?

Kofi has got me a Ghanaian mobile, and I phone round as many of the contacts I've got from James and Amanda as I can. As I sit in the shade outside the hospital, playing ball with Michael's son aged three, one of them hoves into view. His name is Nii, and he runs a group called the *Tima' tuma Theatre Project*. In translation, this means 'well done', because, he explains, theatre in Ghana tends not to be a full-time job, and people deserve a proper reward as they get for work. I ask if he's managed to make it a full-time job for himself. No, he's also an advertising executive. I tell him he's in good company: lots of the best theatre-makers in India are also advertising people.

Nii's work is largely in plays about African history: they've just made one called *Nkrumah-Mandela*, which is about parallels in the lives of the two leaders. This is intriguing for me, with my on-ice Mandela piece stirring into occasional life. Sadly, they're not in production at present. However, he is the first person to come up with a name of an actress who might be suitable for what I'm doing: Mary Yirenkyi. I should be able to follow this up tomorrow, since she has links to the University Performing Arts Department.

We're still chatting when a driver arrives in a blue pick-up, which Ama Ata Aidoo has arranged to bring me to her office. We take another disorienting trip through various bits of Accra, and eventually I meet her. Smaller than I'd imagined, leaning on her stick and feeling a bit the worse for a recent bout of asthma – but bright with energy and excitement, and very funny. She takes her agent (a young man called Eli) and myself for lunch – my first taste of fufu. I give her a copy of *The Handmaid's Tale* as a present. She knows it backwards, of course – having taught it as part of a course in post-colonial literatures: but this fact in itself gets us onto interesting ground. The idea of Canada as post-colonial was apparently considered very radical by students and colleagues. Only the 'Third World' was post-colonial. We are happy to agree on the absurdity – if post-colonial is to mean anything at all, then it has to be about a history which is global: it has to be about understanding where we are right now as the aftermath of a colonial past which isn't only the affair of the poorer nations (to say that is simply to marginalise them again). The inheritance of the colonial period, of slavery, of economic exploitation, is still with us, and the post-colonial discourse has to be about how the globalised world which is the direct result of that inheritance can be inhabited. Which, of course, is exactly what *The Dilemma of a Ghost* is about. Certainly what it will be about in 2007 London.

I talk about some of my ideas for the production, none of which seem to faze her at all. She's actually quite humble about the whole thing, as writers often are when you want to do their work. She talks about when *Anowa* was done at the Gate in 1992 [directed by the late Dele Charley, Eds], and about how brilliant the actors and director were. But she was also very disappointed that the production didn't 'go anywhere'. Sounds familiar. The other production she remembers very fondly is the first production of *Dilemma*, which was staged in the open air at the University in Legon, when (astonishingly) she was still a student. I find it incredible that this should be the work of a 22-year-old: the play really should have been in the BITE Young Genius season last year. (That season included Soyinka's *Lion and the Jewel* in a production by Chuck Mike with Collective Artists. Soyinka was certainly more than 22 when he wrote the play.) The open-air thing is interesting: this relates to my sense that we may be looking for unconventional, non-theatre spaces (don't hold me to this!), and to my sense that the play is (amongst other things) very like a Greek tragedy, with its chorus of women surrounding and commenting on the central action, and its language which moves so subtly from naturalism into poetry.

Most importantly, for me, Ama Ata doesn't seem to think it odd that a white British male director should want to do this piece. Good – she also talks in terms of a shared history, an awareness that the political problems we face require dialogue, require a cultural solution. So the idea of collaborating with Ghanaian actors who can bring the sense of the spiritual and of the cultural depth the play needs makes sense to her. But she doesn't know who either. 'I'm only a writer', she says.

She's keen to come over when the play is on, which will be a good publicity boost (as well as moving and powerful in itself). We leave it that I will phone her again early next week – by which time I hope she'll be feeling fit enough to talk in more depth about some of the details in the piece. But the key contact has been made. We connected.

We come out of the restaurant after a two and a half hour lunch. Eli hails me a taxi and does the haggling over price. As he does so, Ama Ata reaches up an arm, and we embrace under the burning sun.

Friday 14th July

In the Performing Arts Department at the University of Ghana, there are 2,500 full-time undergraduates. Plus a few graduates. It blows my mind. Awo Asiedu, my contact at the Legon campus, tells me that when she graduated (not that long ago) there were only about twenty in the year. Something strange has happened. 'We're just kidding ourselves' she says: 'we can't teach so many'.

It's a great campus, though – with the open air theatre in which *Dilemma* was first performed, a bookshop which sends any Afrophile into a frenzy, and tutors' offices in little whitewashed quadrangles. Plus a Barclays that (guess what?) doesn't cash travellers' cheques – precipitating another mad dash to the

1. *The Bird of the Wayside (Adeline Ama Buabeng), Dzifa Gilikpoe, Agnes Depaah, Anniwaa Buachie), in* The Dilemma of a Ghost *(Border Crossings 2007)* (Photo: Neil Libbert)

head office before it closes for the weekend, exiting with a wad of cedis the size of a big dictionary.

At Legon, I meet John Collins – the legendary Professor of Music, whose conversation is an entrancing journey into incredible facts about African culture. In less than forty minutes I discover:

1. that West Indian musical influences made their return to West Africa as early as October 1800 (I love his precision on the month), and that this form – called Gumbe – became pan-African and pan-Caribbean.
2. that folk-rumour in Ghana decided that the Europeans must be taking the enslaved people to eat them, because they never came back. Ironic given that the Europeans were also erroneously accusing the Africans of cannibalism.
3. that Kwame Nkrumah kept a court jester, whose name was Ajax Bukana. Ajax was encouraged to leap in to Cabinet meetings and express the comic view on any issue. He always wore black-face, which amongst African and black American performers was never considered racist – it's simply the make-up of the Ghanaian clown, just as white-face is worn by the European.

John puts me in touch with a few more artists and musicians, and as I take the taxi across town I phone them all, arranging yet more meetings.

Meetings, meetings.... Awo's head of department, John K. Djisenu, who lets us use their premises to audition former students from the 2,500 a year who might be useful talent. I keep mentioning that the cast shouldn't really be lots of young people – and gradually I start to get some contacts for older actors. Here, as everywhere in the world, it seems that theatre is largely a young people's affair. But the play is actually dominated by older characters; which is startling given Ama Ata's age when she wrote it. It's a sign of the culture-clash at its heart, of course, which is also a generation clash. The younger people in the play are so much more Westernised. This is why it's so crucial that I link up with older actors here – people who retain a real link to cultural traditions.

The first actor I meet, however, is younger. Akofa Adjeani-Asiedu, who has several times received best actress awards for her film work, sends a car to bring me to her (side-line) restaurant, where she sits in what feels like a fortune-teller's tent, covered in jewellery, draped in a red kaftan and sporting a spiky vertical hair-do. Her whole appearance is an amazing re-invention of what it means to be African in the 21st century. The conversation is full of laughter, as happens with extrovert personalities, but there's also a sense of a very serious artist here, and somebody very conscious of her nation's image in the wider world. When I ask her what sort of projects she prefers, she says that she like to do work which shows what is positive in Africa. That she's fed up with images of violence in Rwanda and famine in Sudan governing the world's perception of a deep and living culture. Now *that* I can work with.

She drives me back into town herself. Very fast. I'd phoned the Arts Consultant I was due to meet next to say I'd be late … and arrived early. His

2. *Shonel Jackson as Eulalie and Seun Shote as Ato in* The Dilemma of a Ghost *(Border Crossings 2007)* (Photo: Neil Libbert)

name is Akunu Dake – and he's co-ordinating the British Council's creative response to the big anniversaries next year. Again, the conversation seems fruitful – when he shakes my hand at the end he calls me a 'fellow conspirator', which often feels right. And he names a male actor who John also suggested, and an older woman who'd also been mentioned by Akofa. I tend to believe in the double recommendation. Back to the phone, I go. What would I have done without Kofi's phone?

I stay in the British Council for the evening, because there's a performance. A bunch of young English people walk in. I'd seen them earlier today at Legon, where they are rehearsing *Dick Turpin* ... Yes – a joint UK-Ghana pantomime. On closer investigation, they turn out to be gap-year students, who have themselves raised the funds to come here, including what budget there is for the show. This is the perennial problem of African theatre: because it's so under-resourced, it ends up depending on Western donors in their many shapes and forms, and so voicing their concerns, rather than the real cultural needs of Africa. Pantomime is one form of cultural imposition; theatre for development is all too often another. I'm determined that our project will reach beyond that, and be about genuine dialogue.

The play is an adaptation of Ayi Kwei Armah's novel *The Beautyful Ones Are Not Yet Born*, presented by *Abibigromma*, which is the resident company in the School of Performing Arts at Legon. Awo explains that there was originally only one theatre company (at least in the Western sense) in the country, and that this was based in the university. When the National Theatre arrived, much of the company transplanted there as the National Drama Company. *Abibigromma* is the residue at Legon, and is run by a full-time director called Agyeman Ossei, who has an office on campus. The programme says the company dates from 1983; so I suppose that's the date of the schism. The rhetoric suggests that it's a full-time ensemble of 25 core members.

Judging from tonight's performance, I'm not sure that's quite the reality of the situation. There are actors in there who are wonderful (notably Samuel Dawson Assam Jr, who plays the leading role of the Man) – but there are also a lot of people who seem under-rehearsed, or who turn up in crowd scenes as if they're not sure that this is the moment. The sets are cardboard cut-outs, sitting uneasily in the British Council's rather lush but decidedly untheatrical hall. The whole event feels very disjointed: which may be the consequence of trying to adapt a novel, however strong it may be. The novel is episodic, and depends on narrative and comment for its unity. Ossei's adaptation includes long narrative passages, as he tries to link what become a series of sketches. It all feels rather undramatic, untheatrical and long. Three hours plus with no interval.

Tuesday 18th July

In *The Dilemma of a Ghost*, the ghost's dilemma is whether to go to Cape Coast or Elmina. It's a pretty grim choice, even for a spectre, since these are the two huge slave castles that tower over Ghana's coastline. Not one for dilemmas, I visited both of them over the weekend. Video camera in hand, I was able to shoot some amazing images, which may or may not appear in the final production: especially on Sunday morning, when taking an early taxi out of Cape Coast got me to Elmina before 9 am, and I was the only person in the castle for a full hour. Being in the total darkness of the slave dungeons, and walking to the 'Door of No Return' is an intense experience. I twice got genuinely frightened – once because I really couldn't see where I was, and once because I was suddenly surrounded by bats. In the dungeons of both castles, there are wreaths which have been laid by African-Americans, who return here to see something of their history. The messages are very sad, but also strangely beautiful. The guide at Elmina (who arrives a bit after 10) says that the Castle must be preserved so that people can take from it a renewed humanity. I like that.

Fears of being stranded on the coast (I arrived there on Saturday to discover the last bus back to Accra on Sundays is at 3, and is already full) are allayed by the appearance of a school bus from Takoradi, containing none other than Rebecca and Kate from the Theatre Royal in Plymouth: here to work on their three-year link-up project. (During 2005, a production of *A Midsummer Night's Dream* was presented in Sekondi–Takoradi, Ghana, and Plymouth, UK, with a cast of students from both countries, under the direction of Rebecca Gould. For 2006, the production was Efua Sutherland's *The Marriage of Anansewa*. This was prepared and performed in both Takoradi and Plymouth.) Over dinner back in Accra, we meet up with one of their students from last year; a young man called Williams. Shooing them away with a 'some things are for men only', he takes me in to his confidence, and tells me how much he admires these two women and their work. Last year's production was clearly the best experience of his life, and has changed him profoundly and positively. It's incredibly heartening to be reminded of theatre's power to do this.

There was another reminder this morning, when I (horribly late – thank you email, thank you Accra traffic) was able to see something of *Theatre for a Change* in action with the fishing community in James Town. In a delapidated shack (the grandly named *James Town Community Theatre*), a group of about thirty people of various ages were improvising stories about domestic violence, and looking at ways to deal with the issue. [See www.theatreforachange.com/interacting.html (JG)] Between these scenes, they play silly games and sing songs which involve a lot of bottom-wriggling. It's all strangely playful, and yet they are clearly talking about things which matter very deeply to them. Theatre at its most paradoxically beautiful again. Amongst the group, there was a young girl who could really perform. She is absolutely tiny, and has crooked bones in her back and limbs; probably the result of polio, I guess (there are posters in the streets saying 'Get Polio Out of Ghana'). She also moves extraordinarily, and radiates joy from her face. I kept thinking of Abey Xakwe from *Third World Bunfight*. I begin to wonder if I shouldn't do something really extreme in the casting of *Dilemma*.

The ideas are slowly working themselves out. I had a rash of meetings breaking out all over yesterday and today, spending a Ghanaian fortune in taxi fares and a lot of time stewing in the perpetual traffic jams. But some key contacts have now been established:

- Osei Korankye, who plays me his *seprewa* (a sort of harp) and sings in his strong, high tenor: this is music of contemplation, which was traditionally played to chiefs by a sort of bard or troubadour as an aid to meditation – ideal for transporting an audience to a plane of ritual and spirituality.
- Mohammed Ben-Abadallah, who wrote a play called *The Slaves,* and is full of fascinating insights into the Ghanaian theatre, and is deeply generous with his advice on performers and companies.
- Evans Oma Hunter, a Falstaffian figure whose finger is in many pies, and significantly works with UNESCO here, touring work to rural communities.
- George Hagan, director of the National Commission on Culture, who listens to my ideas with a constantly repeated 'Wonderful', and promises that crucial thing, official endorsement, as well as making some helpful suggestions about outreach and even funding!
- And, perhaps most helpfully of all, the amazing Dzifa Glikpoe: former director of the National Drama Company (the ones who left Legon, and are now homeless and dormant while the National Theatre is restored) and a truly inspiring performer. With this woman there is an instant rapport, and she understands exactly what I want to do. She also reads the text superbly. We talk about how, with George's endorsement, this could be a co-production between Border Crossings and the National Drama Company, in which case it would make sense to rehearse here in Ghana, perform and tour (?!) before transplanting to the UK. Done like this, with Western-trained actors in the Westernised roles, the culture-clash will be so real.

This afternoon Dzifa came to meet me again at Legon, bringing two performers she recommends. The three of them together are a riot: we talk in depth, but we also laugh a lot, and they perform songs and dances for me. Or maybe it isn't for me – maybe it's for one another and for themselves. Song seems to emerge from the conversation of these women totally naturally. One of them is called Agnes Dapaah: she's very intelligent and very aware of the play and its political meaning. The other, who speaks far less English, is an older lady called Aunty Ama. I'm not too bothered about the language issue – and neither, it seems, is she. What matters is her rootedness in the culture, her demeanour, her grace, and her incredible energy. As we talk, I realise exactly who she is. She came from a village background, and started performing as a teenager, where she was spotted by the late, great Efua Sutherland. Since her parents were not around, Efua contacted the grandparents, and told them that she would like to adopt her as her own daughter, undertaking to educate her at the same time as nurturing her performing talent. Even today, she lives in the same house as Efua's daughter Esi Sutherland.

I thought before I came that the key aim in this trip would be to find somebody who was talented enough and sufficiently rooted in the culture to play Nana. I think that's been accomplished. Now all we have to do is make it happen.

Wednesday 19th July

The morning was spent at Legon, where Awo has arranged an open audition for students and former students. A goodly dozen young people show up, plus the ever-supportive Dzifa, and Samuel, who I saw in the *Abibigromma* play on Friday night. It's very interesting to see how he, in his early 40s, and the older ladies I've been meeting over the last few days, have so much more sense of themselves as physical performers than the students, even those who are studying dance. It's as if the new generation is losing touch with African culture on every level, and has very little sense of its own identity. This leaves the young actors floundering. When I ask them to create something, the only images which have any real energy to them are associated with violence. Otherwise it feels so lacking in that depth of culture and spirit I've seen in Dzifa, Agnes, Aunty Ama and the rest.

I meet one more of these fabulous female actors today: Mary Yirenkyi. For 17 years she taught at Legon, and she's also studied in Leeds and Exeter. As she reads from the text, and dances for me, I'm back in the real world of the play and of the Akan culture. It's like two different worlds, one full and one empty. All the more reason to do this project.

Awo drives me up to the top of the hill to see the amphitheatre, where the play was first performed in 1964. It's a lovely space, somewhere between the Greek theatres and the African village clearing. There are always big problems with the open air, of course, but for this project it may be right.

I spend the afternoon with Ama Ata, delving into many of the key issues in producing this play. Two crucial things we establish:

1. The production doesn't need to be set in 1964. This is a relief to me: the thought of researching period accuracy, which would only alienate an audience, is anaethema. As Ama Ata says, shaking her head, so little seems to have moved on that this story could happen just as easily now as in the Nkrumah years. Which makes it very timely to revive it in 2007, as we ask how the West's relationship with West Africa might evolve after 1957 and 1807.
2. It doesn't have to be completely in English. Ama Ata says she never thought of writing the play multi-lingually – though to me the use of English even for passages where the characters are clearly speaking Fanti is a stroke of genius (and she did it 16 years before Brian Friel used the same trick in *Translations*). She knows Aunty Ama as a great performer, and had wanted to write a radio play for her, but felt her own Fanti wasn't strong enough. But for Aunty Ama to play Nana in a mixture of Fanti and English excites her enormously. Brilliant.

Thursday 20th July

The last day in Accra. It begins at 6am, with Kofi banging on the door. I'd rather foolishly said that we could go and meet his Auntie Efua 'first thing in the morning', forgetting that African definitions of the day's beginning are very different from European ones. Still, Auntie Efua is a joy, sitting among nursery children in a collection of Madina 'halls and chambers', and flicking through *Jane Eyre*.

The day's timetable is meant to be simple, but of course Ghana isn't like that. At 11 am, I see Amanda at the British Council again. She's highly excited to hear about the plan for a co-production across both countries, the involvement of the National Drama Company, and the list of performers I'm proposing. Thank you Dzifa, thank you James, thank you Awo! The key, of course, is to make all this happen, and this is where I hope the British Council might come on board. Amanda asks me to come back at 4, to meet the director, John Payne.

In between, I need to scout out the National Theatre building, as an alternative venue to the Legon Amphitheatre, and one which I know Ghanaian collaborators are likely to prefer, if only because of its central location. It's a huge, very modern structure, very well equipped, and totally at odds with its far more modest surroundings. This is because it's one example of the enormous Chinese investment in West Africa: as I walk backstage, I can see Chinese characters on the windows. China has spent a huge amount in this region: all of which is clearly intended to promote trade and political links. These are emerging powers we should not ignore.

The National Theatre is currently closed for refurbishment, and I'm led round by a young man called Francis from George Hagan's office. The leading is quite literal, because there are no lights, and several times he takes me by the hand to get me around. There's no qualms about men holding hands here – even people who've just met! The only way I can get any idea of what this theatre might look like is by flash photography. It seems to be a barn of a place. 1500 seats. But well-equipped, and central. If we end up here, we'll have to work hard to make things feel rough enough.

I just get time to buy some amazing paintings at amazingly low prices before seeing John. Odd how, after so many productive discussions, you always end up with the middle-aged white man in the suit talking about money. Not that John is a typical suit: like most British Council people, he's anxious to make real exciting collaborations happen, and can see beyond the stale rhetoric of his political masters. I think we will need to make some quite specific cases in quite specific ways, but he gives me enough hints for me to feel we have a friend here. I phone Dzifa to let her know, and thank her for all she's done. I have to leave her with a warning – I won't be touching this project for a while, given the imminence of *Dis-Orientations*. But, come the autumn, we'll make this happen. Roll on 2007.

Postscript

I arrived back in the UK on 21st July, and set about funding applications, venue discussions and meetings with potential collaborators. The key to the whole project, to my mind, is the relationship with the National Drama Company. In practice, this means Dzifa Glikpoe and people she works with regularly: but this ad hoc arrangement is actually not that different from many UK companies, including Border Crossings (which, for all its institutional aspects, is a one-man band between projects and board meetings).

POSTSCRIPTS

Wednesday 1ˢᵗ November

… Starting to move ahead with *The Dilemma of a Ghost* too. I met Ivor Agyeman-Duah at the Ghana High Commission yesterday. There's a clear contrast with China: here there is very little bureaucracy, and very little money – though there is a real enthusiasm to promote Ghanaian artists. He promises to broker some meetings. More meetings. I really need to get some administrative help with this company. I spoke to Nick about it, and he was quite helpful on ideas for core funding, though there won't be any sign of even a tendering opportunity from ACE for at least a year, and then it's all likely to be reduced funds (as I predicted in this blog, the Olympics are already making a big dent).

Monday 4ᵗʰ December

Saturday's *Independent* has an article on the 50 leading figures in contemporary African culture. Ama Ata is in there, as she should be. I email the link to all our prospective venues, in the hope it will make a few people sit up and take interest. It seems to be working.

BIBLIOGRAPHY

Aidoo, Ama Ata. *The Dilemma of a Ghost* and *Anowa*. London: Longman, 1987.
Anquandah, Kwesi J. *Castles and Forts of Ghana*. Accra: Atalante/ Ghana Museum's Monuments Board, 1999.
Anyidoho, Kofi. 'Dr Efua Sutherland: A Biographical Sketch.' *FontomFrom, Contemporary Ghanaian Literature, Theater and Film*, Amsterdam: Rodopi, 2000, 77–81.
Armah, Ayi Kwei. *The Beautyful Ones Are Not Yet Born*. London: Heinemann 1968.
—— *Fragments*. London: Heinemann, 1969.
Azoda, Ada Uzoamaka & Wilentz, Gay (eds). *Emerging Perspectives on Ama Ata Aidoo*. Trenton: Africa World Press ,1999.
Briggs, Philip. *Ghana*. London: Bradt Travel Guides 2004.

Buabeng, Adeline Ama. Drama in her Life, interviewed by Esi Sutherland-Addy. *African Theatre: Women*, Edited Jane Plastow, Oxford: James Currey, 2002, 66–82.
Duerden, Dennis & Pieterse, Cosmo (eds). *African Writers Talking*. London: Heinemann, 1972.

INTERNET SOURCES

www.bordercrossings.org.uk
www.theatreforachange.com

EDITOR'S POSTSCRIPT [JG]

Michael Walling blogged during the production, and drew attention to on-line reviews that appeared. The following posting for Thursday, November 22, 2007 catches some important notes:

> The audiences have been getting bigger and bigger, and more and more enthusiastic. Standing ovations again at the Africa Centre last night, I'm told. Lovely. And Saturday's show is virtually sold out already.
>
> Just before the pick-up, a very interesting director from Scotland, Maggie Kinloch, came in to see the play. Talking to her afterwards, I found myself bemoaning the difficulty of getting broadsheet press to respond to the company's work, even with a National Drama Company as co-producer, and the resulting uphill struggle we always seem to have with marketing. Here's what she emailed to me the next day:
>
> It was great to meet you too; I enjoyed the show very much and have thought a lot today about (it) and about your work in general. You are doing really vital and dynamic work and I know that it can be hard when you don't get the press interest and subsequently the audiences are not what they should be. But your work really matters you know. It really does.
>
> There have been lots of 'Wonderful' and 'Brilliant' comments on our audience feedback sheets (plus, at last, one negative comment – 'too long' – our attention span is only 45 minutes'!!) – but I think of all the feedback we've had, Maggie's words are the most valuable to me. She'll help me move forward to the next piece and, as Beckett used to say, 'fail better'.

Introduction to
Our House

Jos Repertory Theatre

The issues discussed in this play were identified in a workshop in Jos, Plateau State, Nigeria on 23–30 of March 2004 by the following: Eucharia Egah, Osasogie Efe Guobadia, Joyce Kelechi Onuoha, Binta Salma Mohammed, Bunmi Obasa, Emmanuel Degri, Tunde Awosanmi, Alkasim Abdulkadir, Adegboyega Olomodosi, Francis Onwochei, Austin Okonkwo, Ismail Garba, Akinpelu Awofeso, Patrick-Jude Oteh and Grace John from Administration The workshop was funded by the British Council and facilitated by Biyi Bandele.

The following took part in the scripting phase in Kano from 14–22 February 2005 and was facilitated by John Binnie, Bunmi Obasa, Binta Salma Mohammed, Joyce Kelechi Onuoha, Toyin Bifarin-Ogundeji, Reuben Embu, Tunde Awosanmi, Akinpelu Awofeso, Alkasim Abdulkadir, Ismail Garba, Patrick-Jude Oteh.

Our House opened at the Professor Luka Bentu Indoor Theatre in Jos, Plateau State, Nigeria on 25 March 2004 at the first Jos Festival of Theatre with the following cast:[1]

Actors:

Nancy   Eloyi Ocholi
Annie   Ewarewah / Efe Sogie Guobadia at alternate performances
Emmanuel Degri
Godwin   Ogbaka
Nelson   Orah

Production Team:

Music: Tongak Deshi,
Producer: Gillian Belben, Director, British Council,
              Kano, Nigeria.

Director:	Patrick-Jude Oteh
Set Design:	Lateef Rasheed
Choreography:	Bose Tsevende
Light Design:	Ayo Gladstone Salako
Production Stage Manager:	Austin Okonkwo
Administration:	'Nife Oteh / Grace John

The Jos Festival of Theatre is sponsored by the Ford Foundation; *Our House* was funded by The Connecting Futures New Theatre project of the British Council.
Note – This text is not the final definitive text of *Our House*.
All enquiries to:josreperthea@yahoo.com
© JOS REPERTORY THEATRE, 2004

The script of *Our House* as it appears here reflects the fact that scenes were prepared in different contexts, and shows the marks of the first production. The layout makes extensive use of the names of the actors in the original company, each of whom played several characters. On some occasions the actor's name is only given in the stage-directions and on others the name of the character appears without an indication as to who played it. The original production was performed by five versatile actors (2 female; 3 male).

Our House

JOS REPERTORY THEATRE
in collaboration with the British Council

CAST

CHINUDU	Degri
JIDE	Ogbaka
YUSUF	Nelson
UDUAK	Annie
CHUUNDANG	Nancy

(*Stage open with cast, one as a narrator, one as a troubled fellow at centre stage. The other three characters acting gnome-like. Flute in the background.*)

Narrator The winds are tearing me apart.
My tears have drowned me in the sorrows of my soul.
Where is the food on my table?
Where is the roof over my head?
They have stolen my mind.
They have hammered my conscience.
The winds are tearing me apart.
My tears are drowning me.
I came into this world crying. (*Cries from an actor*)
Several years on, I'm still weeping.
Where are the laughters I was promised? (*Laughter from the actors*)
The dance my feet yearn for?
This house with flowers of pain.
This house with portraits of deprivation.
Our house of changing colours.
Who will stop these voices in my head?
(*Screams and shouts with weird movements by the three gnomes harassing the lady on stage*)
Who? Who? Who?
Help me, My life has lost its soil.
The winds are tearing me apart.

My tears are drowning me.
(*Sings:* 'Oh! My house')
Oh! My house (2x)
When shall I see my house?
When shall I see my only house?
I'll never forget my house.
Ya yaku zo
Ku zo ku ji
Labarin Nigeria
Mutane ku zo.

(*Spiraling movement by the cast*)

Nelson   Look at this, just look at this, it is still ticking, after all this years, it is still ticking.

Annie   Oh! Oh! We've been away from the house for so long.

Ogbaka   Oh! Oh! Look at this, who can tell me, look at this television, who can tell something about this television?

Annie   And the stains, you remember this stains?

Nelson   I can still remember how a whole lot of people would come into this old parlour to watch this television.

Ogbaka   You are very right. Look at where you peed and Mama gave you the beating of your life.

Nelson   Please don't start it. Look at the scars, they're still there.

Degri   They are still there!

Nancy   And you? You were beaten the day you poured palm oil here, the stains are still there. (*All chorus 'yes'*)

Nelson   Me? It's a lie.

(*They all go on admiring the house*)

Degri   Papa's chair.

Ogbaka   I can still imagine Papa on this chair.

Nelson   Papa and Mama are no more, but these stains on this brown rug are still present after these years.

Degri   That reminds me. Talking about scars and stains takes me back to what we experienced in this house. The scars and stains that are left on our minds several years after. Do you remember the ancient city walls?

Annie   The ancient city walls, what about them?

Degri   They are tearing them down.

All   Bringing it down?

(*Drumming and spiraling movement to different positions. Alhaji supervises 'labourers'. They mime tearing the walls down*)

Alhaji   Look, my friend, be fast about it. I don't have time.

(*Continues breaking the walls*)

(*Another man comes to stop the breaking of the walls*)

Ogbaka   Who is this man? Stop it! Hey you!

Alhaji   My friend, can I help you?

Man   Yes, Alhaji, you can help me in, I am very sure you are the one who ordered them to bring down this wall.

Alhaji And what if I did.

Degri You know Alhaji you can't. This is our ancient city wall. This is our history.

Alhaji Look at who is talking? Do you have any history? My friend, of what significance is this old wall? I am trying to bring this old thing down so that I can build at least thirty, perhaps fifty, shops. Is that not community development? Is that not progress?

Degri Alhaji, are you alright? You cannot, for selfish reasons, for your selfish interest, bring down this wall. This is one of the famous legacies our fore-fathers.

Alhaji You are going bananas.

Ka na da ayaba a cikin kokoluwan ka

(*To the labourers*) Be quick about it and let me get out of here. (*Looks at his wrist-watch*)

Degri You are mad. You are all mad. We are all mad! And to think that no one wants to stop him and the likes of him in this town, in this house.

(*Spiraling movement*)

Nancy Imagine!

Degri That is what is happening to our ancient city walls

Nancy Ah!

Nelson Our city walls

Annie Our heritage

Ogbaka Our defence. Our security.

Nancy Those things that held us together!

Degri Are being town apart for selfish reasons.

Nelson Hey, look at these, just look at these!

Degri What is that again?

Nelson (*Reads from frame on the wall*) Love binds us all. Do you know what? This reminds me of when I met my first love

Degri What?

(*Spiraling movement. An undergraduate assistant is seen sweeping his room. He is wearing a singlet.*)

Voice over Get a grip on yourself, man, it is just a visit. (*Contemplating his last words*) No, this is not just a visit, Vera is coming today, and what she thinks about this place will make or mar what we share. (*Stops to think again*) How can I ever think of bringing a woman into this desert of a room? How can I ask her to leave a life of luxury to join me in my wretchedness. I think something is wrong with me. All the guys we graduated with eight years ago have made it big, but I'm still struggling (*pause*) an ordinary graduate assistant with take home pay that doesn't even take me home.

(*He fidgets around the house, cleaning and arranging the little furniture available i.e. a single chair*)

Calm down, boy. (*He sighs*) She will either say 'yes' or 'no'.

(*A knock on the door. Tony opens it*)

Tony Come in. Hey Vera! (*Vera enters. They hug*) I was afraid you were not going to come.

Vera And miss an appointment with my love? That's impossible! My car broke down and I had to take it over to the mechanics. It's okay now.

Tony Oh! I see. So what can I offer you?

Vera Not to bother.

Tony (*Looks aside*) Thank God! There's nothing at home. Vera, I would like to take you somewhere very special, very spectacular. I know you'll love it

Vera Where could that be?

Tony Wait for me and let me get dressed. Please sit down. (*She looks around the room*)

Tony (*Enters, dressed up*) So, how do I look?

Vera Charming, handsome …

Tony Let's go….

Voiceover And that is the beginning of our story.

(*The young people walk into the garden*)

Vera What a beautiful place! The trees, the singing birds, the water …

(*Accompanying background of appropriate sounds*)

Vera (*Raises up her legs*) I can't wait to feel the running waters on my feet.

Tony (*Takes her foot and gives it a kiss*) Do whatever you wish. Your wish is my command.

Degri And the story continues.

Tony Can you still remember the first time we met? It's almost seven years ago, but it seems like yesterday. I can still remember your mother. She never liked me, she always chased me out of the house.

Vera Come on Tony, don't let me remember those times. Don't let me remember those horrible moments when I had to fight it out with my mother. You remember Chief Amadi? That rich trader she wanted me to marry me to.

Tony A bald-headed, pot-bellied old man.

Vera But parents can be very shortsighted you know? Thank God all that has passed. She saw your present, but I saw your future.

(*She moves close to him, and he embraces her*)

Tony There is something on your forehead.

Vera Oh! What is it? (*She makes a move to touch her forehead while he stops her midway*)

Tony Let me do that for you.

Vera What for?

Tony Close your eyes and let me do it for you.

Vera (*She closes her eyes*) My eyes are closed.

Tony (*Takes a ring and slips it on her fourth finger*) Now, open your eyes. (*She looks at the ring and turns away*)

Voiceover for Vera I would be mad to leave my father's mansion to marry this poor lecturer. I can't even think of telling my father the true position of his pocket. Larry, hmm, he just inherited a business empire from his father. But, I can't marry Larry, he is just a proud brat. But, what would my friends say? I am not used to struggling. I would have to start from scratch with Tony. I can see that saying 'yes' would be signing my life to misery … but I love him. No one knows tomorrow.

Vera Ehm! Tony I …

Voiceover for Tony (*He turns to face her*) I know she will say 'No' Why would she want to marry a man like me with such meagre prospects? I know she has lots of toasters. She has admirers with duplexes. And fleets of cars. Uhn, but if I lose her now when will I find true love and where? I might as well go back to the village. Bringing her here was a silly joke. (*Pause*) But … wait a minute, if she can't marry me the way I am, then she is not worth me.

(*Tony turns to face Vera*)

Vera Tony, I love you. The ring is beautiful and I want you to know that I am yours forever. This is the happiest moment of my life.

Tony (*Goes down on his knees*) I will love you forever and ever. (*He stands, and sweeps her into his arms*)

Cast Ay … Ayrrrrrrrr (*Ovation from the cast. They all dance to the Anya song*) Anya o Nigeria, song and dance

(*A revolving movement takes them back to 'the house'. They all laugh*)

Ogbaka Whao!

Degri I never knew you could play such a romantic role.

Nelson You wan' try me? Just leave me with one of your girlfriends and you'd see what I'd do to her.

Degri Aha!

Ogbaka Don't you think that is the kind of love we need in this house?

Annie Yes, the type that will bind us together.

All As one, yes.

Nelson Oh.

(*The others move around still checking things up*)

Degri Come and look at this!

Ogbaka What is it?

Degri An old newspaper.

(*They all move towards him to see it*)

Degri It's so dusty.

Nancy (*Reading out the date on the paper*) 3rd March, 1957, ehe e!

All Ah!

Nelson Look at this: Alhaji Mustapha Bako makes £20,000,000 from the sale of groundnuts.

Annie What!

Nancy Eh!

Ogbaka Hold it, hold it. (*Finding another shocker*) Chief Olowolagba makes $7,000,000 from cocoa.

All Eh! Are you serious? Incredible!

Nancy Wait, see Mazi Okoro earns £12,000,000

Annie From the sale of …

Nancy & Annie Palm oil!

Nelson (*Moving away from the others*) No, no, no, no, this is impossible, I mean it is incredible. If they made so much money, why did they stop farming?

Nancy Exactly what happened to the groundnut pyramids, the cocoa farms and the palm oil?

Ogbaka That's a very good question.

Annie Yes.

Ogbaka What happened to them?

Annie Just imagine what things were like before oil was discovered.

(*Turning around movement into the days of groundnut pyramid … Nelson as groundnut merchant, changes into the costume of an Alhaji and moves downstage right*)

G.M. Asalamalekun jamaa, yes …? Na gaisheku duka. You see, I am Alhaji Mustapha Bako, yes, I am the groundnut farmer. I farm and farm groundnut very well. In fact, you are seeing the owner of one of the groundnut pyramids in Kano. Walahi talahi, I am in billions of pounds from them. Thank you very much.

(*Degri dressed as an Ibo businessman moves down centre stage*)

Degri (*Laughs*) Eh, e e! I am Mazi Okoro, the one and only Mazi Okoro in this town. I make £12,000,000 from the sale of palm oil.… And do you know one interesting thing? I will never leave this business o, ekene mu nu, eh e e e.

(*He laughs and moves up stage centre while Ogbaka as cocoa farmer moves downstage left*)

Ogbaka Ehn, e ku ijoko o, mu kiyin o, I am Chief Olowolagba, the richest cocoa farmer in the world. As all of you know, cocoa is the fastest yielding agricultural crop in Nigeria. Mo dupe lowo yin o. (*Laughs as he returns to his first position as Alhaji and Mazi join in an embrace. They discuss their business*)

All Ah a a a a

(*Annie and Nancy, as oil prospectors, roll in the barrel of crude oil*)

Nancy & Annie This is crude oil!

Ogbaka Ehn?

Degri & Alhaji Ah

Ogbaka Ewo tun ni crude oil? What is crude oil?

Degri Gini bu crude oil? (*Lines to be delivered in the Ibo language*)

Alhaji Menene crude oil? What is crude oil? (*Lines to be delivered in Hausa*)

Annie This is the fastest way to make money.

Ogbaka Ehn ehn, in what currency does it come?

Annie Pounds and …

Nancy Dollars.

Nelson You want to tell me that this one is faster than farming. Look, I am a groundnut farmer fa, I make millions. You want to tell me that this one is faster?

Annie Exactly!

Nelson Hakika, hakika!

Degri Ehn e, my people, I think I like this business.

Ogbaka Yes.

Degri I already deal in oil, palm oil, so, eh ee, let me take this for good business. (*He bends to lift the barrel but is stopped by the others*)

All (*Shouting*) Ole, barawo. Drop it! Stop!

Alhaji Look, look, excuse me, excuse, walahi talahi okoro, I dey stupid, I dey craze. Let me tell you fa, I am a groundnut farmer. I can feel the texture of this oil fa, kuma ga shi nan walahi kuma, the texture is the same things as that of the groundnut oil. Kuma you know I farm groundnut. So I think I will be in the best position to handle this business. Thank you, thank you, thank you (*He bends to carry the barrel but is stopped by the others*)

Ogbaka (*Stopping them*) My people, there is no need for us to quarrel, unh unh. (*Laughing*) As all of you know that I deal in cocoa. And from cocoa you can get cocoa … oil. I will beg you to help me carry this oil to my backyard when it begins to yield interest, I will now settle all of you. O ya bami gbe, bami gbe. (*Struggling and shouting again as he is forced to take his hands off the barrel*) Ah, I want help you …

Nancy Help who, help who? Abi you want to help yourself!

Alhaji Kun ji balarebe fa.

Degri Onye ara.

Nancy We discovered this oil and we will control it.

Annie And whatever we say is final!

Okoro Nbanu, my people ehn, I volunteer, let me go and make a good sale out of this business. After the sales ehn, (*turning to the cocoa farmer*), I'll give you 10%. (*Turns to the Alhaji*) I'll also give you 10 per cent. (*Turns to the two oil prospectors*) And I'll give you … 5 per cent. I volunteer to keep 75 per cent for all of us.

(*They protest and push him off the barrel as he attempts to lift it*)

Nancy Let us carry our oil and go.

Annie They don't deserve it.

Degri Where are you carrying it to? (*Lines in Ibo language as he follows and strikes the oil carriers from behind. The Cocoa farmer, who has been following them, strikes the Ibo man and he, in turn, is hit from behind by the Alhaji. Seeing that they all are down, Alhaji carries the barrel downstage centre and sits on it. He starts eating fruit. Martial music ushers in the soldier, played by the other four, who attack and drive Alhaji off the barrel. One of the soldiers takes over. He laughs as the opening bar of the national anthem is heard and he sits on the barrel eating fruit. One of the other soldiers now acts as his ADC while Nancy comes in as his mistress. She massages his shoulders and dishes out pecks and kisses intermittently. The leader gives out some largesse from the fruit tray to the lady and the ADC. The other two actors come in as hungry Nigerians begging for food*)

Nelson I'm hungry.

Annie Give me food. (*The leader throws 'crumbs' to Annie and as she is about to eat it, Nancy snatches the fruits and gives it out to the ADC to eat*)

Nelson I'm starving.

(*The same gesture is extended to Nelson by the leader while he laughs but he is forced to give it to the ADC*)

Annie I need food. (*They laugh again*)

Nelson's Voiceover And he ate and ate and ate and after several years, he was neither satisfied nor tired but something got into him and so, he decided to step aside. But for who?

(*The leader stands up and steps aside looking round at the beggars and at his mistress, he is seeking for a new leader. He considers them one by one until he gets to the ADC whom he enthrones. The new leader (Degri) puts his gun down and exchanges his military uniform for mufti. He goes to shake hands with the former leader. The introductory notes of the national anthem, played on a xylophone, are heard*)

New leader (*Laughs as he sits on the barrel*) eh eh eh!

(*The actors now rejoice, dancing around the stage. They perform Berom and Ankwai dances from Plateau State. The leader dials some numbers on a phone. It rings and Ogbaka picks it up at the other end*)

Ogbaka Hello.

New Leader Boy.

Ogbaka Ah! (*Prostrating*) Good morning, sir!

N.L. Boy, you are stupid.

Ogbaka Yes sir! (*Still prostrating*)

N.L. You are very very stupid.

Ogbaka Yes, sir. Thank you, sir!

N.L. What is good about the morning? (*Pause*) I said, what is good about this morning?

Ogbaka Thank you, sir.

N.L. What happened to the barrel of oil we produced, ehn?

Ogbaka We sold it and arrived at 12.5 billion dollars (*His secretary brings in a file for him to sign as he answers the call*)

N.L. (*Laughs*) Eh eh, I like that. Send the money to my Swiss account urgently!

Ogbaka But sir, we have not paid salaries, sir.

N.L. Oh o o that is very good of you. Eh eh I know o. I have not been given my salary. (*Laughs*) Send it to my Swiss account urgently!

Ogbaka Not your salary sir, I mean the workers' salaries.

N.L. Are you stupid?

Ogbaka Thank you, sir.

N.L. You are very stupid, send it there. When it yields interest, we'll pay them. We are owing them for about 10 months now isn't it? Good, when it yields interest, we'll pay them one or two weeks' salaries and life will be easy for them and sweet for all of us.

Ogbaka But what about the ministers and the commissioners?

N.L. Not to worry. We'll make sure we organize some workshops and seminars for them. We will find them some transport allowances and life would be easy for them too and sweet for all of us.

Ogbaka Sir, the masses, the masses are planning to carry placards.

N.L. They are planning to do that?

Ogbaka Yes, sir.

N.L. Not to worry, do crocks grow teeth? (*Laughs.*) uh uh

Ogbaka Crook, sir?

N.L. Are you calling me a crook?

Ogbaka No, sir.

N.L. Are you stupid?

Ogbaka Thank you, sir.

N.L. Did I hear you well?

Ogbaka Yes, sir.

N.L. You are stupid!

Ogbaka Yes, sir.

N.L. You are very very stupid!

Ogbaka Yes, sir.

N.L. I said do crocks, do crocks grow teeth?

Ogbaka Yes, sir.

N.L. Do you think the school I went to in Toronto is useless?

Ogbaka Yes, sir. No, sir.

N.L. You are very stupid young man. Ehn ehn, by the way, I'll see you when I'm back from Japanese. ehn?

Ogbaka But sir, what about me and my family?

N.L. I said I will see you when I'm back from Japanese.

Ogbaka Alright sir, thank you, sir.

N.L. (*Laughs*) Eh eh e e. (*He ends the call and looks at apparatus*) G.S.M. dividend of democracy. (*Laughs again*) eh eh.

(*Nelson enters with a list; addresses the New Leader*)

Nelson Good morning, sir. Sir, this is the list of seven hundred and seventy four community leaders waiting to see you, sir.

N.L. What! 774 leaders waiting for me alone?

Nelson Yes, sir, for you.

N.L. (*Laughs*) Eh eh, impossible, my dear, impossible. Tell them I'm going to Chinese.

Nelson China, you mean to say, sir?

N.L. Are you alright?

Nelson Yes, sir.

N.L. You are stupid! You are very, very stupid!

Nelson I said Chinese.

N.L. Are you questioning my authority?

Nelson No, sir.

N.L. Get out of my office!

(*Nelson dashes out of the office*)

N.L. Stupid boy!

(*Turning around movement; back to the house. The leader character laughs*)

Nelson (*Mimicking the leader*) Did you hear him? Do crocks grow teeth? What are crocks? (*Laughter from all*)

Ogbaka As if I was seeing my president, I went down on my knees and said good morning, sir! (*He kneels down and prostrates on the ground*)

Degri As the landlord of this house, anything I say either wrong or right, right or wrong it is still right! (*Laughs hard*)

Nancy With your Toronto certificate.

Degri (*Laughter*) Oh God!

Nelson (*Bends and points to a music box*) Look at this, look at this! An old music box. Papa's gramophone.

Nancy (*Walks towards Nelson and holds his hand*)

Annie (*Excited*) Yes! His favourite.

Degri (*Walks up to Annie, touches his head with a finger and holds her by the shoulder*) Ahm! That reminds me, Papa used to play James Brown. (*He uses his hand as a trumpet and sings*) James Brown, I'm black and proud. (*Drumming accompanies this demonstration, they dance bending back and forth, Nelson walks as he dances and climbs a table*)

Degri Ehn! Guys you know what: Papa and Mama used to rock and rock. (*He dances a little*) And rock it on.

Nelson Ah! Papa was a good dancer.

Annie Mama was better.

Ogbaka You guys, but you know I take after Papa. (*He sings and dances with his right and left legs one after the other*)

Nelson (*Looks at him in mockery*) With your two left legs. (*Laughter from all*)

Nelson This old music box has given way to new machines like CD players, DVD's and the rest of them.

Annie Yes, new generations! And sometimes, I wish we humans could be like this you know. The old generations in this house do not want to give way to the younger ones. (*She bends a little to emphasize her point*)

Nancy (*With her leg on the table*) And maybe, just maybe, that is what is stopping our growth in this house.

Ogbaka (*Standing, arms akimbo*) But, but whose fault?

Annie I think it is the fault of the old ones.

Nelson (*Aggressively*) No! I think it is the fault of the younger ones!

(*Drums and they do the turn around movement. An elderly civil servant walks into his office, his secretary walks up to him*)

Secretary (*Bends down to greet him*) Papa, welcome, sir, I hope you had a nice rest last night, sir?

Papa Thank God. Eh! Please prepare for me a bowl of tea, very thick and go to my car and get my pillow and the blanket

Secretary (*She turns to go but stops*) Papa, there's this young man who has been waiting to see you since morning.

Papa Let him in.

Secretary Ok, sir. (*Ushers young man 'in'*)

Young man Good morning, sir.

Papa Yes! Good morning.

Young man Sir, I am actually looking for the director of this office.

Papa Yes! I am.

Young man Oh! I … I … I … see sir. (*Surprised*) I actually came to see if there's any vacancy for any job, sir.

Papa And ehn! Did we place any advert that, eh, there was a vacancy for you in this ministry?

Young man No, sir.

Papa So then … get out of my office.

Young man (*Gesticulating*) Sir, I need this job! I desperately need this job, and sir as a matter of fact I work very very hard. In fact sir, my working speed is as fast as light, sir.

Papa   And ehm (*Secretary enters with a file*)

Secretary   Papa.

Papa   (*Turns towards her*) Yes!

Secretary   (*Holds the file out for him*) A document for you to sign, sir.

(*He searches for his glasses*)

Papa   Where did I leave my glasses?

Secretary   It's in your pocket, sir.

Papa   Oh! Thank you.

Secretary   You sign here. (*She shows him where to sign*)

Young man   Oh! He can't even see! He can't see.(*Pointing to the old man*) Even with thick lens glasses. He can't see. (*Moves away as soon as the next young man*)

Degri   Good morning, sir.

Papa   Good morning, young man.

Degri   I was the boy who came here about two weeks ago and dropped my CV with the ministry. (*Smiling*) You asked me to check this week, sir.

Papa   Sorry, there is no vacancy for you in this ministry.

Degri   (*He kneels down*) Please sir, I beg you in the name of God. I've been out of school close to twelve years sir, and there's no job for me, sir.

Papa   And ehm, should that be my business?

Degri   (*Pleads*) I was hoping, sir, that you could help me with a job, sir.

Papa   Young man, now get out of this office

Degri   I beg you, I beg you, take a good look at me, look at my shoes. They are all worn out due to trekking, sir.

Papa   And who told you, I am a Bata shop? Get out of my office now!

Degri   I did not say that.

Papa   Get out of my office!

(*Degri leaves the office while Nelson takes up the narration*)

Nelson   He drove him away. He drove him away, a tall, intelligent, well-built, promising young man. He drove him away.

Papa   And who told you, I am not a tall, handsome, promising young man as well?

Nelson   No! Baba you were promising, but right now you are bent.

Papa   Ah! Ah! Have you come here to insult me this morning?

Nelson   No, sir.

Papa   And ehn, if I may ask you, which of the universities did you attend?

Nelson   (*Proudly*) I went to Our House University.

Papa   (*He laughs*) I can imagine.

(*Drums. Nelson turns around, to act as a JAMB candidate*)

Nelson   Yes! I must pass this exam. Whether you like it or not, or whether I like it or not. I must definitely pass this exam. I will pass and must get into the university next year. These are my 'expos'. This is English. (*He hides it in a trouser leg*) This is Maths. (*He hides it in the other trouser leg*) This is Economics. It is going to be here. (*He hides it in his right armpit*) And this is Agric. It is going to be right here. (*He hides it in his left armpit*) See you in the exam hall. (*As he moves away, another student, Annie, sees him*)

Annie Hey. Mugun, how now?

Nelson Look at this mumu girl.

Annie I am fine thank you. How was preparation for the exams?

Nelson As you can see, I am well prepared.

Annie But why you stand as if na motor jam you. Abi you wear POP?

Nelson I am prepared for exams, that's all. (*She attempts to touch him*)

Annie I hope no be expo you carry o?

Nelson (*Stammers*) Abeg, abeg, I don't want your wahala this morning o!

Annie Eh! I care, that's why I ask.

Nelson Wetin concern you and wetin no concern you. (*She walks off to the exam hall, where a policeman is on guard*)

Annie Officer, peace of the Lord.

Police Offr You dey craze. Na for your mouth dem go pour the pis. No try me o. (*Pointing his baton at her*) Make you open up make I search now.

Annie Officer small small harsh now.

(*He makes her stretch her hands and he glides his hands down the front part of her body*)

Annie Officer now!

Police Offr You dey craze, e dey worry you. (*Points a finger at her*) No teach me my job. (*He reaches down and touches back of her leg*) Na wetin be this?

Annie Na my leg!

Police Offr Na your leg strong like this?

Annie Na so dem born me.

Police Offr Ehn! Ok . No problem. I go dey watch you from here o. Oya enter.

Nelson Hey, Officer. (*He walks hands stretched down*) Area, I dey look for where I go shit. I wan shit, one kind hot shit. As a matter of fact, I dey look for tissue paper. I know no if you get tissue paper, Officer?

Police Offr You dey craze …

Nelson I mean this kind of tissue paper. (*He brings out money*)

Police Offr Make una see this stupid boy, na exam e kon write e dey ask me tissue paper. Ol' boy, if I, if I … (*He turns away to check if anybody is looking and collects the money*) O boy na which kind tissue paper you dey carry so? You dey craze o. Enter fast. I dey watch you from here.

Annie (*Walks on stage rejoicing in her success in the exams*) Hey, I made it, I cannot believe my eyes, 240 – Accounting, University of Our House, here I come. Hey! Aah!

Nelson (*He removes the 'expos' flings them away and cries*)

Annie Some people dey cry, dey say make una read una no gree, olodo, 240 Accounting.

Nelson See mumu. (*Points at her*) Na 240 na im dem give you, na im you dey happy. They over pass me, 540 and to worsen the matter na two courses dey give me at once. Finance and Banking. How I go cope now, how I go c o o o p e?

Papa Keep quiet, how can you cope, when you bribed your way through the university. You youths of nowadays, all you think of is a short cut to everything in life. Hmm. I wrote the London GCE, gained admission to Oxford University … into the Cambridge University for my masters, and came back and got a job in this ministry. I was sent to China, UK, Japan, Yugoslavia, and Iceland, where I learned how to make ice, so that we can be producing ice in this ministry. I was truly equipped with knowledge and experience.

Nelson I am still saying the same thing. I mean if you don't employ me and send me on courses, how will I get this experiences you are talking about, sir? You are an old man. Why don't you go home and relax, retire, employ someone like me into this office? And I am sure your pension would be better than the present salary. Think about it.

Papa I think what this young man is saying is correct. I should go home and rest. But do they pay pensioners? I will rather sit on this seat and at the end of the month I will collect my salary. If I collapse and die, they might give me a state burial.

Secretary Papa.

Papa Yes.

Secretary Have you seen this?

Papa What is that?

Secretary It is a list of director generals – in the presidency. Which of the young men in this office do you have in mind to recommend?

Papa Have you included my name?

Secretary Baba, it is not a retirement list o.

Papa Yes, I know. Include my name as the Director General of Finance.

Secretary Baba what about the young man here?

Papa Am I not young? Include my name and send it to the presidency. (*He laughs. The secretary walks away disappointed*)

Nelson Thinking that I had convinced him. (*He points to Baba*) And yet how do you expect me not to get angry? Why will I not get angry? Why must I not be angry? Baba! Baba!! Just respect yourself and quietly leave this office or else I will do it violently. Leave this office oh! Baba.

Papa Be careful oh! Be careful young man.

(*They start struggling and quarrelling. The turn around movement is performed and they return to the house*)

Nelson Oh! Why did you not allow me push him out of the office?

Degri Do you want to commit murder?

Annie Violence is not the only way out.

Ogbaka But there is a problem, and whose fault?

Nancy The younger ones are looking for short cuts, while the older ones are just being selfish. Wahala dey this house oh!

Nelson I think it is high time we started sweet talking all these old, old people out of the offices.

Ogbaka You are very correct. You are very correct.

(*The men are seen trying to converse together; the girls walk towards them*)

Nelson I mean just we, the young men.

Annie & Nancy Yes, all of us.

Ogbaka What is all of us? What is all of us, I ask you?

Annie What about the women?

Ogbaka The women you said. Do they count in this house?

Nancy Hey!

Degri They don't matter!

Nancy (*Clapping her hands in shock*) And what is that supposed to mean? (*Arms akimbo*)

Nelson Look we are discussing something important here and you are coming to join us. What is that supposed to mean? Go back and sit down and be plaiting your hair and gossiping. That's the best thing you can do. Now go.

Ogbaka Yes, please, go.

Nelson (*The three of them stop to hear him*) As I was saying strategy number one. (*He pauses as Ogbaka opens his mouth in a wide yawn. Degri rubs his belly to signify hunger*) Ehm by the time! I can see you guys are hungry, I am also hungry. Let us eat first of all so that we can reason better.

Ogbaka So what do we eat? (*He touches Degri on the shoulder*)

Degri Ehm! Pounded yam and egusi soup.

(*They all walk towards Nancy and Annie*)

All Three L–A–D–I–E–S. (*All smiling*)

Nelson We are hungry, why don't you just go into the kitchen and cook for your brothers?

(*Annie is shocked, she claps her hands*)

Nancy O ho! (*Standing up*) Na wa for this house o. (*Walks towards them*) I thought it was a serious issue. (*Pointing at them*)

Degri Ehen.

Nancy Is food not a serious issue?

Degri That is why you are here?

Ogbaka We are hungry now.

Nancy Go to the kitchen and cook for yourselves. Macho men!

Annie I thought I heard you say women don't matter in this house? When it comes to doing the laundry, or preparing the meal, it is the work of the women. When a woman gets married in this house and there is no issue in the family, it is also the fault of the women! (*Crying*) I don't blame you. (*She goes to Nancy and cries on her shoulder*)

Nancy Just like our sister.

Ogbaka Please don't let us talk about the dead, please I beg you, don't let us talk about the dead!

Nancy (*Moves forward and holds Ogbaka*) We must talk about her.

(*They do the turn around movement*)

Annie (*She kneels and starts to pray*) Papa God, you dey answer prayer, I know, I accept my miracle oh. I get faith, I thank you, I know dey vex. Say you give me six girls oh! I happy, I thank you for those ones. But, Papa God, I beg now, na only one boy I beg for. Abeg now just do this for me, I be your servant o, anything wey you say make I do for you, I go do am. (*She stands up; in a frenzy*) But I go remind you, God, if na girl dey here make you change am to boy for me o. All my enemies wey say e no go better for me, na dem e no go better for. Fire and brimstone. Fire and brimstone!!! All my enemies wey say e no go better for me ...

Nelson Mama Bisi! Na pray you dey pray abi na cry, or you dey quarrel with somebody. Tell me. I wan know.

Mama Bisi Papa Bisi, I no see my thing for this month, na im I enter here I dey pray say if na girl dey here make e change am to boy for me.

Papa Bisi Oh! Oh!! You no see your thing na im you just dey cry like this. Mama Bisi, come, come no be cry. Shebi na me put am. I know wetin I put there, na boy! No be any kin boy oh! Na boy wey resemble me, n aim dey inside here.(*He touches her belly*) And if you no trust me, we go kuku go hospital now now. We go scan am. (*He touches her belly*). Ah! E dey kick my hand. Dis one go sabi play football like Okocha. (*Mama coughs as she comes in*)

Papa Bisi Mama!

Mama Bisi Mama, good afternoon, I dey greet you mama.

Papa Bisi's Mother (*Not answering the greeting*) Hei! (*She claps*) You and who? I say you and who, for this house? Six! Six girls na im you don born for this house. Strength wey women dey get. (*She demonstrates the strength with her hands*) To take born man-pikin you, you no get. I know know where you come from, so so girls, girls, girls, girls hee heee! Iya girls e chouu! (*She walks up to Papa Bisi*) If una reach there and dem talk say na girl make you make sure say dem comot am. (*She eyes her*) Make she no come back here o! I no want trouble o, I know want trouble at all. (*She pulls his ears*) Your Papa property dey there, abi you want make im brothers sit don on top im property. I no want trouble. I no want trouble at all at all.

Papa Bisi Make we dey go! (*He walks towards Mama Bisi*)

(*At the hospital, she is praying while the doctor is on the left side and Papa Bisi is on the right side. All lights are off as the doctor illuminates Mama Bisi's face with a torchlight that depicts scanning*)

Doctor Madam, you are carrying a baby girl.

Papa Bisi Comot am!

Mama Bisi Eh!

Doctor Madam, you are carrying a baby girl.

Papa Bisi Comot am!

Mama Bisi Eh!

(*This routine is repeated thrice at different locations on stage which depicts three separate abortions. Lights come on sharply as Mama Bisi sits on the chair centre stage after the third abortion*)

Mama Bisi Baba Bisi, na so you and your mama dey make me dey comot belle. This one na number ten. You know oo Ehn. Doctor talk say e dey risky and apart from that e dey pain o. Me? I no dey do again hmn ahh.

Papa Bisi (*Pointing at her*) See o! I sorry for you, na di person wey dey give abi na the person wey dey receive? No be me dey give? No be me put am? I dey give dem dey comot, I go give dem dey comot. I go give dem dey comot and you dey get mouth talk. I dey sorry for you. Make you stand up make we dey go house now. Make we know how we go take put anoder one o. And me, I sure say na boy I go put inside there. But if you turn am to girl again, dem go still comot am. Make we dey go. (*Mama Bisi turns her back to him*) Make we dey go o.

Ogbaka Uhn, the women in this house are really going through pains. They are suffering.

Nancy That was how she died ... after the tenth abortion. (*Nelson pulls her to himself*)

Nelson Come to think of it (*moves to take Annie with the other hand, now holding the two ladies to his sides*), it's so unfortunate that I could do nothing to help her. I'm sure the same thing will not happen to the two of you.

Annie & Nancy Amen.

Nelson At least you have a big brother beside you. You don't have to be afraid. Now girls, (*looking at them*) why don't you go into the kitchen and cook something for your brothers?

(*Immediately, the girls move away from him, hissing*)

Annie (*Hisses*) Get away I beg.

Nancy You must be joking.

Nelson (*Now alone*) What is this now? Ehn, what is all this? (*Moves towards the other two actors*) For God's sake, all I'm saying is that while we are here working, discussing and strategising.

Degri & Ogbaka (*Laughing*) Yes!

Nelson (*Turns to the girls*) You people will be inside the kitchen working and cooking and later we can meet together and share ideas, so that we can move forward.

Annie Just listen to yourself.

Nancy Listen at him, like a politician trying to sweet-talk us with his manifesto.

(*All laugh as Degri moves to him*)

Degri Ahhhhh you are right my sister. You see, if I were a community leader, you would have won my heart and that of my people, ehn en, with the way you talk, I think you would make a very good politician.

Ogbaka Ehn?

Degri A very good politician (*turns to Ogbaka*). You know there is a style in which he places his words.

Nelson You think so?

Degri Yes.

Nelson (*Turns to the ladies*) You think so?

Ladies (*Chorus*) Yes.

(*Turning around movement into the campaign scene. Nelson as the politician and the others, the crowd. A small riser is carried to the apron (stage-left) as platform for the politician*)

Politician (*Climbs the platform*) I have a dream. Well ... I had a dream last night and my grandmother said to me 'Boy you will become a very successful politician'.

Crowd (*Shout*) E e e e e.

Politician A. I. P.

Crowd Power.

Politician A. I. P.

Crowd Power.

Politician Power to the people.

Crowd A. I. P.

Politician Let me go straight to my manifesto.

Crowd Yes.

Politician The first item on my manifesto is this: talking about food.

Crowd Yes.

Politician As soon as I get into power – and as soon as the power gets into me, I'll make sure that there is food on everybody's table.

Crowd (*Shout*) E e e e e e.

Politician A. I. P.

Crowd Power, Power.

Politician Power to the people.

Crowd A. I. P.

Politician Listen carefully, listen carefully. The second item is this: talking about education. As soon as we get into office, I mean as soon as the office gets into us, we will make sure there will be free education from the kindergarten level up to the university level – and from the university level back to the kindergarten level.

Crowd (*Shout*) E e e e e e.

Politician A. I. P.

Crowd Power. Power.

Politician Power to the people.

Crowd A. I. P.

Politician Listen carefully, this is very very important. It is of great significance. As soon as I get into power, I mean as soon as the power gets into me, I will make sure that we assassinate all our opponents.

Crowd (*Shouts and screams*) E e e e e e , you don win.

Politician A. I. P.

Crowd Power. Power.

Politician Power to the people.

Crowd A. I. P.

Politician This is a very sensitive one.

Crowd Uhn.

Politician It is a very touching one.

Crowd Uhn.

Politician It is for the beautiful mind.

Crowd Uhn.

Politician For the women.

Crowd Uhn

Politician Listen carefully, our beautiful women. (*The ladies beaming with smiles become seriously interested*) As soon as I get into power. As soon as you give me your mandate, as soon as I have your mandate, I will make sure we empower the women so that they can be empowered. (*Suggestive movement of getting women impregnated*)

Crowd (*Shouts and screams especially from the women*)
Women 1 A I P.
Crowd Power.
Women 1 A I P.
Crowd Power.
Women 1 Power to the women.
Crowd A.I.P.
(*They all sing the AIP song*)
Give Democracy na AIP.
Politician I say e e e e.
Chorus E e e e.
Politician I say o o o o.
Chorus O o o o o
(*He dips his hands into his pockets and starts spraying crisp naira notes as he continues with the song. The crowd is seen scrambling and struggling to gather as much money as possible with shouts of 'You don win' 'you don win'. As the shouts continue, the men in the crowd take up the roles of thugs cum area boys*)
Thug 1 Baba alaye, alaye baba.
Thug 2 Area father.
Thug 1 Na so o.
Thug 2 Father, father, born in Naija, brought up in abroad.
Thug 1 Na so.
Politician Boy, boys, I've been in politics for a very long time.
Thug 2 E dey show for your face.
Politician Boys, when I give a job, I want it to be properly executed.
Thug 1 Na that 'executed' na im be our name.
Politician The road to that office, I repeat, the road to that office. (*Bends and looks straight into the audience*) I don't know whether you can see the road. I can see a lot of obstacles in my way. Boys, how do we clear all this mess up?
Thug 2 Baba alaye, you no get problem at all. Se you see all these obstacles wey you see dey look you so. (*Laughs*) Eh ee, as we don dey do our own side, we go dey clear those timbers and calibers wey dey the road.
Thug 1 One after the other, yes.
Thug 2 Na only your banker go talk, your pepper, na im go dey talk.
Thug 1 That one na im we dey talk say your money talks and the bullshit work.
Politician Money has never been my problem, but how to spend it. How much do you guys want?
Thug 2 Na 15 milla. (15 million naira)
Politician What do you small boys want to do with 15 million ehn? Boys come on let me give you one million. One million is okay for you kids.
Thug 1 Ehn?
Thug 2 Say wetin happen.
Thug 1 I beg bobo, make we dey go.
Politician Okay, okay, wait. I'll pay you a cheque for 10 million. (*He picks out a cheque and begins to scribble on it*) Right now I will give you one hundred

and fifty thousand naira and then give you the balance later. Whom do I give?

Thug 1 Attacker, collect the thing.

Politician Do a nice job done for me.

Thug 1 & 2 Oga no worry, job don do.

(*Turn around movement. Shift to home after politics scene*)

Degri You'd make a bad politician.

Ogbaka Did you hear? We'll empower the women so they will become empowered.

Degri What kind of empowerment is that?

Nancy That's the best kind of empowerment. (*Laughter*)

Annie That isn't funny you know. Has it occurred to you all that the women in this house are unfairly treated?

Nancy Yes, they use them anyhow for anything, then dump them. And it is still happening to this day.

(*Turning around movement*)

BANK MANAGER'S SCENE

Jessica Good after, sir.

Bank Mgr Why not sit down?

Jessica I'd rather remain standing.

Bank Mgr So have you finally made up your mind?

Jessica Yes, sir, here is my resignation letter. I can't stoop so low just to meet a target.

Bank Mgr No, Jessica, don't be insensitive. Don't be irrational with your decisions. I believe any woman with your kind of beauty will reach any target she sets her mind to. You know you have this kind of beauty that speaks volumes. So what do you say?

Jessica Sorry sir, but my mind is already made up.

Bank Mgr Now Jessica you go home and sleep over this – and I'll see you tomorrow when I hope to get a positive response from you. Good day Jessica.

(*Jessica remains*)

Bank Mgr Good day.

Jessica (*As she exits*) Good day, sir.

MAMA'S KITCHEN

Jessica Good afternoon, mama.

Mama Ooh good afternoon Jessica. You're home so early. Come let me hold you. (*They hug*) Is everything alright? No work today?

Jessica Mama I'm thinking of resigning from the office. The pressures are too much for me.

Mama Are you out of your mind Jessica? Where would you get another job that pays as well?

Jessica You don't understand Mama. They want me to meet outrageous targets of 50 million naira every week and that is impossible.

Mama And why is that impossible?

Jessica Mama, I'll have to do absurd things to meet this target. Things you didn't teach me. Things that are just not me mama. I have to preserve my womanhood.

Mama Are you the only lady that was asked to meet this target?

Jessica No mama, there were lots of us.

Mama Ooh! I thought you were the only lady and the others were men.

Jessica Aah! Mama, you need to see the terrible things the other girls do – just to meet their targets. They open their legs w-i-d-e for all sorts of men. Mama, I cannot descend that low. God forbid, you know now how you brought me up. (*Snaps her fingers*)

Mama Jessica, I did not ask you to open your legs w-i-d-e. (*Big arms gesture*) for all sorts of men like the other girls do, that is bad.

Jessica Yes, mama.

Mama But you have to keep this job. Why not open it … s-m-a-l-l, just a little.

(*Jessica pulls away shocked. She talks to herself*)

Jessica I don't understand, I had to battle with the decision of maintaining my integrity and womanhood, thinking my mother would say 'oh Jessica, what an excellent decision', but I was wrong … God, what do I do? Where do I go from here? (*Pause as she thinks. She decides to return to the office*)

BANK MANAGER'S OFFICE

Jessica Good morning, sir.

Bank Mgr Good morning Jessica, sit down.

Jessica Thank you, sir.

Bank Mgr So have you reached a decision?

Jessica Yes sir, I'm willing to do anything just to meet this target, sir.

Bank Mgr That's my girl. That's more like it (*He comes behind her*) I've always known from the very first day that you are ingenious and enterprising. You are so well endowed. Now you go out there and make full use of everything at your disposal. Because your best is our best and our best is your best. I'll see you later Jessica.

Jessica Have a nice day, sir.

SEDUCTION SCENE

(*Jessica with her back to the audience removes her shirt revealing a tight-fitting black top underneath. She turns and applies lipstick. She seduces Nelson, SR with her dance and body gyrations*)

(*Same with Degri centre-stage*)

(*Same with Ogbaka*)

(*The body gyrations are evocative of sex*)

(*Puts on her costume again*)

BANK MANAGER'S SCENE

Jessica Hello. (*She hugs Bank Manager*)

Bank Mgr Oh Jessica, how did it go?

Jessica Guess what, I have finally surpassed my target.

Bank Mgr You did?

Jessica Yes.

Bank Mgr Oh Jessica my dear, I knew it. That is wonderful news. This calls for a celebration. Oh Jessica, I don't know what to do with you. I feel like squeezing you … I … I … What do I offer you? (*He goes to the imaginary bar*) Champagne? I've got Don Simon, Don Money, Don Target, Don Gwape.

(*Jessica gasps in pain*)

Bank Mgr Are you alright Jessica?

Jessica I think I have a fever.

Bank Mgr Ooh you must be so tired. I understand the hassles you go through trying to meet your target. Why not go to the bank's clinic and take care of yourself?

Jessica Alright, sir.

Bank Mgr And Jessica, I hope you don't mind working late tonight?

Jessica Not at all sir! (*She winks*) And don't forget to go through my file.

Bank Mgr I won't Jessica … And I think you're due for promotion.

BANK MANAGER'S OFFICE

(*Bank's clinic Doctor enters*)

Doctor Good afternoon, sir.

Bank Mgr Good afternoon, my young man. Can I help you?

Doctor Sir, the lady you sent to the clinic.

Bank Mgr Oh Jessica my darling, the target meeter. What target has she met again?

Doctor Sir, she's HIV positive.

Bank Mgr What? HIV? What a waste. Such a young, enterprising, beautiful woman with all her life in front of her. Where is her file? (*Gets out her file*) Make sure she gets this.

Doctor A sack letter?

Bank Mgr We don't need her services anymore… or do you need her? By the way did you touch her? (*Doctor looks suspicious*) Aah, I see, where is your file?

Doctor No! I never touched her

Bank Mgr You make sure she gets that. Now get out of my office

HIV DANCE

(*Jessica with her back to the audience has removed her top. She applies lipstick. She dances to Nelson SR and repeats the same motions as before and whispers into his ears*)

Jessica HIV.

Nelson Aah, I can't, I'm black. I'm strong. It can't get me.

(*She dances to Degri centre-stage*)

Jessica HIV.

Degri Ooh! Its impossible, I'm manager of my company.

(*She dances to Godwin SL*)

Jessica HIV.

Ogbaka Ooh! But I'm married with four children. Aah! my mother, my family, what am I going to do?

HOME

Nelson Poor Jessica.

Annie What she had to go through.

Ogbaka The women in this house are really suffering.

Nancy So are the men ... because of the insecurities and uncertainties in the house, some of them go abroad to seek greener pastures.

Degri As if the grass over there is greener than the ones we have in the house.

Nancy Remember Femi and Emeka?

LONDON TOWN

Femi & Emeka London Bridge is falling down (*Song*) Falling down.

Femi I am in London. Olorun ose O!

Emeka Femi, we are in London. Chineke, I thank you O.

Femi Emeka, let us go to the West of London.

Emeka Femi, look the East of London is better. There will be better business opportunities there. Come and see.

Femi No. Emeka, come and see a building like cocoa house in the West of London.

Emeka Eh! You have come again. Because you are from the West of OUR HOUSE, you want to go to the West of London!

Femi What of you? Because you are from the East of OUR HOUSE you want to go to the East of London!

Emeka If that is the case then let everyman go his own way.

Femi Yes, everyman for himself, God for us all.

Emeka Ah! You will suffer in this London.

(*They make to fight*)

Annie (*As narrator*) On getting to London, Femi and Emeka after parting ways − get themselves all kinds of odd jobs ranging from helping school children cross the streets, to mowing lawns, to dishwashing, to ...

Emeka Have a nice day!

Annie To making French fries and getting rid of refuse. They worked for a minimum of 100 hours a week until Femi gets himself into trouble and is sent to jail for dealing drugs. Emeka being the good boy he has always been never forgot his people back home.

Emeka Have a nice day.

Annie Especially his mother.

EMEKA'S LETTER HOME

Nelson (*As narrator*)

Dear Mama,

I'm very sorry not to have written for a long time now. Mama it's due to the pressure of my job but not to worry, all those pressures will soon be taken care of. Mama, I have good news for you, I'm now the Deputy Director of the company which I work

for. How are my younger ones? I hope they are all fine. I miss them especially Chidi. Tell him to continue reading his books. Mama, I am enclosing 15 pounds in this letter. I want you to make use of it as I will send more very soon. Until then, bye bye. Yours sincerely
Emeka Okoronkwo
P.S. Mama, I also enclose the picture of me and my latest car – a Lincoln Limousine. As you can see, I was waving, I was actually waving to the President of London when he stopped to greet me. Mama, you can see your small boy is now a big man. Bye bye.

Indian Lady Where in blazes is that naughty boy? … (*Emeka saunters in*) Boy where exactly have you been? All the French fries have been burnt to cinders and you obviously were no where to be found. No, no, no, don't bother explaining, I've gotten another illegal immigrant to take your place. I want the best for my customers … and you obviously are not the best. Out of my office. You are fired. Out before I call the police … Ramesh, take over.

Emeka Hey! I don die! Which kin suffering be this one? From helping school children cross the road to making French fries, to … Yee! And it is so cold here! (*Gathers his arms around himself and shivers from the cold … The other actors mime Europeans who cross him on the street … it is winter …*)

Nancy Who is this?

Annie Another miserable beggar! (*They leave. Emeka turns back to face Nelson*)

Nelson Hey! Blondie make way for me. (*He waves Emeka off and as he turns he comes face to face with Ogbaka*)

Ogbaka Go back to your country …

Emeka Hai! These people have killed me. Me, Emekus, Emekus … I will go back to my country before this people will kill me!

HOME

Nancy Why did you come back to this house?

Nelson Why did you come back to this roofless house?

Ogbaka This house where there's no food in the pot?

Nelson This house where the foundations are shaky?

Annie No electricity.

Ogbaka Cockroaches everywhere.

Nelson Mosquitoes everywhere.

Nancy Can't you see cobwebs all round.

Nelson No water to flush the toilets.

All Why? Why? Why?

Ogbaka I am a young lawyer. My colleagues and I have all graduated but there is no work for us. This house renders us jobless and hopeless. What am I going to do?

Annie It's upsetting to think this house is unfair. I'm treated differently because I am a woman. As a woman artist, I am rated second class. No one takes me serious and if they do, they want something in return. I do not have the same rights as a man. How can I stay in this house, where it is almost impossible to prove that I am as good as a man.

Nelson I once saw a man who wanted the best for his community. That there was electricity in that community was due to his efforts. That there was pipe borne water in that community was due to his efforts. And because he loved his community, he decided to contest for a political post. But his opponent, who was from a different tribe connived with men from the underworld and killed him. This resulted in tribal warfare. Lots of blood shed.

Nancy I took a walk down the streets the other day. And under the bridge was a helpless woman, with a sick child. There was no money to buy food neither was there money to buy drugs. It was such a horrible sight. I went back home and returned a few days later. But the woman was gone. Who knows, may be they are dead.

Degri But this is our home. It is safe here and it is peaceful. Remember Papa's gramophone and the stain on the rug and Papa's chair. We belong here. This is our home, not 6000 miles from here. Let us come together and move our house forward. Our house... our house.

Degri (*As narrator*) At the twilight of our stay in this house, Mama and Papa are no more. Except for the quietness of the place and the dust, it is still amazing how nothing has changed.

Nancy We need good landlords

Ogbaka We need men and women of vision.

Nelson Arise stability!

Annie Arise honesty!

Nancy Arise integrity!

Ogbaka We need accountability!

Degri And upright people!

All Let us arise together and move this house forward!

(*They sing 'Nigeria'*)

    Nigeria yi ti gbogbo wa ni

    Ko ma gbo do baje

    Kosi bo miran ti a le lo

    Ajo ole da bi ile

    E ja ka sowo po ka fi mo so kan

    Gbe ke mi gbe (*Repeat 2x*)

(*Drums roll and all lift hands together and lights out*)

SONGS AND INTERPRETATION

Lop lop – oh	
Lop lop – mu ne soja } 2x (*Chorus*)	
Dama fura dam dam	
Wani boro – eh!	One idiot – eh
Ya sata mana doya	stolen our yam
Dama fura dam dam	Mix the fura well
Doya nan – eh!	This yam – eh
Ya kawo masa zawo	Made him to purge
Dama fura dam dam	Mix the fura well

Zawo nan – eh!　　　　　　This purging – eh
A ka dutse aka yi ta　　　　was released on a stone
Dam fura dam dam　　　　Mix the fura well
Dutse nan – eh!　　　　　This stone – eh
Ya kamo da wuta　　　　　Caught fire
Dama fura dam dam　　　　Mix the fura well

(*Repeat chorus*)
Mutane ku zo　　　　　　Come people
Fada ma ku labari Nigeria　Let us tell you the story of Nigeria ⎱ 2x
Ku zo ku ji　　　　　　　Come and listen
Labari Nigeria　　　　　　The story of Nigeria
Ku zo ku ji　　　　　　　Come and listen
Labari Nigeria　　　　　　The story of Nigeria
Mutane ku zo　　　　　　Come people
Fada ma ku labari Nigeria　Let's tell you the story of Nigeria

IDOMA
Anya o, Nigeria　　　　　Thank you, Nigeria (3x)
Aje k'ole adam o　　　　　My father's land
Nigeria ah ah Nigeria
A hum'otu i'ibi Nigeria　　I love you so much Nigeria
A hum'out I'ibi Nigeria　　I love you so much Nigeria
ah ah ah ah ah ah　　　　ah ah ah ah ah ah
Aje k'ole adam o　　　　　My father land

GLOSSARY

Barawo	Hausa word for 'thief'
Hakika	An Hausa exclamation that means 'precisely' or 'definitely'
Me ne?	What is?
Kuma ga shi nan	I can feel the texture of this oil 'see it here'
Walahi kuma	I swear again
A salam alekum	An Arabic word for 'greetings' or 'peace'
Na gaisheku duka	I greet you all
Ka na da ayaba a cikin kokoluwan ka	You are going bananas
Mugun	A slang term in Yoruba meaning a 'fool'
Mumu	Hausa word for a 'fool'
Expo	A shortened word for 'exposition' used as a slang term for examination leakages
POP	Plaster of Paris
Piss	Broken 'pidgin' English for urinating
Olodo	Yoruba word for a dullard

Book Reviews

Mervyn Millar. *Journey of the Tall Horse: A Story of African Theatre*
London: Oberon Books, 2006, 277 pp. Foreword by Basil Jones (pp. 7–10).
ISBN: 1 84002 599 9, £15.99

From the outset, it is clear that this book is not an academic exploration of a theatre production or company, there are no titles to chapters, no bibliography or index. However,
it is a significant and exciting book, especially for scholars interested in intercultural
theatre practice because of how it traces the collaboration between South Africa's
Handspring Puppet Company and the Malian Sogolon Puppet Company. It also
contains the 2005 version of the script developed through this collaboration, and many
fantastic photographs of the work in progress, with direct quotations from the key
figures involved.

    Not much has been published about either company's work. Apart from *Ubu and the
Truth Commission* (1998) none of the texts adapted by the Handspring Puppet Company
have been published; and video or film of their work is limited to tantalising thirteen
minute promotional videos. In 1998 the Société des Expositions du Palais des Beaux-
Arts de Bruxelless published a compilation of work: *William Kentridge*, to accompany a
travelling exhibition of much of Kentridge's line-drawings and short films, including
drawings and stills for *Woyzeck on the Highveld*, *Faustus in Africa!*, and the Ubu projects.
The short bibliography suggests how little this work has been documented, mainly
because this company works by a collaborative process of improvising adaptations of
classic European texts with actors and puppets against the art work of Kentridge, which
is back projected to create performances that address contemporary African issues that
have emerged from the postcolonial experience.

    The Sogolon Troupe, which performs in the Malian Bamara tradition under the
direction of Yaya Coulibaly, the leading exponent and custodian of Bamara puppet
theatre, is even less accessible to most of us than is Handspring. This is because it is profoundly part of the Bamana tradition, an animist belief system that incorporates
puppetry in all levels of initiation into the various societies, for both men and women.
At these mask and puppet performances both the attendance and those performing pro-
gressively narrow from the whole community to only initiated men and women, and
finally only mature men. The performances range from the sacred and ritual, through
the semi-sacred performance, to traditional and popular theatre. Janni Donald, who
curated the *Patrimony* exhibition of Yaya Coulibaly's collection of Malian puppets in

Cape Town in 2004, explains the place of puppets in the sacred and ritual ceremonies in the accompanying catalogue: 'The initiation ceremony is a nightlong performance of the puppets, masks and [fetish] objects.' (*Patrimony*, 2004: 8). Although popular theatre is unrelated to initiation and religion, there are nevertheless strict rules about how the puppets may be handled and are carved. Little is generally known about this work outside of Mali, and thus Millar's reference to Mary Jo Arnoldi's *Playing with Time* (2001) is useful to the reader.

I write this rather long contextualisation of the work of both companies to highlight the uniqueness of Millar's documentation of theatrical work that is primarily defined by the lived moment of the rehearsal process and performance event.

Millar traces this exciting collaboration from its initial brokering by Alicia Adams of the John F. Kennedy Center in Washington, to its revisited and reconceptualised first workshop in Cape Town in February 2004, with funding from AngloGold Ashanti and Business & Arts South Africa. It then details a seven week rehearsal period from July 2004 at the University of Stellenbosch, to the first performance at the Baxter in Cape Town. Despite being an assistant director in the project, Millar documents the experience as an outside observer who traces the complex realities of intercultural collaboration; both its exciting potential, and very real challenges.

The story is based on the historic account of a giraffe, Sogo Jan, that was captured in Africa and taken to France in 1826 as a gift for the King's menagerie; as a bribe from Mehmet Ali, the Ottoman viceroy of Egypt, to dissuade the French from involving themselves in the Greek War of Independence. The personal aspect focuses on Sogo Jan's relationship with her handler, Atir, a freed African slave who is forced to accompany this giraffe as she will trust no-one else. It is explicitly about the exoticism of Africa as the 'Dark Continent' brought to 'Enlightened Europe'. The story is told from an African perspective; thus we see the French aristocrats who 'fawn and flutter over their living curios' (p. 12) through African eyes. The director, Martinnus Basson says: 'The starting point was an extraordinary animal going north. Something that people have not seen. So you have the familiar, from our point of view, travelling into the unfamiliar' (p. 120).

The documentation begins with a week long development workshop in Cape Town, where the creative contributors come together for the first time to sketch out what will be rehearsed five months later. The international team are: project originators Adrian Kohler and Basil Jones from Handspring Puppet Company; Yaya Coulibaly, the puppet-maker and director from Bamako, Mali. They are joined by Koffi Kôkô, a celebrated choreographer from Benin; script-writer Khephra Burns from New York; as well as Marthinus Bassoon, Jaco Bouwer and Warrick Sony, the director, video artist and composer, from South Africa. During this week they get to know one another, explore and develop the script, test some of the visual pieces and show their work to one another. At the end of the week they present a work-in-progress to their main supporter, AngloGold Ashanti.

The next phase is the seven week rehearsal process. Millar traces the challenges of this project – twelve performers from different cultures who must master skills that are completely new to them: ranging from puppetry to stilt-walking, dancing and particular kinds of rhythmic singing. Then too, there is the profound challenge of language. The four Malians speak French and Bambara among themselves. The eight South African performers, the director and video animator speak fluent English, but their mother-tongues are Xhosa, Afrikaans and Zulu. Kephra Burns has created a complex, witty text, including Latin jokes, which must be spoken in English and French, with no inherent reason beyond the performers' choice as to which lines are spoken in which language.

The director is very articulate and signals fast redirections in English which not all the Malians understand. The styles of teaching and working are also very varied. Each key player demands something particular and often new from the performers: Kôkô teaches a particular use of energy and presence in the body on stage; Yaya Coulibaly and Adrian Kohler teach the performers how to make the puppets breathe and to direct their own energy through the puppets, but each puppet type demands different handling, and there are sixty puppets in the show. Basson creates spectacular images and layers on stage. Each of these men's demands must be reconciled with the others to create a coherent and powerful narrative of performers, images and actors on stage. The complexities of the production were summed up by Basil Jones: 'We've been through very hard times with this project. And very dark times when it seemed totally impossible. I feel that it's much more within the bounds of possibility. Now, it's much more ... you know, its easier to control. But it's still terribly difficult. We've got fourteen different types of puppet, and people that are not used to them. And a director that likes [stage] business... It seems like a thousand layers.' (p. 51)

However, the significance of the project, and this documentation of it, lies in these very difficulties. This book is not a dry description of some timeless African tradition that is venerable and distant, being translated into an accessible form. All the aspects of this performance art are alive, fluid and need negotiation. This begins with the language; as multi-lingual South Africa meets French-speaking West Africa, with a text written by an African-American. The companies had to negotiate cultures, languages, traditions, techniques; and this in itself produced innovation – Kohler allowed his puppets to be painted, whereas previously he worked only in natural wood. And the Malian *castelet,* the basic design for the giraffe, was combined with the Handspring use of rods and contemporary materials for the neck. All have learnt, adapted and shared knowledge and experience. Yaya Coulibaly says '*Tall Horse* is not the project of one individual. It belongs to all of us. No-one can say "It's mine." This is an encounter between people with the same desire: to make a piece of work.' (p. 167) Ultimately this seems like a key to successful intercultural exchange – the willingness to make the work, even at the expense of one's own initial conception, knowledge or tradition.

Millar tracks all the excitement and tension with a sense of openness and honesty. He asks clear and often difficult questions throughout. These include questions about the choices being made, the styles of the various directors, and the techniques being used. Ultimately such documentation reveals the real issues of intercultural performance practice, not so much what happens to the art form, but how one negotiates power, input and fairness of ownership and voice, how one learns to trust and understand the other. Millar sums this up at the end where he says:

The progress of *Tall Horse* has been challenged constantly, by miscommunication, by difficulties to do with place, distance and language, by contrasting styles struggling to find a common rhythm. Like the two puppeteers in the giraffe, strapped together in a cage, the collaborators in *Tall Horse* have sometimes pulled against one another and come close to falling. They've needed to find an instinctive connection to walk on stilts successfully. But in 2005 it began to feel as if the companies were walking in step. Each time a run of *Tall Horse* is set up, the collaboration is renewed, these artists trust each other a little more, and the connection between the groups, on and off stage, becomes stronger. (p. 231)

Ultimately this is an inspiring read. It is much more than a new play, or a write up of a project. It is an account of a process that inspires one to want to read and know about the various performance traditions, from Bambara to Banraku puppetry. It reads like an adventure that you cannot put down because you have to know what happens next. It also evokes a profound sadness in me that I couldn't be a part of this magic process, even as a fascinated spectator.

Yvette Hutchison
University of Warwick

Loren Kruger: *Post-Imperial Brecht. Politics and Performance, East and South*
Cambridge: University Press, 2004, xii + 379 pp.
ISBN 9780521817080, £55/ $95

This book sheds in some ways new light on Brecht's role in the histories of twentieth-century performance culture. Grounded in a strictly historicising approach it carefully dissects Brecht's conception of the arts and theatre practice in various concrete historical contexts/circumstances in which they have developed and 'operated' since the 1920s. The book is deliberately directed against a 'habit, all too prevalent in the Anglo-American world, of treating Brecht's method as a timeless set of tools that can be applied to anything from political theatre to advertising.' (p. 16) Most importantly, Loren Kruger offers a new comparative look at both the role of Brecht's works and the impact of his theory on theatre in the 'East' and in the 'South' after 1945, exemplified by a close reading of performance in the GDR from the late 1940s to its demise in 1990, in the unified Germany thereafter, and in South Africa under and after apartheid. This is to critique the European priority in studying Brecht, stressing that his 'legacy should not be mapped only on a West/East or only on a North/South axis.' The book is to show 'the intersections of the Cold War axis', between West and East, in the 'same plane as the post-colonial axis', between affluent North and impoverished South. (p. 15)

   In the first chapter the development of Brecht's political, philosophical and aesthetic stance before 1945 is laid out. Outlining his role in the controversy among European critical and Marxist intellectuals such as Lukács and Adorno over the character and possible function of a 'proper' critical and/or, respectively, revolutionary socialist litera-ture, Kruger emphasises that Brecht's approach was premised on the primacy of produc-tion over theory, 'and thus of experiment over prescription in the realm of social as well as artistic transformation.' (p. 46) Chapters two and three deal with Brecht's attitude, manifested in his theatre practice after 1945 and his theoretical interventions, toward the 'actually existing socialism', particularly in East Germany. Chapter four discusses *inter alia* 'the decline of Brechtian futures, as well as opportunities for critique' (p. 176) or, in other words, his 'legacy' after 1989 in the unified Germany. Of particular interest are the passages on Brecht and Heiner Müller, both Brecht's most eminent 'successor' and most insightful, productive, forward-looking critic, in the GDR. In a well argued implicit, and at times explicit, critique of superficially binary (old Cold War style) assumptions about their relationship with the socialist project in general and the then East Germany in particular, Kruger interrogates the changing roles some of Brecht's and Müller's major productions played in changing historical contexts from the late 1940s through 1989, that is the history of the GDR. I particularly recommend reading the passages on Müller's plays and theatre productions *Der Bau* (Construction Site), *Der Lohndrücker*, in David Bathrick's translation *The Wage Buster*, and especially on his adaptation and radio-production of Brecht's *Fatzer* (Fragments). The book provides valuable insight into complex socio-cultural realities and the 'real history' of Marxist-oriented critical intellectuals and their highly contradictory, conflict-fraught relationship with the historical project they had opted for.

Chapter five traces the Brecht-reception in apartheid South Africa. It focuses on the role of Brecht's theory and plays in the anti-apartheid theatre movement. A look at the Serpent Players' and Athol Fugard's collaboration on the production of *The Caucasian Chalk Circle* in 1964 sets the tone. The Players used 'Brecht's elucidation of gestic acting, dis-illusion, and social critique, as well as their own experience of the satiric comic routines of urban African vaudeville.' (p. 217) Chapter six, entitled 'Realistic Engagement', returns to the East and the limits of solidarity: Athol Fugard in (East) Germany'. Touching, for instance, on the difficulty East German theatre had in coping with impersonating black people on stage, mostly resorting to 'blackening up', Kruger implicitly prompts the reader to examine a much wider-reaching issue, namely not only the limitations of leftist and humanist-liberal Europeans solidarity with Africans but of their virtual neglect, at least their lack of and, arguably, their rather sluggish interest in understanding African and other 'Third World/South World' cultures, histories, and 'things' in general. Going on from her analysis of Fugard's impact on the GDR theatre, another essay or even book could and should, for instance, discuss Müller's unique position as regards genuine concern for cultures of the 'South', especially Africa, unique at least in German-speaking countries, a deep interest to be traced from his translation of Césaire's piece on Lumumba, *Une saison au Congo*, in the late 1960s through to his dramatic text and production *Der Auftrag*, translated by Kruger as *The Mission*, in 1979/80 to *Anatomie Titus. Fall of Rome*, his version of Shakespeare's play, in 1985. Such an essay could and should, of course, take into consideration the Brecht reception in the whole of Africa and at the same time problematize Brecht's apparent lack of interest in thematizing the 'otherness' of non-European/non-Western socio-cultural contexts such works as *The Measure Taken* and *The Exception and the Rule*.

The last chapter on 'Truth, reconciliation, and the ends of political performance', treats trends in performance in post-apartheid South Africa. Brecht's impact, Loren Kruger states, became more indirect although the Brechtian impulse of an enlightening theatre would be clearly seen in various attempts at forms such as AIDS-fighting 'Theatre for Development' (p. 339). Referring to the fragmentary *Messingkauf*, Brecht's incomplete chief theoretical work on theatre, and Raymond Williams' Brecht-reading, she turns to a critical analysis of the theatricality of the Truth Commission hearings. It's a little surprising that she does not mention and thus elaborate on Brecht's conception of the theatricality of the whole range of non-aesthetic or 'indicative', a Williams- and, by the way, Victor Turner-designation of societal communicative activities, or the 'natural' or 'everyday theatre', or 'applied theatre', as Brecht put it in 'Die Straßenszene' in 1938, one of his pivotal essays. The essay is connected with the *Messingkauf* enterprise as one of the entries in his journals/diary in 1942 testifies:

> For the *Messingkauf* the subject of the *applied theatre* needs to be worked out […] it is of the utmost importance to recognise that what people do when they usurp or arrogate social rank to themselves, accommodating their expression and bearing to more or less prescribed custom etc. is (partly unconscious, but nonetheless real) theatre. (p. 258)

On 6 December 1940 he had already written:

> After the studies in the *Street Scene* other kinds of everyday theatre ought to be described and other examples of theatre in real life identified, in the erotic sphere, in business, in politics, in the law, in religion, etc … I have already done some work on the application of theatrical techniques to politics in fascism, but in addition to this the kind of everyday theatre that individuals indulge in when no one is watching should be studied, secret 'role-playing' … the *Street Scene* constitutes a big step towards making the art of theatre profane and secular and stripping it of religious elements.
>
> (Brecht, Bertolt. *Brecht Journals*. p. 115, Ed. John Willet. London: Methuen, 1993)

The book is a highly recommendable contribution to both comparative Brecht studies and comparative analyses of African (performance) cultures and, particularly, their role in the North.

Joachim Fiebach
Berlin

Annabel Maule, *Theatre Near the Equator: The Donovan Maule Story*.
Nairobi: Kenway, 2004, 295 pp.
ISBN 9966252266, £16.95.
(Distributed by African Books Collective Ltd, Oxford)

Sybil Thorndike said 'You've got to be a little mad to get anywhere in the theatre, and you two are the most delightfully mad people I've ever met.' (p. 73) She was talking to Donovan Maule and his wife, Mollie, who, in 1947, went to Kenya to set up a professional theatre. This they managed to accomplish against great odds and the Donovan Maule Theatre operated as a repertory company in Nairobi until 1979. The theatre survived, and sometimes flourished, becoming a significant business enterprise. For example, in 1967, it had its own theatre building, with facilities that included twelve flats, and it employed forty people, some twenty of whom were expatriates (p. 122). In January 1971, the Maules' daughter Annabel, an actor and all round Woman of Theatre, became Managing Director (p. 153), fighting the exhausting battle to keep the theatre going for the last eight years of its existence. During that time, in true 'staying on' – end of the Raj – fashion, she also had to play a supporting role as her parents' health declined.

Theatre Near the Equator is a colonial and post-colonial narrative with a quintessentially English activity – a repertory theatre – centre stage and the changes that convulsed East Africa between 1947 and 1979 flickering across the cyclorama. Buffeted by changing economic and political fortunes, the Donovan Maule Theatre, 'the D.M.', was eventually sunk by a combination of factors that included pay for actors (UK Equity rates), 'duds' (unsuitable texts), 'pigs in pokes' (actors recruited in London who proved unsuitable in Nairobi), and increasingly burdensome government regulations. It was also sunk by the Maules' own narrow perceptions of theatre, and their distance from the community in which they lived.

The list of D.M. productions, a remarkable 350 in all, is fascinating. All three Maules were well aware that, since they had no Arts Council funding or similar, the Nairobi Box Office was always going to tell them the brutal truth. It revealed that the profitable plays were 'almost always light comedies and thrillers' (p. 77), or what John Counsell, Managing Director of the Theatre Royal Windsor, referred to as 'Good, light escapist entertainment.' (p. 92). Despite this, the Maules, perhaps touchingly, occasionally picked up plays that had created a sensation in London irrespective of the constituency they played to there. In some cases the choice represented a real 'dud', a bridge too far for the Nairobi faithful. For example, we read, without surprise, that *Look Back in Anger* 'did very poor business' (p. 86). We are not told the reaction to *Beyond the Fringe* or *Loot,* but can imagine the response of those members of the audience whose expectations of the theatre were somewhat to the right of 'Disgusted' of Tunbridge Wells. However, we are made aware that the 'colonials' could take some productions with bite: apparently *Who's Afraid of Virginia Woolf?* provoked some angry letters but attracted 3,169 patrons. It had a good run. (p. 119)

The book draws on the copious and detailed records of the theatre kept for many years by Donovan Maule himself and then continued, and preserved, by Annabel. These records include the Authors' Royalty Books in which ticket sales were meticulously noted. This means that if you ever went to the D. M. you were counted and are part of the story this book tells. Though not presented in an academic format, this briskly written book is based on access to meticulously compiled data, and infused with a profound involvement on many levels in the story it tells. It is informative, authoritative, and a 'labour of love': Annabel's account of the theatre is the history that her father never seriously got round to writing.

One of the most vivid passages concerns an ambitious international tour of *Bell, Book and Candle,* by John van Druten, undertaken at the end of 1952 and beginning of 1953. Though based in Nairobi, the D.M. company aspired to take professional drama to the theatres, some of them 'garrison theatres' left behind after the war, used by the drama societies attached to the expatriate clubs. Annabel Maule interrupted her career in the English theatre to travel to Kenya and act with her parents' company in towns in Kenya, Uganda and Tanganyika. The 17-performance, 7-week tour, coincided with a State of Emergency – the Kenya Land and Freedom Army was active, but despite this, and an actor dropping out at the last minute, the first ever 'fit-up tour' of East Africa went ahead. For the record, the performers travelled with footlights, house curtains, twelve frames of production photographs and a 'huge crate of programmes with other necessary stationery'! (p. 37) Intriguingly for those concerned with recent developments in theatre in the community, the tour was seen as having a definite purpose: part of its justification was to 'take settlers' thoughts off their worries for an hour or two'! (p. 37) The company travelled 2,384 miles and played to 4,185 paying customers. In her account Annabel comes across as a chip off the dogged, determined Maule block. A 'good trouper', she also did quite a lot of running around, sometimes 'sprinting'. (pp. 38, 39). From time to time, however, she reveals the considerable distance between her and the lives lived by the majority of Kenyans. In describing moments on the tour, she records that 'Africans' were amused by some of the more extraordinary fixes that the members of the company found themselves in. She is preoccupied with their 'grinning black faces with flashing white teeth' (pp. 52, 55). One is not surprised that later she gets into trouble over a carelessly worded letter in which she refers to 'slaves'. (p. 133)

For Annabel, as for her parents, London and the English theatre provided inspiration, and this focus persisted even when connecting with drama as studied in Kenyan schools provided commercial opportunities. Sometimes the D.M. put on plays that were on the school syllabus, and to its credit, Caltex, the Kenyan subsidiary of Chevron, South Africa, was prepared to subsidize special matinees so that school children could see their set-texts brought to life. On at least one occasion an African actor had an important role in one of these production: Donald Kiboro played the Common Man in Robert Bolt's *A Man for All Seasons* (p. 106). With support from Caltex and young audiences that production ran for a remarkable six weeks. But African actors were not sought out, and possible links with schools were not fully exploited. The example of Shakespeare provides a case in point. We read that *Scenes from Shakespeare*, acted by Donald Wolfit and Rosalind Iden were popular with pupils (p. 88) who attended matinees in 1959, and learn that Caltex subsidised seats for 250 school children to watch *The Merchant of Venice* in 1964. But Shakespeare was rarely performed at the D.M. Annabel indicates that the Bard's plays were considered too expensive because the large casts required 'extra guest artists', that is to say more British actors flown in and paid Equity rates. Moreover the tights for the men attracted nearly 100 per cent in taxes! (p. 106). The unwillingness to use local actors, to improvise and adjust, that lies behind these complaints indicates why, for all its determination, the D.M.'s days were numbered.

If the founding father, Donovan Maule himself, had been less in tune with settler values and with the theatre values of the manager of the Theatre Royal Windsor, if he had, for example, been more of a 'Shakespeare Wallah', the history of the theatre that bore his name might have been different. Again and again, one senses that the Maules, parents and daughter, couldn't move towards the African actors who could have been found in Nairobi or towards the African audiences that surrounded them. They were not able to move sufficiently far from 1947, to engage adequately with the local audiences and to broaden their ideas of theatre. If things had been different then the D.M. might have lasted longer and have left a greater legacy. As it is this readable, well-informed book, packed with information and attitude, reveals the strengths and weaknesses of two generations of a 'mad' thespian family who, for part of the twentieth century ran a Theatre Near the Equator.

James Gibbs
University of the West of England

Wole Ogundele and Gbemisola Adeoti (eds) *ÌBÀ: Essays on African Literature in Honour of Oyin Ogunba*
Obafemi Awolowo University Press, 2003, 274 pp.
ISBN 9781361360, £19.95/$22.95
Distributed by African Books Collective

Oyin Ogunba was for many years Professor of English at Obafemi Awolowo University, Ile-Ife, Nigeria, having commenced his academic career, both as a student and a teacher, at Ibadan. His major written work, as relevant today as it was when first written, is *The Movement of Transition: A Study of Wole Soyinka's Plays*, published by Ibadan University Press in 1975. In his foreword to this collection of essays, Dapo Adelugba recalls the 'incident' at the launch of this volume when Ogunba was criticised by young scholars in what the editors call the 'heady days of political and intellectual idealism' in which

Ogunba's rational, well-researched and perceptive study of Soyinka was regarded by his critics as lacking in political correctness! Disarmingly, Femi Osofisan, one of the most forceful and articulate of the youthful critics at the time, takes the opportunity of the opening essay in this collection to reflect and reassess, recalling Ogunba's dignity under assault and his enduring 'humaneness and humanity'. Oyin Ogunba's career and scholarly interests were not, of course, confined to drama, and this volume of 22 essays covers the novel, poetry, language, and cultural issues, as well as the drama and performance. (One gem is Niyi Osundare's 'The Rhetoric of Lament: A Socio-Stylistic Study of Obituaries and Memoriams in Nigerian Dailies'.)

The essays on drama and performance are substantial. Mabel Evwierhoma offers an assessment of Ogunba as 'a pioneer critic of the Nigerian Theatre', noting his interest in festivals as well as literary drama. Remi Raji-Oyelade offers a detailed study of the early plays of Osofisan and of Bode Sowande (an important playwright who rewards attention). Gbemisola Remi Adeoti, in a stimulating essay, shows how a range of playwrights – Soyinka, Rotimi, Irobi, Yerima, Tomoloju, Onwueme and others – have engaged with the 'political imperative' of creating democracy and good governance in Nigeria. Tejumola Olaniyan contributes a discussion of suicide and ideology in Nigerian drama, which visits not only the more obvious candidates (Clark, Ogunyemi, Ladipo) but also a playwright new to me, Oladejo Okediji. Dele Layiwola's typically impressive essay on 'dilemmas of identity' centres on Clark (*Song of a Goat*) and Rotimi (*The Gods Are Not to Blame*) and also – importantly – on Ebrahim Hussein (*At the Edge of Thim*), another playwright who deserves more exposure. Femi Fatoba offers a subtle reading of Soyinka's *Death and the King's Horseman*, looking at language and symbols of time and transition, and Uko Atai celebrates the 'festive comedy and the spirit of man' in the Cameroonian Oyono Mbia's *Three Suitors, One Husband*.

Other essays in the collection discuss dance, Sola Olorunyomi asking *What is Contemporary African Dance?*, and Mathew Umukoro on the 'dance metaphor' in Nigerian theatre, a performance analysis of a number of contemporary plays that would very usefully inform and stimulate any staging of them.

This is an affectionate tribute to Professor Oyin Ogunba, but it is also a substantial collection of important essays on mainly – but happily not exclusively – Nigerian drama.

Martin Banham
Professor Emeritus, University of Leeds

Emelda Ngufor Samba, *Women in Theatre for Development in Cameroon: Participation, Contributions and Limitations*
Bayreuth: Bayreuth African Studies Series, 2005, 245 pp.
ISBN 3-927510-86-6, Euro 25.95

John Tiku Takem, *Theatre and Environmental Education in Cameroon*
Bayreuth: Bayreuth African Studies Series, 2005, 192 pp.
ISBN 3-927510-92-0, Euro19.95

Women in Theatre for Development is a detailed sociological and technical study that provides a compelling circumstantial investigation of the fate of woman in contemporary Africa, as opposed to the often unfounded and incantatory generalizations on the predicament of the African woman under the vicissitudes of patriarchal regimes. The study is informative for the general reader who desires a more situated report on the gender situation in Cameroon, as well as the more specialized reader interested in the dynamics – 'the ways and means' – of Theatre for Development (TFD). Relying on active field experience and literature Samba imbues her study with an appealing freshness, especially when contrasted with the voguish theses on the endangered 'African Woman'. What emerges in *Women in Theatre for Development* is a rare marriage of theory and practice and a style which has the engaging appeal of prose narrative. There is no doubt that this is a study by an expert in the discipline, and her claim of involvement in over twenty of her case studies seems irrefutable.

The first two chapters offer an overview of the history of gender relations in Cameroon, with emphasis on the rural and semi-urban spaces, and identify the genesis of the most problematic issues confronting the typical Cameroonian woman. Although not overtly feminist (or 'womanist'), these sections proffer invaluable positions on the feminist agenda which should be particularly beneficial to mainstream feminists. First, Samba stresses the challenges which the Cameroonian woman faces and argues that these, rather than being homogenous, are inflected by class, culture, geography, education and religion. Then she locates the complication, and indeed the genesis, of these problems in foreign presence. For instance, on the exclusion of women in the inheritance and ownership of property, she observes that in the pre-colonial era; 'both men and women had usufruct and temporary rights to land [and] women did not have to be attached to a husband to gain access to farmland' (p. 43). However, Islamisation, colonisation and capitalisation have changed all that 'to the detriment of the African woman' (p. 43). The same factors are identified in the other issues, such as the com-modification of women through the practice of bride price, marginalisation of women in access to western education, and the peculiar problem of the dehumanising widowhood rite which is not essentially an importation but is particularly inflamed when it is 'transposed from their natural abode to more sophisticated and multicultural milieus' (p. 49). She does point out that ironically 'women, more than men, reinforce widowhood rites' (p. 49). Particularly profound, although inevitably brief, is her socio-logical study of the peculiar identity of the Mbororo woman whose problem is com-pounded by illiteracy, religion and an insular lifestyle.

The other chapters proffer specialised exploration of the mechanics of Theatre for Development. They examine the various approaches, with adequate field examples, identifying their individual merits and demerits. Observing the under-representation of women even in most women-focused TFD programmes the study locates this difficulty in faulty methodology. Rather than adopting the 'unidirectional', it submits that the better suited methodology is the 'participatory' for it affords full involvement of both change agents and target groups in the entire process. In practically all the case studies discussed in the book the participatory approach was applied. The individual programmes are examined in detail, ranging from the profile of participants, through consultations, analyses of collected data, devising of performances or plays, methodologies, to post-performance discussions and follow-up programmes. Song texts and the language of performance also receive detailed analyses. Notably outstanding is the acuity of the visual aids in the form of photographs, linear representations, maps and tables. The tables especially offer a quick composite picture of the individual programmes. For instance, 'Table 1: Inheritance and Ownership of Property' itemises, under four different sections, the 'Problems', 'Short-term possible solutions', 'Long-term possible solutions' and 'Resolutions and recommendations'. This summarises the entire project at a glance.

Women in Theatre for Development in Cameroon is not simply a well grounded imaging of the troubling gender inequity in a particular post-colonial setting, it offers a narrative of hope in the agency of women to remedy this imbalance. The pages resonate with the author's passion for the development of not just her gender but her entire community. It is also written in flowing, confident prose, thus instancing the need for accessibility in the literary production of the socially-conscious academic whose work is for the betterment of society rather than the shelves of sundry academic libraries.

John Tiku Takem's *Theatre and Environmental Education in Cameroon* examines the way environmentalists employ theatre to raise awareness on the need to conserve the perennially endangered rain forest of South-West Province of Cameroon. Takem observes that the Cameroonian rain forest is rated amongst the most endowed in bio-diversity, but is also one of the most endangered. The factors which constitute this danger include unwholesome farming methods, increased land cultivation and deforestation to sustain a rapidly growing population, and commercial logging activities which destroy young plants without replenishing them. The crisis is exacerbated because of the lack of any decisive state policy to guide the exploitation of natural resources. Even where such a policy is formulated it is either selectively implemented or not at all. Although the activities of commercial loggers constitute the greatest threat to the environment the political structure which privileges the 'big and powerful' has meant the focus of environmental protection attention has fallen almost entirely on the rural population, while encouragement in the form of concession rights are given to wealthy individuals and local and international companies to harvest timber.

This is the backdrop which has necessitated the formulation of diverse strategies by environmentalists to conserve the rain forest. One such strategy is theatre, with projects sponsored by Non-Governmental Organizations (NGOs), and financial and technical support from international organizations, such as WWF, GTZ, Living Earth, WCDS and ODA. It is, however, ironic that both the devastation and the preservation of the rain forest are colonial legacies, one originating in the policy of extraction adopted by the German colonial administration, the latter in the designation of 'protected areas' in such places as parks, botanical and zoological gardens, and forest reserves.

For the environmental theatre practitioner this terrain poses many challenges. The most significant is how to operate without falling foul of the state whose repressive strategies could range from an outright ban to a threat to the very life of the environmental activist. In this context the best strategy is not a confrontational anti-establishment posture but covert subversion.

Chapter Four undertakes case studies of five selected Theatre for Development (TFD) projects, identifying their challenges, objectives, methodologies, successes and limitations in the campaign for ecological health. It puts to the test the claim that TFD leads to empowerment and liberation of the populace within particular socio-political contexts. Although the practice of TFD is not procedurally defined its definitive format entails a participatory engagement of the target audience in the analysis of problems, composition of plays, performance, and post-performance dialogues. In this respect only one of the case studies, the Bole Butake-led Bamendankwe campaign, succeeded in actually engaging the participation of the target audience. Some of the factors responsible for this general failure include the imposition of a theme selected in advance on the people, lack of a thorough study of the target audience, and the lack of follow-up action to assess and monitor the results of the projects. The majority of these ventures seemed to lack innovation and ingenuity, and a proper mastery of a workable field methodology. In concert with the overarching socio-politically repressive regime these people-oriented developmental projects merely 'participated in the domestication of the people in the oppressive patterns of environmentalism, rather than articulating pathways to sustainable ecological consciousness' (p. 175).

Theatre and Environmental Education in Cameroon is a critical investigation adopting more of a literary than a sociological approach. In this respect it clearly underscores the inter-disciplinary nature of TFD and its sensitivity to the temperament of the socio-political landscape. Particularly stimulating is its theoretical mapping of the practice within the postcolonial tradition of decolonization, routing it via the socio-cultural concerns of pre-colonial traditional theatre and the socio-political engagement of post-colonial literary theatre. Consequently, Takem succeeds not just in positing a well researched analysis of the fortunes of TFD in Cameroon but also in producing outstanding documentation of the social, methodological and political theory of postcolonial African theatre.

Chukwuma Okoye
University of Ibadan, Nigeria

Terence Zeeman. *Finding Feet Conference. Theatre Education and Training in the SADC Region*
Windhoek: New Namibia Books, 2005, 118 pp. n.p.
ISBN 99916 31 82 8

This report by Terence Zeeman details the process and resolutions of an unusual conference held by the Southern African Theatre Initiative (SATI) in Namibia in 2003. The aim of the event was to bring together personnel from universities, theatre training centres and community arts initiatives across the SADC (Southern African Development Community) region to see how they might work more closely across disciplines and national borders for the benefit of theatre training for all. The event was facilitated by Robert McLaren, a South African and long time resident of Zimbabwe, and was attended by 54 delegates from Botswana, Lesotho, Malawi, Mauritius, Mozambique, Namibia, Seychelles, South Africa, Swaziland, Tanzania, Zambia and Zimbabwe.

What was immediately unusual about the event was its structure. McLaren explained that:

> The main aim is to avoid an academic talk-shop where people listen to long papers being read and at the end of it everyone goes home fatter, less fit but more motivated to try to attend another workshop soon in the future because the hotel and the food was good. (p. ix)

Instead this would be a participatory workshop for what was conceived as a theatrical 'family', with the three groups divided up as a 'cast' – university staff as 'gowns', theatre school personnel as 'dreads' and community arts practitioners as 'hoes'. The theatrical metaphor was sustained throughout. 'Setting the stage' on day one was about identifying an ideal situation and then analysing strengths and weaknesses in the community. On day two the focus was on 'character descriptions' where the three groups were examined before going on to 'character analysis' on day three. 'Plotting the action' consisted of groups in a number of configurations coming up with an 'Action Plan'. Finally on day five a 'script', the 'Finding Feet Action Plan', was adopted.

Zeeman is very much the reporter in this lively little book, and resists any commentary on the event. Instead of chapters we have days, followed up by the various action plans, and appendices giving the texts of the few keynote speeches allowed. What is fascinating to those working in this or related areas is the insider view we are given of the concerns of this diverse theatrical community.

First it is quickly apparent that in terms of access to resources, opportunities, and training we are in very unequal world. In South Africa there are numerous well-equipped universities offering a wide range of theatre courses, including extensive developments with complex theatre technologies. Contrast this with the situation at the University of Malawi where David Kerr stated that:

> In his department there is only a single computer – there is so little money that they cannot photocopy or staple documents. If there is a printer, then one must provide one's own paper. (p. 18)

Vocational theatre training centres are very thin on the ground in the region with institutions operating only in Namibia, South Africa, Tanzania and one just being established in Zimbabwe. Bagamoyo College of the Arts in Tanzania is by far the oldest, with a history dating back to 1962, and the most prestigious, with substantial government and NGO support, and a programme of training, consultancy and production as well as its international annual Bagamoyo Arts Festival. In South Africa and Namibia the Market Theatre Laboratory and the College of the Arts are much smaller training colleges and are still working to develop recognised curricula and secure on-going funding.

Representatives from the Hoes are possibly the problematic category in this conference. It appears that with the exception of representatives from companies in Namibia, most of the attendees in this category were leaders of cultural organisations. They speak eloquently on behalf of the poverty and lack of training and recognition for their members but one has little sense of the actuality of life for community practitioners at the grassroots. It would have been good to have heard more experiential evidence of what one knows are the considerable struggles of such artists.

Notable also is the lack of representation of women. The workshop does repeatedly recognise this problem and calls for greater opportunities and representation of women, but nowhere is there any analysis of why the problem exists and just what needs to be done to address it. If there is a lack to the action plans emerging, I would say that it is most notably this absence of any plan for just how to assist women theatre artists in the development of their careers and profile across the region. Simply noting the problem is going to do nothing to resolve it.

As we hear from each of the three groupings it becomes evident that university staff are sometimes seen as too separate from the communities they serve. Andre Strauss, the Deputy Director of Namibia's Ministry of Basic Education, Sport and Culture goes so far as to say that:

> The aim of this workshop – to marry what happens in universities, theatre schools and in the work of individual practitioners – is in my humble opinion quite a daunting one … I hope it will work. I hope so, since I have not been convinced by the professors at our universities that they even regard themselves as Afrikans (sic). (p. 91)

It does not appear to me that the tenor of this conference substantiates such a gloomy analysis of theatre academics, but common perceptions of divergence in status and wealth are a real and recurrent issue for participants.

Other issues that dominate proceedings are the need for exchanges between professionals across national boundaries to ameliorate considerable problems of regional ignorance of theatre training modes and curricula; the question of how to incorporate professionals with considerable practical experience but few education credentials into teaching programmes, and the related problem of how to allow access in theatre training to young enthusiasts who have not had the educational opportunities that would give them an entry point to higher education. In what comes across as a still quite socialist grouping delegates discuss problems with conservative bureaucrats and the dangers of on-going dependence on foreign funders. (At the time of the conference SATI's funding by Swedish government agency SIDA was coming to an end.) There is a wonderful 'vision' at the end of day three that includes, 'Rich black companies; graduate Hoes driving home in their cars from a successful, independent theatre', but also one where audiences are 'paying only a little and filling all sorts of available spaces'. Theatre is envisaged as contributing 'to the struggle against global imperialism' (p. 46). This is only a vision but it is definitely predicated on socialist ideologies that are woefully absent from most SADC government circles, and such forms of independent theatre could surely only be developed with levels of government funding that show no sign of emerging anywhere in contemporary Africa.

McLaren, himself a socialist visionary if ever there was one, keeps trying to focus the workshop on achievable aims in the present day, with a tight schedule using SWOT and SMART analyses lifted from business and development practice. The final action plans concentrate on issues of networking, lobbying, accreditation, quality training, Africanisation, and nod towards gender equality.

One can't help wondering what, if any, concrete developments emerged from this obviously radical and energetic participatory conference, especially as it emerges that the umbrella organisation, SATI, has had problems in convening activist national chapters. Has funding continued to the organisation? Are there any more women in it? Has substantial networking taken place? Perhaps I don't really want the answers to these questions, since previous international African efforts at artistic cooperation have so often evaporated once workshops and conferences conclude. Nonetheless the Finding Feet Conference was evidently a real attempt to engage across barriers of status and nationality, and the energy and urgency of the organisers and many participants is well reflected in the form and style of Terence Zeeman's presentation.

Jane Plastow
University of Leeds

Jane Plastow (ed.), *Three Eritrean Plays. A Village Dream* (Mesgun Zerai), *The Snare* (Solomon Dirar), *Aster* (Esaias Tseggai)
Leeds: Alumnus, 2005, 64 pp.
ISBN 1901439046, £5

Forged in the struggle

All three playwrights featured in this volume were *Tegedalay*,[1] the Tigrinya[2] term for a freedom fighter. Between them they notch up over 40 years in the Eritrean People's

Liberation Front (EPLF).[3] During the conflict, the longest war of liberation in modern African history, both sides saw culture as an important tool in the propaganda war. It is within this context that Solomon, Esaias and Mesgun[4] began writing; with the independence struggle and the wider aims of the EPLF being of paramount importance to their work.

A Village Dream, Mesgun Zerai

Unusually for an Eritrean play *A Village Dream* contains writing that is highly stylised and employs music and dance, which lend the play a dreamlike quality. Underneath this facade, however, is a strong socio-political agenda. Women have traditionally been subservient to men in much of Eritrea and it is domestic oppression that Mesgun is concerned with.

Before the actors even enter, the set alludes to the traditional hierarchy of village life. In the foreground are laid out a pestle and mortar, a milk churn and a grinding stone; tools African audiences will immediately associate with female labour. As the play begins the women rise, notably before any men; take up the tools and begin a dumb show of milling grain, washing clothes and other domestic chores.

When the men finally appear, having risen late, they laze about drinking coffee and grooming their hair. Whilst humour is certainly intended, the contrast between these two morning rituals leaves the audience in no doubt as to who bears the brunt of the workload. The only exception to endemic male apathy is a character simply called Old Man. He takes his grandchild from his daughter, Dehabe, and offers to help. It is at this point that Dehabe articulates a question central to the play:

> **Dehabe** Why are we women suffering too much? We fetch water, we cook, we collect firewood…we do everything without any help from our husbands. What is our sin father? (p. 28)

The Old Man's reply is cryptic. He tells his daughter that the village women work so hard because 'they want to', and that an old story called 'The Women's Sin' explains how this came to be the case.

The audience don't get to hear this story until much later because the village women decide to teach their husbands a lesson by running away to the mountains. This happens at night and the following morning a comic scene follows as the men ask one another whether anyone has seen their wives. Men like Ijugu cannot bring themselves to believe their wives could show such initiative:

> **Ijugu** You know my wife can't even piss without asking my permission. (p. 31)

The men then repeat the mimed sequence that began the play, but this time with disastrous consequences.

For the reader much of the humour has to be imagined as Mesgun provides only an outline of the action in the stage directions. This is typical of the playwright's craft as learnt during the struggle. It was expedient for there to be a good deal of improvisation when developing new plays and writers collaborated closely with actors. Hajait Mendal, a veteran actress, described working methods in an interview with me in 1995.

> Anybody who had the ability to write was free to do so, but we usually worked together. We all felt free to give suggestions and comments or advise alternatives. (Warwick, *New Theatre Quarterly*, No. 51, 1997)

This does not suggest that the writing is unimportant. Broad brush strokes have been employed in a parts of *A Village Dream*, but elsewhere the writing is detailed and powerful. One example is the lament the women sing as they head into the hills. The rhythm of the writing is gently evocative of the endless toil they hope to escape, while the lyrics paint a hauntingly sad picture of their suffering. In the second stanza Mesgun describes the exhausted nights the women spend in their husbands' beds, their love-making drained of all passion by the burdens of the day.

> Day becomes night, night becomes day,
> Work without rest.
> I come to you and beside you I lie.
> Another labour I find,
> Another price to pay,
> My body knows no pleasure.
> I slave for him whom I desire.
> I have scrubbed, and chopped
> And ground and hauled and dug
> And washed my love away. (pp. 29–30)

For an Eritrean playwright to address sexual relationships in this way is exceptional and it makes a powerful point.

The first time we see one of the women after their escape it is Abita, sneaking back to visit her boyfriend, Rogie. As she returns to the mountain next morning she sows a trail of grain for her lover to follow. The image, as in a fairytale, is the mechanism that will usher in the play's denouement. Following a series of dreams heralding the arrival of the men, the women wake to find that they are surrounded. But the men have not come with an altercation in mind. They have come to seek resolution.

Dehabe then tells the story of 'The Women's Sin'. Many years ago the village men did the work, and they then ran away in protest. The women atoned by agreeing to take over all the village work. Mesgun is demonstrating that another turnaround is not going to suceed. Instead he champions the need for a solution that breaks the cycle of oppression and revolt. Dehabe makes this explicit when she calls for all to share the workload equally and leads the village and the audience in a dance of reconciliation.

The Snare, **Solomon Dirar**

The Snare is built around three characters. Sheka Haile, an Eritrean collaborator, Demsas, an EPLF fighter, and Ghebre, an Eritrean Everyman caught between the two. Demsas has assassinated an Ethiopian official and is now hiding out in the woods near Sheka Haile's house. Sheka Haile and Ghebre have told him they will help him escape but Sheka Haile reveals to Ghebre that the Ethiopian authorities have offered a 10,000 Birr reward for the capture of the assassin. He is plotting to betray Demsas for the money and much of the ensuing dialogue centres on his attempt to persuade Ghebre to help him. Through this conversation Solomon explores an ideological dilemma faced by many civilians during the Ethiopian occupation: to profit from collaboration or to remain loyal to the struggle.

For a piece of propaganda the characterisation of Sheka Haile is surprisingly well balanced. He is suitably villainous for the audience to find him reprehensible, without the playwright undermining the character to the extent that we are unable to appreciate the point of view he expresses. The fact that Sheka Haile and Ghebre are cousins sharpens the predicament further. Family ties are very strong in Eritrea but in *The Snare* the need to support the struggle is seen to override everything else. Ghebre, who does remain loyal to the cause, eventually betrays his cousin and hatches a counter-plot with Demsas that results in Sheka Haile's downfall and execution. To western audiences this may seem brutal, however the play must be viewed in context. During the struggle 'in towns and cities a covert war was being conducted every bit as bitterly as the war in Sahel' (Plastow and Tsehaye, p. 47). For a wartime audience the play served as a stern warning to would-be collaborators and a reminder of the responsibility everyone had to shoulder if the liberation struggle was to succeed.

Given that *The Snare* is a propaganda play it is unexpectedly honest about the difficulties of living up to these responsibilities. Ghebre is exactly the kind of Eritrean civilian that the EPLF fighters depended on for their survival and precisely the kind of Eritrean who would have been sat in the audience. Even so, Solomon's examination of his position does not shy away from uncomfortable facts. The play acknowledges the suffering of the Eritrean people and accepts that this hardship could be made worse by not collaborating with the Ethiopian regime. It recognises the dangers involved in supporting the fighters and sympathises with the divisions this may cause within families. Sheka Haile's underestimation the Eritrean Everyman is not one that Solomon shares, and his play is all the more persuasive for it.

Aster, Esaias Tseggai

Like *The Snare*, *Aster* is set in the midst of the independence struggle. Its tone, however, is entirely different. When we first meet Dawit his war is already over. Once a platoon leader, we discover him in a military hospital facing a future in a wheelchair. Esaias confronts his audience with what is often a taboo subject by placing the injured veteran in the limelight: '*Up stage, a mountain. Stage right, Dawit, in a wheelchair. He remains lit throughout the play*' (p. 53).

Dawit's constant presence on stage forces the audience to juxtapose his paralysed body with the rest of the stage action; particularly the heroic descriptions of him as a fighter. Dawit's presence powerfully articulates the gulf that exists between the poetic ideal of the warrior and the harsh reality of becoming a casualty. Tragically, it is this distance that proves unbridgeable for Dawit; a gap into which he has all but disappeared by the end of the play.

Throughout *Aster* Esaias describes the bravery and suffering of the fighters in intensely poetic language. This communicates to the audience the deeply ingrained EPLF code of valour, and helps to establish just how embedded in the war effort the *Tegedalay's* sense of self was. Understanding this is crucial if one is to fully appreciate the enormity of what Dawit has lost. Certainly his injuries are terrible; doubtless he feels unmanned. He may even feel guilty about being able to play no further role in the fighting. But his injuries have a further psychological impact – and this is what Esaias wants us to grasp. Dawit's very identity has been blown apart.

> **Dawit** I am crippled! Staring at death, I am dissolving slowly. Don't you see? I am nobody. (p. 60)

The play is also about love: Aster is Dawit's comrade/wife, and Esaias asks us to consider what place love might have in the midst of conflict. The really profound question posed by the play is encapsulated in Dawit's admission that he was 'afraid of love, not war'. What has happened to a man who is afraid not of war, but of love?

Aster's arrival at the hospital is one of the most powerful moments in the play. The long pause that precedes any speech is almost unbearably painful. Dawit can no longer envisage a future for himself, and though he still loves her is determined to set Aster free of him. 'Everyone knows that I am finished – I am blind, I can't see you. *Ciao*. I love you' (p. 60). In the conversation that follows we learn that Dawit's injuries have left him incontinent and impotent. Metaphorically these injuries suggest another dreadful effect that this war has had on those that fought it, that the chance of a normal family life has been for ever taken away from them as a result of their experiences.

At its deepest level *Aster* is asking the audience to consider to what degree humanity can survive war. There is a cruel symbolic value to the nature of Dawit's injuries: once a warrior who has taken the lives of others, his impotency means he now cannot create life. He believes himself incapable of having any kind of loving relationship, and in a final, heart-rending act of belligerent self-sacrifice he sends Aster away for ever.

> **Dawit** I love you too. Don't make me nervous. We are the junction of love and hate. Aster, we can't reconcile them, we are not special. I am empty. I am lost. *Ciao*. I love you but *ciao*. (p. 63)

Esaias' play is a raw and painful testament to the scars that the fighters bear, both physical and mental, but like the other plays in this collection *Aster* is not just a play about the past. Dawit's line, 'we are at the junction of love and hate' has a chilling significance both in the light of Eritrea's more recent conflict with Ethiopia and the current, uneasy peace. Perhaps it also contains a warning. If, like Dawit, people cannot reconcile themselves to what they have suffered and seek resolution, no matter how unjustly they have been treated, they will remain locked in the past, trapped in a world of hatred and death, and forever cut off from the future, life and love.

NOTES

1. *Tegedalay* is the Tigrinya term for a freedom fighter. The rendering here is a phonetic approximation used in the playwrights' translation. For simplicity I have ignored gender cases.
2. Tigrinya is one of the Ethiopic branch of Semitic languages and the most widely spoken of Eritrea's nine languages.
3. The Eritrean People's Liberation Front (EPLF) was an armed organisation that fought for the independence of Eritrea from Ethiopia. It emerged in 1970 as a group that split from the Eritrean Liberation Front (ELF) and eventually won independence in 1991.
4. In Eritrea people are known by their first names. I have followed Eritrean rather than European usage in this article except where people share the same name – when I have used both.

BIBLIOGRAPHIC REFERENCES

Plastow, Jane and Solomon Tsehaye, 'Making Theatre for a change: Two plays of the Eritrean liberation struggle', *Theatre Matters*, Richard Boon & Jane Plastow, eds, Cambridge: Cambridge University Press, 1998.

Warwick, Paul, 'Theatre and the Eritrean Struggle for Freedom: the Cultural Troupes and the People's Liberation Front', *New Theatre Quarterly*, No. 51, 1997.

Paul Warwick
Theatre director

Ahmadu Kurfi, *The Barons*
Ibadan: Spectrum Books Limited, 2005, xiii+442 pp.
ISBN 9780295437, £9.95/$16.95

Olu Obafemi, *Dark Days are Over?*
Ibadan: University Press PLC, 2005 xvii+51 pp.
ISBN 978030956X, n.p.

Ahmed Yerima, *Yemoja*
Ibadan: Kraft Books Limited, 2002 63 pp.
ISBN 9780390669, £9.95/$14.95

The Barons and *Yemoja* are both distributed by African Books Collective

Ahmadu Kurfi's political satire, *The Barons*, is a dramatic tall order. A play in 58 acts! The grand design creates a real structural problem for the author: how to shape such intractable material into an effective, living drama. This would be a stunning feat even in the hands of an accomplished dramatist; and for someone new to the trade there is bound to be a problem of form. The ostensible historical time frame is the fifteen years of military rule that preceded the present Obasanjo regime, that is, the dark days of the military dictatorships of Generals Buhari/Idiagbon, Ibrahim Babangida, and Sani Abacha, from 31 December 1983 to 29 May 1999. But the book is a mine of information on Nigeria's political history. Every milestone in that history is talked about and each one of them is good enough material for a play: Lord Lugard's conquest of the north at the end of the nineteenth century, the Kano riot of 1953, the first general election of 1964, the first military coup of 15 January 1966, the Gowon era and its demise (1966–74), Obasanjo's first missionary journey as military head of state (1976–79), the Shagari administration (1979–83), the Gideon Orkar coup of 1994, the Saro-Wiwa execution of 1995, the aborted Oladipo Diya coup of 1997, the June 12 election debacle of 1993, the Ernest-Shonekan 82-day interregnum of 1993, etc., etc.

The author is at pains to order such a vast material into a workable drama. And because this hasn't been quite forthcoming, we have here a sprawling piece of amorphous dramatic experiment. The key players in the drama are the old-breed politicians from the north, called 'the barons'. Anyone familiar with Nigeria's political history can guess the identity of the political ancestry of the barons, or the originals upon whom they are modeled.

In spite of the author's disclaimer in the preface, the barons are the descendants of the well-known, powerful but notorious 'underground' political institution in the north known as the Kaduna Mafia. They are the scions of the Hausa-Fulani oligarchy who see it as their divine right not only to be kings but also kingmakers in Nigeria's political status quo. They are rich, privileged, spoiled, arrogant and relentless in their pursuit of power. The original qualification for membership was Hausa-Fulani lineage, underscored with affluence and political influence, but they have expanded their tentacles to admit into their cabal the moneyed class, the military class, the mercantile class, and any nobody who has some ill-gotten wealth to display. Under their tutelage, the north has produced rulers for Nigeria for 34 out of its 38 (as of the time of the play) years of existence as an independent state.

Although the old north has been split into about 20 states, the Mafia has never lost sight of the golden age of its history, the Sarduana-of-Sokoto era of the 1960s. This golden age is drummed about in the play as the barons sing the Sarduana's praise-song. In real life, the Mafia has laboured hard to keep the north intact for its political interest in spite of its balkanization through state creation. The allegiance of any politician from the new or old north must be north first, and Nigeria second. This, indeed, is the theme song of the barons: 'Our motto is 'Unity in Diversity at the federal level' and 'One North, One People, One Destiny' in the North' (p. 191). They want to keep the North perpetually in a position of political power. This can be accomplished by any means. 'Politics is in my blood and we do not mind shedding blood to achieve our objectives', boasts one of the barons (p. 117). The play captures this consuming drive for power and how it is feebly resisted by politicians from the South.

We must credit the author with some degree of satirical insight as the barons make a caricature of themselves through their own statements. Here is the testament of one baron:

> I have blue blood running in my veins, a patrician to the core. Wheeling and dealing in politics is my stock-in-trade. We make and unmake, we install and destool; we enrich and pauperize political actors at will. We are the uncrowned kings at times or kings at occasions. (p. 118)

The play documents, then, the manoeuvrings of the barons to consolidate and perpetuate an agenda for their political domination of the country. As history, the book records faithfully the events of those anxious years; but as drama, the play fails to move. Long, tedious orations masquerade as dramatic speech, and there is no major dramatic action. Action consists only in meeting after meeting convened by the barons to address issues of political interest to the north, but these meetings serve as forum for exchange of low jokes and display of the egos of the baronial overlords. Agenda matters are often bypassed altogether and discussions are often inconclusive. This is part of the author's intention to satirize the indolence and messianic pretensions of Nigeria's political elite.

The language is cliché-ridden; nearly every page teems with irritating jargon, and sometimes the author allows his imagination to run wild. What else could have motivated the unnecessary allusion to Julius Caesar in Act 57, Scene 2 and the rush to [mis]interpret the Latin adage, *veni vidi vici*:

> Veni vidi vici. So said Julius Caesar, the Roman conqueror of England and Angleland. For the benefit of those who did not study classics including Latin, Caesar's remarks meant we came, we saw, we conquered. (p. 424)

Caesar comes up again in the final act of the play in the several misquotes of one baron who is eager to impress his listeners with his reading:

> When the poor cried, Caesar hath wept: ambition should be made of sterner stiff [sic] … O judgment, though [sic] art fled to British beasts [sic]. (p. 438)

What Shakespeare wrote, I believe, was that ambition should be made of sterner 'stuff', and that the better judgment of those who approved of the assassination of Caesar had fled to 'brutish beasts': but both allusions smack of pedantry. There is high comedy in the testament of the barons cited above from Act 14, but such dramatic moments are rare. The play remains, not good drama, but good satire, and a good historical document on Nigerian politics.

Olu Obafemi's play, *Dark Days are Over?*, is a sprightly piece of theatre in three movements addressing the issue of cult activities in our university campuses. The play's thesis is that social unrest, whether on campus or in the larger society, is a complex problem that must be addressed at source for it to be eradicated. The root cause of the problem is corrupt leadership. Cultism and violence, asserts the dramatist, are the only option for university graduates who have no job to fall back on. They have no job because funds for stimulating the economy and generating jobs have been misappropriated by those in privileged positions of leadership. And if we must imprison the common campus criminal, we must also imprison the real robbers who, with a stroke of the pen or the power of the gun, command billions of dollars into their foreign accounts. This, the play asserts, is real justice.

There is nothing new about this thinking but the dramatic unfolding of the idea is admirable. Obafemi springs surprise upon surprise upon the reader. The chief judge trying Yepa 1 for rape at the Court of Law is the same chief justice who bribed the DPO to set Yepa 2 (Yepa 1's accomplice in crime) free from detention. To right this wrong, the People's Court replaces the state Court of Law, and a judge chosen on stage by the people takes up the trial. Yepa 1 is, of course, convicted, but not without a long homily delivered by Agbe, the People's judge, on the injustice of our judicial system. *Dark Days are Over?* is a delightful agit-prop play energized with campus language and the moral indignation of a participating audience craving for instant justice.

Ahmed Yerima's beautiful play, *Yemoja*, transports us into the arena of the drama of the gods. It celebrates the beauty, the gentle nature, and maternal qualities of Yemoja as the goddess of the river, of fertility and bountiful harvest, and her ultimate glorification as the goddess of the sea. All the familiar figures in the Yoruba pantheon are evoked through dance as the movement of transition, but they end up as witnesses to Yemoja's final apotheosis: Olodumare (the supreme god), Obatala (known also as Orisa-nla, the god of creation), Orunmila (the god of wisdom and divination), Ogun (the god of war), Esu (the trickster god), Sango (the god of thunder and lightening), and Oya (his wife).

The gods are here humanized and shown to be prone to our normal human weaknesses. Their weakest point is excessive sexual drive. 'Women remain the greatest wonder of Olodumare's gift to the world', Orunmila tells Yemoja (p. 47). Nearly all the gods are in love with Yemoja, and seek her hand in marriage. This introduces the play's love subplot. Yemoja rejects Esu because of his inconsistency of character. She wants to marry Ogun in spite of his fiery temper. Ogun's dancing feet charm her and compensate for other negative aspects of his character. But at the final contest for her hand in marriage between Ogun and Sango, Queen Yemoja rejects both men to pursue an independent existence as the queen of the sea. This decision is a dignifying one, making her, perhaps the forerunner of modern feminism. Of course, Esu, the god of evil machinations, is behind every frustration of Yemoja's intention to marry.

The play orchestrates extensively the ritual metaphor of dance. Dance is the dramatic idiom for the summoning of the gods from the land of the dead, in what is sometimes known as the movement of transition. Each god manifests whenever his particular ritual dance is performed. We have also dance as the language of courtship as when Ogun dances for Yemoja, who also tries to persuade Obatala to dance for her. Several other interpretations are given to the metaphor of dance, and the dramatist insists so much on them that they cannot be missed.

Yerima's is the most beautifully crafted of the three plays discussed in this review. I think that the medium he has chosen to work in is responsible for this distinction, making his work a ritual drama that appeals through the dignity of its poetic language, the gentle tempo of its movement, and the stark dignity of its classical structure. The only problem is that the vernacular theme songs are not translated and this can become an obstacle for the uninitiated reader.

Obi Maduakor
University of Nigeria, Nsukka
Tyndale University College, Toronto

Index

172

Printed and bound by CPI Group (UK) Ltd, Croydon, CR0 4YY

14/04/2025

14656923-0001